Praise for *Whatever Works*

"In *Whatever Works*, psychologist Thalma Lobel shares the surprising and unexpected ways small tweaks can have a big impact on our performance and success at work as well as our general job satisfaction. From mind hacks for increasing concentration to tricks for boosting creativity, there is a lot here for employers and employees alike. The great watercooler talking points alone are worth their weight in office cred. Fun, practical, and important!"

—Guy Winch, author of *Emotional First Aid* and three-time TED Talk speaker

"Simple, accessible, profound. This book will help you introduce small changes to your environment that can make a big difference in your life. Thalma Lobel provides a blueprint for increasing levels of happiness and health, as well as success."

—Tal Ben Shahar, *New York Times* bestselling author of *Happier*

"*Whatever Works* challenges the notion that 'anything works.' It presents a wonderful opportunity of using a growing body of research in an effort to improve life and work in simple but very effective ways."

—Efrat Dagan, head of talent at Next Insurance and former head of talent at both Google and Lyft

"Professor Lobel has written a quite *unputdownable*, highly accessible, and personal book. The range of topics covered is very wide and she weaves together studies from many different areas of psychology. Most important, the book is strongly evidence-based, which reflects her wide and critical reading. The book rejoices in counterintuitive findings and certainly leads you to rethink many of the things you experience in the workplace. This will definitely be a bestseller!"

—Adrian Furnham, author of *50 Psychology Ideas You Really Need to Know* and professor of psychology at University College London

WHATEVER
WORKS

Also by Thalma Lobel

Sensation: The New Science of Physical Intelligence

WHATEVER
WORKS

The Small Cues That Make a Surprising
Difference in Our Success at Work—
and How to Create a Happier Office

THALMA LOBEL

BenBella Books, Inc.
Dallas, Texas

BENBELLA

BenBella Books, Inc.
10440 N. Central Expressway
Suite 800
Dallas, TX 75231
www.benbellabooks.com
Send feedback to feedback@benbellabooks.com

BenBella is a federally registered trademark.

Printed in the United States of America
10 9 8 7 6 5 4 3 2 1

Library of Congress Control Number: 2019059830
ISBN 9781950665099 (paperback)
ISBN 9781950665266 (electronic)

Editing by Claire Schulz
Copyediting by Scott Calamar
Proofreading by Dylan Julian and Christine Florie
Indexing by WordCo Indexing Services, Inc.
Text design and composition by PerfecType, Nashville, TN
Cover design by Faceout Studio, Molly von Borstel
Cover images © Shutterstock / Paladin12 (texture), Rido (red tie), and Africa Studio (blue tie);
    © the Noun Project (icons); and (c) Pexels / Jeri Tovar (plant)
Select chapter icons © Noun Project: "Door" by Mooms, "Handshake" by Susannanova,
    "Speech bubble" by howadesign, "Pickpocket" by Proletkult Graphik, "Eye" by Petr Papasov,
    and "Drawing" by Scott Kennedy
Printed by Lake Book Manufacturing

Distributed to the trade by Two Rivers Distribution, an Ingram brand
www.tworiversdistribution.com

Special discounts for bulk sales are available. Please contact bulkorders@benbellabooks.com.

To my beloved son Dani
And to my beloved Danielle, Elinor, Natalie, Dean, Libby, and Adam

CONTENTS

INTRODUCTION

Work. It's a fact of life. Between the twin pillars of birth and death, most of us work.

According to a 2018 report by the US Bureau of Labor Statistics, the average man worked 40.8 hours per week in paid employment, while the average woman worked 36.2 hours per week. Add to that the commute and other necessary activities for holding down a job, and you end up with a huge chunk of your waking hours devoted to work.

Aside from sustaining ourselves and our families, work is a massive determinant of our identities. The most common question heard when strangers meet (once the names have been dispensed with) is: "So what do you *do*?" The question is universally understood to mean "What *work* is it that you do?" The response received evokes a cluster of assumptions about the other person and, whether we like it or not, is a marker of social status.

For the lucky among us, work can be a source of great satisfaction, prestige, pride in accomplishment, and a handsome income. On the other hand, for the less fortunate who have no choice, work can be little more than a quotidian duty that takes up a large chunk of the day, and little more. But no matter which of the extreme camps we belong to, or where we lie along the continuum, it is natural that we should wish to increase our job satisfaction and well-being, boost our performance, enhance our creativity, gain recognition, and advance in our careers. This holds true for individual workers—whether as freelancers working alone or as salaried employees—as well as for business owners, organizations, and managers who wish to optimize and incentivize their workforce and thus maximize their bottom lines.

You might ask: "Another self-help book on success in one's work and career? Really?" Well, not really. The vast majority of books focus on one obvious and important subject, methodically laying out its secrets and conclusions. For instance, there are books on changing one's mental attitude and mindset as keys to success. There are books on motivation and books that emphasize human relationships—the people we know and those who we reach out to—as springboards to success in our careers. And there are plenty of niche books that address achievement from narrower angles such as dressing for success, career advancement for women, body language, and so forth.

All of these are wonderful and valuable books, but many of them tend to focus on more obvious factors like harnessing motivation, getting organized, networking, and so on. This book is different.

Based on cutting-edge science and novel experiments, *Whatever Works* focuses on elements that we are less aware of—and even if we are aware of them, we often don't think they matter. These are factors, such as clothing and lighting, that are there all along, virtually under our nose, but that we are less aware of, or whose effects we might have only given a passing acknowledgment to without digging down. Yet they influence our performance, satisfaction, and happiness. The experiments I'll describe in this book uncover unexpected truths about subtle cues in our environments, our teams, and our personal habits. The vast majority of these discoveries are related to the space we work in, some are in our mindset, and some are powerful cues that were hitherto ignored or unknown. Many are truly surprising, and some even challenge our beliefs to the point of saying: "Come on, that can't be true." However, the scientific proof in these cases is inescapable.

For example, much has been written about clothes and "dressing for success." But did you know that dressing in a certain way can increase your cognitive powers? Or that what you wear can distort objective professional assessments of your performance?

Did you know that if you are in a crucial negotiation—in a business deal or negotiating a raise or promotion—expressing anger or disappointment can work in your favor? Alternatively, it can backfire horribly, potentially putting you out in the street. It all depends, and this book tells you exactly when and how to express such emotions to your advantage. Or did you know that placing even a single person on your team who is ethnically different can bring about a quantum leap in the team's creativity, effectiveness, and originality—even if that person never utters a word?

Did you know that simply looking at certain colors can boost your creativity and restore your attentive powers when you really need it? Or that a walk in nature during a work break can significantly reduce stress, help you recover from fatigue, and increase your cognitive powers on the job?

These are just a few of the many insights that recent scientific studies have brought to light. All can be applied to great advantage, by both workers and organizations.

Throughout my professional career, I have always been fascinated by the factors that influence our performance, decisions, and judgments, and make us happier. I studied at Tel Aviv University, where I received my master's degree and PhD in psychology, and where I've been working for many years as a psychology professor. I went to Harvard University for my postdoctorate studies, and I later returned to teach as a visiting professor.

My studies were published in leading psychological journals and were read mainly by psychologists, but I always wanted to write a book for the general audience. There are so many interesting and extremely valuable findings in psychology that should be available to everyone and not just to professionals. So several years ago, I wrote my first book, *Sensation: The New Science of Physical Intelligence*. Published in many countries and translated into many languages, *Sensation* shows how, without our awareness, our decisions and behaviors are influenced by physical sensations such as the color, texture, and temperature of items we hold. I was invited all over the world to talk about this subject. It was so gratifying to see how it drew the interest of numerous people from various professions, and I was happy to hear the positive reactions from readers, and to receive so many emails from people who read the book and told me how they incorporated its takeaways. That inspired me to write this book, on a subject that is so close and important to most of us: the workplace. *Whatever Works* focuses on the factors that influence our performance, creativity, and happiness in the work world.

I am well familiar with the pressures of the work environment—both as a psychologist who has spent years studying the factors that influence our behavior, and as a working mom, who always struggled between career and family. Although my main work as a professor at the university is research and teaching, I do not sit in my ivory tower; I also have a great deal of experience in managerial positions. I was the chair of the School of Psychological Sciences and the Dean of Students at Tel Aviv University, and I was the representative of the professors on the university's board of directors. I also sit on the board of directors of several organizations. In these roles, especially as the chair and the dean, I was in charge of many employees, hiring and firing, handling conflicts among employees, and composing working teams and committees. I have vast experience in interviewing people for various roles, including administrative and research assistants, psychologists, heads of units, financial managers, and even CEOs.

In this book, I bring together aspects of my extensive experience and professional background to show the various cues and factors that we should be aware of to improve our performance and well-being in the workplace.

My goal is to offer individuals and organizations actionable steps that will measurably improve their bottom lines in terms of effectiveness, satisfaction, career advancement, and income. In doing so, I based my approach on recent, cutting-edge experiments that reveal novel insights, "hacks" if you will, which can be used to advantage rather easily.

The book is divided into three parts:

The first part, "Whatever Works at the Office: The Cues in Your Environment," deals with environmental factors, and it brings to light studies that show how our performance, behavior, motivation, and satisfaction are influenced by these cues in ways you would have never imagined. This includes the office layout, its closed or open spaces, light quality (bright or dim, artificial or natural), temperature of the workplace, the existence of windows (or lack thereof) and the effect of the views seen from them, and the influence of nature on our work.

Part II, "Whatever Works for Your Team: Surprising Factors That Change How We Work Together," focuses on the factors that influence the results of interactions at work, such as interviews, discussions with colleagues, sitting with the boss to discuss a job promotion or salary terms, business-related negotiations (and private ones too), team work, and optimal team composition. This part includes chapters that illustrate the effect of mimicry, expressing various emotions, the clothes we wear, our physical appearance, human diversity on team performance, and how others perceive us, as well as how effective we can be as negotiators, to name a few. Each chapter offers valuable insights that will enhance your success in negotiations, teamwork, interviews, and interactions in general.

Part III, "Whatever Works for You: The Power of Our Personal Habits," covers factors that depend on our own choices and habits and affect our individual performance. A chapter on the influence of technology on our work includes important and even surprising ways that we can use our smartphones to our benefit and how to avoid their negative impacts on our work. The chapter on order and disorder explains how organization (or lack of it) in the office or workspace can influence our behavior and performance. Music is the subject of another chapter. The final chapter deals with creativity, which, in the workplace, can present a difficult and even cruel challenge, because we often don't have the luxury of riding the magic carpet of the "muse" when it arrives in its own good time. At work we are sometimes called upon to be creative, virtually on cue, and we must show results in a timely manner, or worse, by a specific deadline. This chapter offers many takeaways, most of them quite unexpected and even seemingly irrelevant, but nevertheless backed by science and available for you to exploit in order to boost your creative and innovative powers.

Of course, there is some overlap between these sections, as the factors and their effects are interrelated. Taken together, the book offers a wealth of little known and novel insights that can be used to your advantage. Exploiting even a few takeaways you receive from this book—on the day you ask for a raise or promotion, enter a crucial negotiation, need to come up with a killer idea or else, or simply perform at your very best—has the potential to help you enhance your performance, well-being, and creativity, and, as a natural consequence, your overall happiness and satisfaction with life. This is my sincere wish for you.

Part I

Whatever Works at the Office

The Cues in Your Environment

The Office Layout

How Your Office Design Influences Your Productivity and Satisfaction

*If you think good design is expensive, you should look
at the cost of bad design.*
—RALF SPETH

Most of us spend much of our life indoors, and apart from our homes, the workplace is our major indoor environment. At work, we find ourselves thrust into an unnatural and artificial setting for the vast majority of our waking hours—and thus our lives. This inevitably affects us; research has shown, and continues to show, that the quality of our indoor environment impacts our health, well-being, happiness,[1] and productivity.[2] This is something we all need to pay attention to. From the employer's standpoint, it only makes sense financially to optimize working conditions in a way that best supports productivity, lowers absenteeism, and increases job satisfaction and well-being of the company's workforce. For employees, once we are aware of the effects of environmental variables that are under our control, we can tweak and make adjustments accordingly so that we are happier, healthier, and more productive at work.

It might not be surprising to hear that the office environment has a big effect, but we might be surprised to learn *how* it affects us. This section of the book deals with the *physical* factors in our workplace environments that influence us. Studies have examined the impact of ambient features in work environments, such as office layout, open and closed spaces, noise, room temperature, lighting, window location, and more, and how these features influence our satisfaction, attitudes, behaviors, and performance. It behooves all of us to be aware of these so that we can make relatively simple adjustments that go a long way toward improving the quality of our working lives, our mental and physical well-being, and the corporate bottom line.

Open and Closed Spaces: Which One Is Better for You?

There are many stories about the suffering of workers that are directly related to office layout.

Over the past century, there have been rapid and dramatic changes in workplace design. Many companies, after having built private offices, transitioned to a layout with individual cubicles for employees. The rationale was that placing workers in cubicles and buffering them from distractions, human or otherwise, would help them to concentrate and perform better. However, cubicles have received a lot of criticism from workplace experts and employees. Evolutionary psychologists assert that our preferences in designing our environments spring from our collective history on the savanna.[3] We prefer settings that comport with our hunter-gatherer legacy, feeling instinctively uncomfortable in situations that would have placed our ancestors at risk. Prehistoric humans felt safest when situated in a secure space with a clear escape from predators or enemies and not isolated from the security of the herd. A modern office worker, sequestered in an isolated cubicle, continually uncertain of the presence of nearby "predators" (bosses, rivals, and other stressors), is in a naturally uncomfortable environment. Cubicles are semiprivate, but people are deprived of sunlight, their views restricted, and they sit in a small space that is sometimes more confined than their bathroom, with backs exposed to limited view. (Scott Adams, creator of the *Dilbert* comic strip, wrote a book about office life called *Cubicles That Make You Envy the Dead.*)

More recently, many companies have moved to open spaces. Walls between employees (if any) are built to a low height. The rationale behind the open space is that it boosts teamwork and the exchange of ideas, leading to innovation and enhanced productivity. Moreover, it saves organizations money; they use less space per person and don't need to spend as much on construction. According to the *Washington Business Journal*,[4] a report by the International Facility Management Association details that "some 70 percent of American office workers now have desks with either low partitions or no partitions at all." Rather than informal interactions being limited to common locations such as the watercooler, coffee corner, or photocopy machine, open spaces provide multiple opportunities for informal interaction and knowledge exchange.

There is a belief among some that open spaces are most conducive to collaboration. However, that perception has been turned on its head; the open space has aroused much criticism. In a study described in a 2018 *Washington Post* article entitled "Open Office Plans Are as Bad as You Thought," researchers examined two companies that changed their office layout to open-space offices with no cubicles.[5] They found that, after the change in layout, workers engaged in 70 percent *fewer* face-to-face interactions and instead had more electronic interactions, sending emails and other messages. Additionally, many open-office workers wear noise-canceling headphones to ignore the sound around them, often at the expense of interacting with colleagues.

A 2014 article in the *New Yorker* entitled "The Open Office Trap" reviewed several studies and concluded that open-space offices also negatively affect performance.[6] In a study conducted in Denmark, researchers surveyed 2,403 office workers to discover how many sick days they took off from work and found a correlation between sick days and the number of people sharing the same office.[7] Employees who shared an office with another person had *50 percent* more sick days than those in a single-person office, and those working in offices with an open-plan design had 62 percent more days taken off for sickness. One might argue that the reasons for this are physical (exposure to other people's germs, for instance) or psychological (dispersion of responsibility—the larger the group, the less conspicuous the absence, and the more available manpower to fill in for the absentee). But regardless, absenteeism costs money to the company and affects job security and employee retention.

A number of studies, most of them conducted by researchers from Sweden and Denmark, found that such a working environment negatively impacts worker satisfaction and well-being.[8] And a study published in 2018 in France found that a full 70 percent of employees were unhappy with the open-space design.[9]

Does Open Space Shut You Down?

Open-space offices are widely believed to be beneficial because they encourage collaboration. However, researchers at Harvard University came to a different conclusion.[10] They examined the transition of two companies from private offices to more open office spaces, and how this change influenced interpersonal communication. Their findings demonstrated that face-to-face interaction decreased significantly, while interaction via electronic means increased. The researchers concluded that in open-space offices, people tend to withdraw from coworkers who are sitting in the same space, and they prefer interaction via emails and messages. Thus face-to-face encounters, which include small talk and visual cues that enhance communication, are reduced and replaced (and compensated for?) by faceless and voiceless electronic exchanges.

Email correspondences do have advantages, but as we shall see in a subsequent chapter of the book focusing on email, there are also disadvantages. These include misinterpreting the tone or intention of the written word—a grievous pitfall that can negatively influence a project or sour a relationship. Therefore, it is highly desirable for both types of communication to coexist and complement each other.

The most common complaints among employees in the open-space office are noise, lack of privacy, and lack of control over one's space.

Too Much Noise

According to a 2017 Gallup Poll entitled "The State of the American Workplace," a full 75 percent of office workers complain about noise in the workplace, and 38 percent say they would change their jobs just to have an office with a door. Without question, open-space offices are louder than closed private offices. Noise has been implicated in multiple ills including disturbed concentration, lowered productivity, reduced worker satisfaction, and subpar physical well-being and performance. Workers who sit in a noisy office perform worse in memory tasks and even in relatively simple math tests.[11] Several groups of Swedish researchers found that excessive noise leads to lower motivation and increases fatigue,[12] and more health problems are reported in a noisy office.[13] One study, for example, conducted at Cornell University, exposed half of the subjects (clerical workers) to noise in an open office for three hours while the other half sat in a quiet room.[14] Participants in the noisy room exhibited far less motivation to solve problems. Furthermore, their stress levels went up as measured by the level of epinephrine (also called adrenaline) in the blood.

The biggest and most distracting auditory villain in the open-space office is human speech, followed by ringing phones, footsteps, and other noisy activities.[15] Studies show that background speech has a negative influence on the performance of various cognitive tasks that are conducted at the office such as proofreading, reading comprehension, and writing.[16] A good portion of the speech we hear in an open-space office consists of phone conversations. Unlike listening to coworkers chatting among themselves, phone conversations are "halfalogues," or utterances and responses by only one of the conversing parties: "Are you kidding?" "What's her problem?" "Then what did he say?" They irresistibly pique our curiosity and seize mental bandwidth as our brains seek to fill in the blanks. When you hear only one side of the conversation, you are naturally tempted to infer what the other person is saying, which pulls your concentration at the expense of other attention-demanding tasks. Comedian Bob Newhart was famous for his hilarious halfalogues to the delight of his audiences who, based on his delivery, *manufactured in their minds* the entire comic scenario taking place. Studies show that people listen more attentively to halfalogues than dialogues, find them more annoying, and exhibit decreased performance when hearing a halfalogue compared with a dialogue.[17] A group of Swedish researchers gave their participants an office-based task that required focus, comprehension, and memory.[18] The participants were asked to perform the task as quickly as possible. There were three noise conditions: a *halfalogue condition*, in which, during the task, participants could hear only one side of a phone conversation; a *dialogue condition*, in which participants heard both sides of the same conversation while they were working; and a control *quiet condition* with no background noise. Each noise condition was either meaningful, and participants could understand the conversation, or meaningless, where the words were twisted so participants could not understand what was said. The researchers found that the halfalogue condition impaired performance more than the dialogue, but only when it was meaningful. When the participants heard an unclear, meaningless conversation, whether it was dialogue or halfalogue, they did not perform worse than when there was no noise at all. A meaningful halfalogue captures our attention and affects our performance.

One way to overcome these noise distractions is by masking sound, which helps to overcome the negative influence of the background speech. Various studies have investigated the effect of several masking sounds such as the sound of springwater, music, and speech babble (multiple talkers in the background).[19] These studies found, for example, that those who heard multiple voices performed better on cognitive tasks than those who heard a single voice. Workers were the most satisfied when both multiple voices and the sound of water waves were used as masking.

Keep It Private

Ask employees to take their private phone calls outside the office. Workers in an open space get distracted by the private calls of colleagues, as they often try to guess the "other side" of the conversation.

While noise usually distracts us and has a negative effect on cognitive performance, one surprising study showed that a certain level of ambient noise does just the opposite—it can actually enhance creativity.[20] The researchers randomly divided participants into four groups and gave them the Remote Associates Test, a task researchers often use to measure a person's creative potential (remember the name—we'll discuss that test again in chapter 14). While taking the test, each group was exposed to a different noise level. One group was exposed to a low level of noise, 50 decibels (equivalent to the level of a quiet suburb or a running refrigerator); one group was exposed to a moderate level of noise, 70 decibels (equivalent to a running shower); and one group was exposed to a high level of noise, 85 decibels (equivalent to a noisy restaurant). In addition, one more group sat in a quiet room and was not exposed to any noise. Surprisingly, those who were exposed to 70 decibels—the moderate level of noise—performed better than the other three groups, including those who sat in a quiet room. In other words, a low level of ambient noise has a positive effect on creativity. This might also partly explain why people seem to focus better with the ambient noise of a coffee shop.

Headphones? Sounds Good!

If you have no choice but to work in an open space and the noise disturbs you, try wearing headphones. You can listen to nature sounds, or coffee-shop sounds, or other sounds that are meant to mask distracting noises at the office. Indeed there are websites and YouTube videos that show you how to listen to coffee-shop noise using your headphones to help you focus and be creative. (For one example, check out mynoise.net.) If your company does have an available private space, try working there on tasks that demand concentration. Otherwise, take a few minutes every hour for a short break to clear your head, with headphones if possible.

Indeed, even a noisy restaurant is a better working environment for tasks that require focus than an open office with a similar noise level. Why? In a 2017 article in *Harvard Business Review*, David Burkus suggests that the reason we are able to work more efficiently in a Starbucks than in an open-space office is that the office continually draws us into conversations.[21] In contrast, the background noise of a coffee shop is mostly irrelevant to us, and we are not drawn into or distracted by conversations (unless of course a juicy one is taking place right next to us or if a disturbance erupts nearby). Here again, it is the *relevance* of the conversations (or irrelevance in the case of the coffee shop) that determines the extent of our distraction.

Privacy (or Lack Thereof)

Aside from the problem of noise, workers in open spaces suffer a glaring lack of privacy. Clearly it is hard to concentrate on your job when a person drops by your coworker's desk, or when you see a coworker flirting with another worker. Such distractions are hard to block out, and doing so requires mental effort.

Workers grumble about lack of privacy both on a professional *and* personal level. We behave differently when we're in a group of people and naturally need to maintain a respectable social face. But what about when we become truly tense and upset? Or when we need to make an important call on a personal matter? Or even scratch an embarrassing itch? True, important or confidential conversations among colleagues, or with the boss, are typically held in a private space, but neutral conversations in the open space can quickly turn to personal matters that cannot be discussed discreetly in the presence of multiple eyes and ears. In some workplaces, employees complain that there is no unthreatening place to go, aside from a private toilet stall or outside of the building. A study published in 2018 examined employees of government offices in the United Kingdom who moved from traditional private or semiprivate offices to large open offices.[22] Not surprisingly, workers' satisfaction was found to be lower in the open-office environment. What is significant here is that women, especially, were dissatisfied, which probably holds true for all open-space offices. Lack of privacy typically exacts a heavier price among women. Women reported that they felt more scrutinized for their appearance in the open office. They felt the stares of male eyes and constantly fussed over their appearance, a source of self-consciousness and irritation. Such self-consciousness made the women think twice about where to go in the office and caused them to consider more carefully how they dress. Another study of five thousand office workers from different types of offices found that women were more negatively affected by office type than men.[23]

I Need Some Privacy

Organizations should provide a private space for employees who work in an open-space office, where they can make phone calls and hold private meetings. This will not only give them privacy when they need it, but it will also enhance the performance of the other workers.

There are of course individual differences, and what is good and comfortable for one person may not be agreeable to another. Introverts feel less comfortable in open spaces than extroverts and often find it extremely difficult to work in such types of offices.[24]

Lack of Control

Another common lament of workers over the open-space office is not having control over room temperature, lighting, personal space, and so forth. Sharing a room with others necessitates finding a temperature that will get the least amount of protest, in other words, a "happy medium" that might not be so happy for some. Air conditioners and heaters keep the office at temperatures that are comfortable for some and can be torture to endure for others. I am personally acquainted with a lovely lady who has shared an office for ten years with three other workers. She suffers terribly from overly cold air-conditioning and on hot days suffers through the entire workday in conditions that are agreeable to her coworkers but hell for her. Her pleas to raise the temperature are sympathetically rejected in order to satisfy the majority. This has been the source of tension every summer and has actually ruined one of her relationships at work (with the colleague she needs to sit next to five days a week).

It's Too Cold, It's Too Warm, and Sometimes It's Too Dark

In an open-space office environment, try to have a small lamp and fan next to each desk. That way workers can have control, to some extent, of the light and the temperature.

The New Model: Flexible, Activity-Based Working Environment

Many major companies like IBM, Microsoft, Boston Consulting Group, and GE have transitioned to designing hybrid offices. This new model takes into consideration that what is good for one type of worker is not good for another. Such offices combine private spaces where employees can sit in a quiet place and work when they need to focus and concentrate on a task with no distractions, many open areas that enable social interaction and networking, smaller open spaces for teamwork, movable walls, and soundproof telephone areas. The idea is to increase individual workers' productivity without overlooking the important social factor. Some enlightened companies have begun to offer soundproof "isolation rooms" and even lounges where technology is prohibited. Some companies have "chilling out" rooms equipped with pillows and cushions where people can rest or sit and read their email. The Salesforce Tower in San Francisco actually has a meditation area on every floor for employees. According to a *New York Times* article entitled "Don't Get Too Comfortable at That Desk," many companies are readjusting their offices to activity-centered workplaces, sometimes called "flexible offices," in which workers are free to migrate to whichever space is appropriate for the task at hand.[25]

How these activity-based work environments influence workers' performance and happiness is only in the early stages of empirical evaluation. The findings are not clear—and are even contradictory. Some studies found that this type of workplace has a negative impact on well-being and productivity,[26] whereas others found a positive influence on workers' health in the long run.[27] In 2019 a group of Australian researchers reviewed seventeen studies with 36,039 participants.[28] They found that activity-based workplaces had positive influences on interaction, communication, and satisfaction, but were negatively related to privacy and concentration. However, the findings related to the association between this type of workspace and mental and physical health were not consistent. More studies are needed to fully evaluate the influence of this type of working environment.

Clearly you cannot choose the exact type of office space you work in.

As we've seen, the open-space office has been shown to be inferior from the standpoint of employees' general well-being, and this continues to be borne out by studies.[29] Unfortunately, many organizations continue to adopt open layouts, despite their shortcomings.

In companies where most employees work in private spaces, there ought to be a common area where people can congregate and talk. Ideally, it should be a pleasant spot, not far from the offices, with a coffee machine and a watercooler where colleagues can sit and interact. This is very important because it is against our nature to sit virtually alone all day, working without social interaction.

Thus the modern trend among serious companies is to make the transition to hybrid offices. This is best all around for workers, as we've seen, and certainly best for the companies in terms of less absenteeism and better worker performance and satisfaction.

If you're "stuck" in an environment that does not work well for you, try to adopt the recommendations discussed above. Bring headphones, a fan, or a heater from home, and hope that one day your work environment will be better designed for your needs.

2

Let There Be Light

The Influence of Light on Our Performance and Well-Being

Learn to light a candle in the darkest moments of
someone's life. Be the light that helps others see; it is
what gives life its deepest significance.
—ROY T. BENNETT, *THE LIGHT IN THE HEART*

When I got my first job at Tel Aviv University, I was assigned a small, windowless office with fluorescent lighting. I really hated that office. Sometimes I went to work in the library to avoid spending time there. The thing that bothered me the most was that it didn't have any windows; I had only artificial light, no sense of what was going on outside, and never saw a tree or even another building, or people walking around the campus—it really upset me. In case you're wondering why I did not say anything at the time—well, I was a young professor, on a tenure track, and at that time I depended on the senior members and the chair of the department, who did not seem especially concerned about us being happy in our offices. They thought that we should be thankful for whatever office we got.

Many years later, when I was the chair of the department, I tried to remember that and to show more concern for the well-being of the young, new professors. Since then things have changed dramatically: new researchers get nice offices and the windowless rooms serve only as labs. My own spacious office today has not one but two windows, though I remember those early days very well.

Only in recent years, when I studied the influence of windowless offices on our health and performance, did I realize how bad it was—it affected much more than I imagined. Many studies have explored the negative effects of sitting in a windowless office; it's not just about comfort level or the lack of an interesting view, but the overall effect on our health, mood, sleep quality, and performance.

A window provides us with natural light and a view. We will get to the importance of a view in chapter 4, but first let's talk about light.

Artificial or Natural Light

It is almost a given that people prefer bright, sunny surroundings to cloudy and dark ones. In a study that asked participants to rate photographs of places, they showed a clear preference for photos of bright and sunny areas.[1] There are several explanations for this preference. According to the evolutionary theory, people preferred environments that were healthier and served adaptive needs. In our early history, we lived in nature, with our activities and survival heavily dependent on daylight. Since there was no artificial light as we evolved, humans were extremely vulnerable in the dark, at the mercy of enemies and predators well equipped to attack at night. Light illuminates our perception of safety-related information, dangers, and the weather. Other theories suggest that the preference for light is learned and culturally based. Even if we are predisposed to choose light over darkness, this predilection is reinforced and shaped by social learning, starting in childhood when children learn that they are more vulnerable in the dark. This preference is also learned due to repeated pairing of light and darkness with good and bad in expressions, idioms, and metaphors such as *there is a light at the end of the tunnel, dark ages, the forces of light and darkness, light of my life, my darkest hour,* and so on. In this chapter we will focus on how light affects mood, performance, and well-being in the workplace.

Overall, people prefer sunlight and natural light to artificial illumination. However, not all workers have that choice. Many people sit in windowless cubicles or offices buried deep inside a building—like I did so many years ago. They work under artificial light that remains fairly constant throughout the day. They can work in a *bright* room with the flick of a switch, of course, but that is not the same as sunlight.

Researchers who study the influence of light on human behavior come from various disciplines and have multidisciplinary expertise, such as architecture, engineering technology, medicine, sleep disorders, and psychology, which goes to show that light has deep effects on diverse areas of our lives.

One collaborative study was undertaken by researchers from very different backgrounds. Mohamed Boubekri, a professor at the Illinois School of Architecture, explores the influence of lack of daylight inside buildings on well-being. Phyllis Zee is a neurologist and the chief of sleep medicine in the Department of Neurology at Northwestern University. Working with a team of researchers from architecture and neurology backgrounds, Zee and Boubekri compared the well-being and sleep quality of people who worked in offices with artificial light and natural light, and they showed the importance of natural daylight exposure for workers.

They gave the workers a self-reported questionnaire that assessed both physical functioning and the person's perception of her or his ability to perform various roles. It also measured general mental vitality (how energetic or tired the person is). In addition, the participants filled out a questionnaire that measured their sleep quality. Compared to those working in offices with daylight, workers in windowless offices reported it was more difficult for them to perform their roles due to physical problems and fatigue. They also reported poor sleep quality more frequently compared to those who worked in offices with windows and were exposed to daylight.[2]

Beyond simply helping their employees lead happier, healthier lives, organizations should be interested in the effect of sunlight. A group of researchers from Qatar and the United Kingdom, headed by Professor Yousef Al Horr from the Gulf Organization for Research and Development in Qatar, reviewed more than three hundred papers to examine the relationship between quality of the indoor environment of an office and workers' productivity. They found that organizations with offices that let in more daylight have higher productivity. Buildings with more natural light have lower absenteeism rates and show an increase in attendance.[3] The researchers give examples of companies like Lockheed Martin and Verifone, which reported a 15 percent decrease in absenteeism in the buildings that supplied the maximum daylight.

Bright and Dim Lighting

Although natural light is preferable to artificial light, the intensity of the light (whether or not it is artificial) also affects our overall health and productivity.

Mental fatigue is a common phenomenon in the workplace, and one way to overcome it is through appropriate lighting. Numerous studies have shown that bright light helps us to feel more alert. For example, a group of sleep researchers in the United Kingdom exposed ninety-four white-collar workers to two lighting conditions; each exposure lasted for four weeks. One was white light and the other was a more intense blue-enriched white light. Those who were exposed to the more intense light reported being more alert, in a better mood, felt they performed better in the office, and were less tired in the evening.[4] Other studies showed that in bright light, participants felt less sleepy and more energetic and alert, and their heart rate increased compared to a baseline; meanwhile, the heart rates of subjects exposed to dim light decreased. These effects were seen both in the morning and the evening, which shows that light is important not only when we're tired or the sun is going down, but also under ordinary daytime and office conditions.[5]

Karin Smolders, professor at Eindhoven University of Technology in the Netherlands, received her PhD in lighting research and environmental psychology. She and other researchers conducted several field and laboratory studies to examine the influence of light exposure on feelings of vitality (alertness and energy). In the field study, they asked office employees and students to wear a light-measuring device for three consecutive days, from 8 AM to 8 PM. Every hour the participants completed several questionnaires. The researchers found that the more people were exposed to light, the more vital, alert, and energetic they felt. Smolders found similar results in a laboratory experiment. In the lab, participants were exposed to either high or low illumination in the eyes. They were asked how alert and how sleepy they were and were given several cognitive tasks. Participants not only felt more energetic and less sleepy in brighter light, but they also performed better on the cognitive tasks in higher illumination.[6]

Feeling Tired at Your Desk?

Tired at work and mental fatigue dragging you down? Try increasing the intensity of the light: make the room brighter. Within a short time, you'll notice yourself feeling more alert and energetic with greater vitality.

In sum, office lighting is important not just so we can see what we are working on; bright light also makes us more attentive, perform better, and feel more energetic. That's true not just subjectively but also in objective terms— studies show brighter light leads to a measurable rise in heart rate. So you might want to consider getting a bright new lamp for your desk. And of course, if you have a window, lift the curtain or shades, even on a gloomy day, and let the daylight in.

You may be surprised to learn the extent of influence light can have—on far more than just our well-being and productivity.

Light, Self-Awareness, and Self-Control

Sometimes we are upset and want to shout at our colleagues or boss (or our children or significant other), but then we get a grip on ourselves and hold back. We can often find ourselves in trying situations where we are caught between following our impulses and exercising restraint. We can choose to "let it all out," or we can try to behave in keeping with social expectations and norms. Some people seem to naturally possess more self-control than others. However, there are also situational variables that influence whether we will act impulsively or control ourselves.

One decisive factor is whether we are alone or in a room with other people. When we have other people around us, we tend to be more self-aware, and there is a better chance that we will curb our impulsive behavior and behave according to norms and expectations. But that's not the only cue at work.

Would you believe that we exercise more self-control in a well-lit room than in a room with dim lighting? An interesting study led by Professor Anna Steidle from the University of Applied Sciences Ludwigsburg, Germany, showed just that.[7] Based on a series of experiments, the researchers found that light and brightness influenced the participants' self-awareness and self-control. In one of Steidle's team's experiments, participants were exposed to various intensities of brightness and were asked to complete a questionnaire that measured public self-awareness (e.g., "right now I am concerned about what other people think of me"), private self-awareness (e.g., "right now I am conscious of my inner feelings"), and awareness of the immediate surroundings (e.g., "right now I am keenly aware of everything in my environment"). Participants who sat in a well-lit room reported a higher rate of *public* self-awareness than those who sat in a dimly lit room, whereas no difference was found in their awareness of their inner feelings or the environment. Thus, it seems that bright light makes us more concerned about the impression we make on others.

Always Bring Things to Light

About to have a conversation or discussion at work that is liable to arouse emotional reactions such as anger? Try to hold it in a well-lit room. People tend to behave less rashly and in a more controlled, socially acceptable, and polite manner in a well-lit room.

The researchers conducted another experiment to examine the association between light and brightness and self-control. Participants believed they were involved in a marketing study. They were asked to wear either sunglasses or glasses with clear lenses and evaluate them. They then completed a seemingly unrelated questionnaire that rated the importance of goals and desires. The idea was that the more impulsive a person was in a given moment, the more importance he or she would attribute to desires, whereas those with more self-control and willpower would ascribe greater importance to duties. The findings showed that those who wore sunglasses attributed more importance to desires than those who wore clear glasses. In other words, the participants who wore clear glasses, through which they saw a more brightly lit room, felt that their responsibilities took precedence over whims and desires, which translates into more regulated and self-controlled behavior. The same phenomenon holds true for the workplace, where there's the occasional urge (and more frequent daydream) to let it all out—shout at our boss or a colleague and give them a piece of our mind. Clearly and despite the temptation, we naturally prefer to maintain control and hold ourselves back. It seems that a well-lit room is the best medium for exercising self-control, which, in the workplace, is a good thing.

Light and Choices

Have you ever found yourself facing a choice between what you want and what you need? We've all been there. We might dream about buying a flashy red sports car, but we know that what we really need is a family vehicle. In other words, we often have to choose between a product that provides us with functional or practical characteristics and a product that may be impractical but enjoyable. Or you might want to spend your free time watching a silly sitcom, but you know that you'd be making better use of your time reading a book or watching a documentary. Or eating ice cream even though you know that it is better to have a healthy shake or fruit.

These types of decisions are called hedonic versus utilitarian choices. The hedonic choices are those that you actually want to do, to enjoy, that are fun and exciting, while the utilitarian choices are those that are more functional, practical, and effective.[8] At work we often have tasks that are not enjoyable, or are boring or tedious, but that need to be done. At such times we might also have other tasks that await us, which we enjoy or find far more interesting.

However, we have to do both and sometimes have to force ourselves to work on the less desirable but necessary tasks.

Apparently, light can influence your choices. A group of researchers examined whether the level of light in the room influences consumers' decisions: In what conditions do we choose what we want, rather than what we feel we should or what other people expect us to?[9] The researchers divided 180 participants into two groups. One group sat in a room with no lights except for a computer screen; the other group sat in a well-lit room. Participants were asked to decide between utilitarian (practical and functional) and hedonic (enjoyable and fun) options. The choices were between a mobile app for work and a mobile app for entertainment, a documentary film and a love drama, a durable laptop and a high-end laptop, and a competent job candidate and a fun job candidate. Participants were also asked to respond on a scale from 1 to 9 to statements such as: "I feel I am free to decide for myself how to live my life," "I feel I can be myself in my daily situations," and "I feel that nobody can tell me what to do." The findings are extremely interesting. Participants who sat in the dark room made more hedonic choices than those sitting in the bright room. They also expressed greater self-authenticity; they responded that they can be themselves, live their life the way they want, and nobody can tell them what to do, more than those sitting in the bright room. The researchers suggest that darkness makes people feel disconnected and distant from others, increases the feeling that they can be themselves and do what they want, and care less about what is expected of them to do. Consequently, they make more hedonic choices.

These findings have significant implications on the personal and the consumer level. If you want to choose what you really want, without thinking of what is expected of you, dim the room, but if you want to make the more practical choices, light up the room. These findings also have direct implications for consumer-oriented businesses. If you want your customers to make more hedonic choices, dim the store lighting. If you want them to focus on the more practical and efficient products, turn up the light!

These results also have direct applications to the work environment. They suggest that a brightly lit setting will motivate workers to adopt behaviors that impress those around them rather than behaviors that might be judged harshly.

Generally, this is a good thing. We want employers and employees to be less impulsive in their interactions with each other and to adopt ethical behavior. An exception is the effect of light on creativity, which we will talk about later on.

So Let There Be Light!

Light is a mood booster that makes us more alert and energetic. In well-lit environments, people perform better and, surprising as it may sound, they will be more self-aware, and therefore more in control and less impulsive.

The Dark Side: Light and Ethical Behavior

We have seen how important light is to get work done and do it well. But light, or more specifically the lack of it, is also related to ethical behavior. Professor Chen-Bo Zhong from the Rotman School of Management, University of Toronto, has conducted many important studies on environmental factors that influence our behavior, including ethical behavior.

Light is associated with safety, and indeed, more crimes are committed under the cover of darkness, when there is less chance of being caught. When people believe they can't be seen, they might have more of a tendency to engage in unethical behavior. However, a study by Zhong and his colleagues showed that people behave less ethically in a darker environment than in a well-lit room, even when in both cases they are sure that they can't be seen and can't be caught.[10] More specifically, the researchers showed that when the lights are dim or when people wear sunglasses, they are more inclined to cheat than when they sat in a well-lit room.

In the first experiment, the researchers recruited eighty-four students from the university and divided them into two groups. One group sat in a very bright room with twelve fluorescent lights, while the other group sat in a room with only four fluorescent lights. All participants were then administered a simple math task; they were shown several matrices with three-digit numbers and were given five minutes to find pairs that added up to ten. The participants were given an envelope with ten dollars and were told to take fifty cents for each pair of numbers that they correctly found. The researchers let the participants check their answers. The participants thought that there was no way to know whether they cheated or not. However, without the participants' knowledge, the researchers could compare their actual performance to their reported performance. They found that those who sat in the dim room cheated significantly more than those who sat in the bright room, but there was no difference in how they did on the math task. Remember, the room was not completely dark, and in both conditions the participants could be seen. Nevertheless, they cheated more in a dimmer room.

In a second experiment, the researchers examined the influence of darkness on fairness and generosity. They divided participants into two groups and asked one group to wear sunglasses while the other group wore clear glasses. They were given six dollars and were asked to divide it any way they wanted with a partner. Of course, if they were fair, they should have divided it equally and given their partner three dollars. If they were completely selfish they could take the whole sum for themselves. The researchers found those who wore sunglasses gave a smaller amount, on average, than those who wore clear glasses. In another study conducted in Taiwan,[11] the researchers divided participants into three groups in rooms with high-, medium-, or low-level lighting. The participants were told that they were each playing a game with another person who was sitting in a different room. They received a certain amount of money and could decide how much to give the other person. They found that the brighter the room, the more money participants offered the other person, the more ethical and fair the behavior. In another experiment, they found that participants in a well-lit room donated more money. These studies show that in general, people behave more ethically or in a way that is more considerate toward other people in a well-lit room.

It seems that darkness gives license to unethical behavior. That may also hold true even when someone is alone in a room, sending an email, or writing a report and is sure nobody can see him or her.

Don't Be Shady

If companies want their workers to be more generous and fair, they should turn up the light. This is true also in negotiations and various interactions. If you are negotiating with another person and you want her or him to be fair and generous, make sure not to sit in a dim room. People behave more ethically and are more generous when their actions are "exposed to the light of day," both metaphorically and in point of fact.

The association between light and darkness and ethical behavior goes both ways. Not only do people behave less ethically in a darker environment, but when they think of an unethical behavior from their past, they perceive the environment they are in as darker. In one study,[12] participants were asked to recall and describe either an unethical or an ethical deed from their past. They were then asked to judge the brightness of the room they were sitting in while remembering. Those who recalled unethical actions perceived the room as darker than those who recalled ethical actions. That is, their physical perception was influenced by whether they did something unethical or ethical.

These findings are one more example of how, without our awareness, our physical environment influences and regulates our behavior. In this case, it is the intensity of the light in the room that affects our self-control, our choices, our generosity, and our ethical behavior. In other words, whether or not we behave in a more socially acceptable manner depends not only on personal characteristics and the social context, but it's also influenced by a seemingly irrelevant factor—the level of light in the room. At the workplace, make sure that at least part of the time you are working in a bright room. As we have seen from the studies in this chapter, a brighter room will make you more alert and allow you to get more work done. Moreover, teams will work better in a brighter room; they will be more considerate, listen to others, and will behave more ethically.

3

I Am Too Cold, I Am Too Hot
The Impact of Temperature

It doesn't matter what temperature the room is,
it's always room temperature.
—STEVEN WRIGHT

Temperature is widely perceived as one of the most important factors in workplace comfort, and studies show that temperature affects well-being, motivation, and productivity.[1] We are usually very conscious of the temperature; it's a typical topic of conversation, and we complain if it is too hot or too cold. Studies that compared responses to light, humidity, and temperature found that workers were more sensitive to room temperature than to light and humidity. There are of course differences between people, and temperature is a subjective sensation that changes from person to person and varies with age, clothing, window location, and mood.

Heat stress has a greater influence on our performance than cold stress. Peter Hancock, a professor at the University of Central Florida, found that when the environment we work in is too hot, it's not only bad for our health, it also affects our ability to work well.[2] Our bodies have greater tolerance for cold than for heat.[3] The question is how the temperature affects our performance: What is the optimal range of temperatures for best performance in the workplace?

Workers in buildings with a central thermostat often argue about the temperature. These disagreements may create an unpleasant work environment, like they did for the friend I mentioned in chapter 1. An article published in the *Globe and Mail* tells the story of a woman who was always cold at work.[4] Her boss's office was controlled by the same thermostat as her workspace, and he did not let her turn the heat up. This created a lot of tension between the two, until her boss finally allowed her to bring in a space heater. This was not an ideal solution, and she still felt very uncomfortable. This is not an unusual case.

It is very difficult to please everyone. A 2015 survey conducted in the United States found that 56 percent of the workers thought their office was too cold in the winter and 42 percent thought their office was too warm in the summer.[5] Nevertheless, there is still an optimal range of temperatures for best performance in the workplace.

Temperature and Performance

Beyond the comfort factor, how does temperature influence our performance? Many studies have examined this question and compared performance on various tasks at different temperature levels. Most of these studies were conducted within the range of around 60°F to 80°F (15°C to 26°C), which is typical in work environments. Findings showed that the best performance was between around 68°F (20°C) and 72°F (22°C).[6] Olli Seppänen, a professor at the Department of Civil Engineering at Aalto University in Helsinki, Finland, investigated the influence of indoor temperature on workers. Seppänen and his colleagues reviewed twenty-four studies, some conducted at the workplace and some in the laboratory. Studies conducted at the workplace measured, for example, the time it took the participants to talk with a customer. Studies conducted in the laboratory gave participants tasks similar to those given at work, measuring speed and accuracy of their performance. The researchers found that performance increased with temperature levels up to 70°F to 72°F (21°C to 22°C), and then dropped when the temperature was above 73°F (23°C).[7] It's not surprising that this study was conducted in Finland, where the winter is very cold and temperatures range between -22°C and -3°C (-7.6°F and 26.6°F). In cold countries, workers tend to heat the rooms, and this study shows that too much heat has a negative influence on performance.

A study conducted at Cornell concluded that there is a clear association between performance in the workplace and temperature.[8] The comfort zone within which performance improved was between 68°F and 77°F (20°C and 25°C), and workers made 44 percent more errors than when they worked in a temperature that was not in the comfort zone. Several researchers developed models that quantify the association between certain ventilation rates or temperatures and workers' sick leave or performance.[9]

A study conducted by researchers from the University of Virginia and the University of Houston showed that warm temperature has a negative influence only on the performance of complex tasks that demand cognitive effort.[10] Participants who sat in a cool room (67°F/19°C) performed better on complex tasks than those who sat in a warm room (77°F/25°C), but the room temperature did not influence the performance in less complex tasks.

Other studies conducted by researchers from the Finnish Institute of Occupational Health, which specializes in well-being at work, showed that high temperatures (around 83°F/29°C) have a negative influence on the performance of some tasks, but not on others.[11] The researchers gave participants several tasks that require different skills such as attention, psychomotor performance, alertness, and long-term memory. The most difficult of these was the N-back task, a memory task that's more complex than just repeating words. Participants are presented with sequences of letters and are then asked whether the letter was identical to the one from n steps earlier. The task has several difficulty levels; in 1-back, for example, the participant has to state whether the letter is identical to the one presented immediately before it, while in 3-back, they are asked if the letter is identical to the one presented three trials back. The researchers found that the only task with poorer performance in warmer temperatures was the N-back memory task, which was also the most complex. The other tasks that required psychomotor performance, attention, and long-term memory were not affected by the temperature.

However, while a slightly warm temperature (83°F/28°C) did not influence participants' actual performance on some tasks, it did have a negative effect on subjective measures like comfort, fatigue, and perceived workload. Participants who sat in a warmer room felt more tired and less comfortable and felt the work was more difficult than those who sat in a cooler room—even when the performance level was the same in both rooms. These results suggest that in warmer temperatures, work takes more of an effort, and people expend more energy to achieve the same results. Consequently, even when the temperature does not influence performance, it might have an influence on subsequent work due to accumulating fatigue.

We can conclude that the optimal temperature for work is around 70°F to 72°F (21°C to 22°C). Within the range of moderately cold and moderately warm (60°F to 80°F/15°C to 26°C), cognitive performance suffers more when it is too warm than when it is too cold, and complex tasks are more affected than simple tasks.

What about individual differences? What is comfortable and pleasant for one person can be too cold or too warm for another. (And of course, that's true almost everywhere you could go, not just at work. At the start of almost every Pilates class I go to, there are disagreements about whether the room is too hot or too cold. Sometimes the arguments get quite heated—if you'll excuse the pun.) A study conducted by researchers from Leiden University, the Netherlands, found that within the range of moderately cold and moderately warm temperatures, subjective temperature (how the room temperature feels to you) is more important than objective temperature (the actual measurement of degrees).[12] The researchers simply asked participants if they prefer warm or cold temperatures and divided them into two groups—those who prefer warm temperatures and those who prefer it cooler. Participants were asked to complete several tasks in two temperatures levels, around 59°F (15°C) and around 77°F (25°C). The participants who preferred warm temperatures performed better in the warmer room, and those who preferred cold temperatures performed better in the cooler room. In other words, within the range of moderately cold and warm temperatures, people know better what is good for them. (These results do not contradict the findings that very warm temperature has a negative influence on performance.)

Gender and Temperature Preferences

I often serve on committees and in board meetings where most of the participants are men. I usually find the room to be cold, especially in the middle of summer when people tend to blast the air conditioner to full freeze. Over the years I've learned to always bring a sweater with me and put it on when I enter the room. If it were up to me, I would raise the temperature in the room, but I notice that most people (men) in the room seem comfortable. Well, apparently, I'm not the only one who suffers this way. Many articles in the popular media, including the *New York Times*, the *Washington Post*, the *Telegraph*, and the *Atlantic*, have discussed the fact that office buildings are too cold for women. As Monica Hesse wrote in the *Washington Post*, "men, in this country's view, are the default temperature setters."[13]

The American Society of Heating, Refrigerating and Air-Conditioning Engineers defines thermal comfort as "that condition of mind that expresses satisfaction with the thermal environment and is assessed by subjective evaluation."[14] This thermal comfort is influenced by various factors, and one of them is gender. Indeed, several studies show that there are gender differences in thermal comfort. Finnish researcher Sami Karjalainen compared the results of many studies that examined men's and women's thermal comfort.[15] This is called a meta-analysis study. The review included both field and laboratory studies from many countries with very different climates such as Australia, Finland, Switzerland, Taiwan, and North America. The field studies were conducted at office and residential buildings, classrooms of schools and universities, commercial buildings, and homes of the elderly. The laboratory studies were conducted in the laboratory where the temperature could be manipulated. Most studies found that women express more dissatisfaction than men in the same thermal conditions. Women were also more sensitive to deviations from the optimal temperature and were especially dissatisfied in colder temperatures. For example, one study conducted in office buildings in the United States found that women were significantly less satisfied with the temperature level in the summer, but not in the winter.[16] Similar results were found by a later study conducted in 2018 in three office buildings in Brazil.[17] A study conducted in Japan found that about 30 percent of women suffer from cold syndrome, while it is rarely found in men.[18]

How can we explain this difference?

Heat production in humans depends on several components: One of them is basal metabolic rate (BMR), which is a function of age, gender, body composition, and body size. Women have lower BMRs compared to men and, therefore, usually have lower heat production. Women also have lower body mass and higher BSA/body mass (body surface area to body mass ratio), which means that there is a lower heat generation.

As explained by two Dutch researchers, office thermostats were designed from a model developed in the 1960s "based on an average male, and may overestimate female metabolic rate by up to 35%."[19] Nowadays, when about half of the people in the office are women, we need to change the model so it will include metabolic rates of females and males as well as body tissue parameters.

Some Like It Hot

Studies show that women are more affected and more sensitive to indoor thermal environments than men. Moreover, women are more satisfied and productive in higher temperatures. Setting the thermostat in the workplace to a higher temperature than the current standard in many places will make things more comfortable for women and increase their productivity, with only a negligible decrease, if any, in the productiveness and satisfaction of males. Another consideration (aside from common consideration) is the cost of overcooled buildings—in energy, money, and to the environment.[20]

Low temperatures in office buildings not only influence the comfort of women, but also their productivity. A study published in 2019 examined the influence of temperature on cognitive performance of men and women.[21] The researchers gave 543 participants a set of math and verbal tasks in different temperatures that varied from 61.14°F to 90.6°F (16.19°C to 32.57°C). They found that women performed better in the warmer temperatures while men performed better in the colder temperatures. However, the increase in women's performance was significantly larger than the decrease in men's performance.

Temperature and Decision-Making

About a year ago I had to make a decision about how to invest a certain amount of money. I was sitting in the office of an investment consultant who gave me several options, and I was trying to decide which one was the best for me. It was not easy since there were several factors I had to consider carefully. I had to decide what risk I was willing to take, understand the financial products, and find the appropriate mix and diversity. I needed to consider my entire portfolio before reaching a decision and choosing the best plan. It was a hot summer day, and the consultant apologized that the air-conditioning in the office had stopped working earlier. I was looking at the papers, trying to systematically examine the pros and cons of each plan, and it felt like an impossible task. I had two options: I could just decide based on what I had been able to process in the hot room, or I could go home and make the decision another day. I was smart enough to leave and not make any decisions that day.

Studies show that, indeed, when we are too warm, it is difficult for us to systematically consider all the options in complex decisions. In one study, marketing researchers Amar Cheema and Vanessa Patrick put participants in two rooms; one was moderately cold, at 67°F (19°C), and the other was moderately warm, at 77°F (25°C).[22] Participants were presented with two cell phone plans and were asked to pick the best plan. The plans were complex, and participants needed to examine them carefully and calculate the cost of each plan in order to realize that one was better and less expensive than the other and provided more free minutes. The participants who sat in the warmer room picked the better plan significantly *less* frequently than those who sat in the cooler room. It seems that even moderate heat depletes and exhausts our available resources and makes it more difficult for us to consider all the options. High temperatures take a toll and we pay a mental price. In high temperatures, we have fewer mental resources for more complicated cognitive functions, such as decision-making. Consequently, we might make decisions that are based on only one aspect of the problem. Focusing on a single aspect is faster and easier but may often lead to irrational choices. Similar phenomena happen with lack of sleep or when we work nonstop and our cognitive resources are exhausted.

Temperature for Best Performance— Avoid the Extremes

Make sure that your workspace is at an optimal temperature (68°F to 72°F/20°C to 22°C). Don't work in a room that is too warm or too cold. A cold room will make you feel uncomfortable and will affect your performance. A warmer room might feel cozy but will decrease your performance, make you feel tired, and might even sabotage your decisions by not allowing you to consider all aspects of a problem.

Temperature and Conformity

Research shows that physical temperature can influence our judgments and emotions. Studies found associations between physical warmth and social warmth, and they showed that metaphors such as "warm personality" and "warm relationships" are more than just a nice way to enrich the language. For example, in a highly cited study published in the prestigious journal *Science*, marketing professor Lawrence Williams and social psychologist John Bargh demonstrated that people who held a warm cup of coffee tended to perceive others as being nicer, warmer people and were friendlier and more generous.[23] Studies also found that those who touched a warmer object trusted others more.[24] A later study conducted in Germany found that people in warmer temperatures feel more similar to others.[25] Warm temperatures increase connection among people,[26] while cold temperatures increase the feeling of loneliness.[27] I discussed these studies in my book *Sensation*,[28] and I showed how the physical sensation of warm temperature activates warm and generous behavior. Here I want to examine how the physical sensation of warmth is related to our behavior in the work/business world.

If indeed physical warmth increases perceived similarity and closeness, does it also increase conformity? We know that some people are more conforming than others, but is it possible that it also depends on the temperature of the room?

A study conducted by a group of researchers from China and Hong Kong addressed this question.[29] In a series of experiments, the researchers found that people in a warmer room perceived the opinions of others as being more valid and were more willing to conform to those opinions, as opposed to people in a colder room. In one experiment, one group of participants sat in a room that was comfortably warm, while the other group sat in a room that was comfortably cool. Each participant was presented with three pairs of items: two sofas, two bicycles, and two handheld GPS devices. The participants were told the market share of each item and then were asked to choose one from each pair. One of the products in each pair had a higher market share than the other, meaning that it was purchased by more people. The participants in the warm room showed more conformity and were more likely to choose the products that were bought by more people, compared to those in the cold room.

In a second experiment, researchers examined conformity in a financial context. They told MBA students that they were participating in a study on stock forecasting. They were assigned to either a comfortably warm room or a comfortably cool room. They were then shown six graphs that illustrated changes in the price of a stock over eight time periods. The graphs were randomly drawn by a computer. The participants had to say whether they should buy or sell each stock. Since they wanted to make a profit, they were told that if they expected the price of the stock to rise in the next period they should buy, and if they thought the price would decrease in the next period they should sell. Participants were told that those who predicted correctly would receive a monetary prize.

Half of the participants were shown the choices most participants had made in an earlier session of the same experiment. They were told that the majority of the participants in the previous session predicted that the price of three of the stocks would increase and the price of the three others would decrease. The other half were not told the answers of others. The results were surprising. Participants were more influenced by the decisions of others regarding the stocks when the temperature in the room was comfortably warm than when it was comfortably cool. For the group that was not told anyone else's opinion, there was no difference between the warm and the cool room. Similar results were found when participants were asked to imagine that they were at a racetrack and could bet on a horse. Participants were more likely to bet on favorite horses when they were in a warm room than when they were in a cold room. The researchers suggested that warmer temperatures increased feelings of closeness and therefore increased conformity and influenced decision-making.

This need to belong and befriend others when in a warm temperature is also evidenced in the way subjects answer questionnaires. A study showed that people who sat in a warmer room were more likely to agree with what they believed was the experimenter's intent, rather than answering what they really thought.[30]

Warm temperature not only increases conformity, it also increases the value we assign to products.[31] Researchers placed participants in two rooms with different temperatures: 64°F (18°C) and 79°F (26°C). The participants were presented with photos of various products that students typically purchase, such as a cup of coffee, a CD, or Dove body wash, and were asked how much they were willing to pay for each of them. Participants in the warmer room were willing to pay more for the products than those in the cooler room.

Get Them to Warm Up to You

If you want people to feel closeness and intimacy and as a result conform more to your suggestions and decisions, increase the temperature in the room. A warmer room can help you in a negotiation in terms of getting the other party to agree and conform to your opinions. Similarly, if you are selling something, make sure the room is warm enough and comfortable. By doing so, it is more likely that the buyer will like your product.

Clearly, physical temperature has an influence on our performance, especially on complex tasks and decisions. Warmer temperatures exhaust our resources and decrease our ability to consider the various aspects of a problem or to concentrate. Within the optimal range of 68°F and 72°F (20°C and 22°C), subjective feeling might have more of an influence than objective feeling. If you can control the temperature in your office, make it comfortable but not too warm. If you can't control it and you feel it is too cold or too warm, bring appropriate clothes so you can control and change your subjective feeling.

Temperature doesn't just affect our performance, it has deeper psychological consequences than you might think. If ambient temperature can increase conformity, intensify the need to belong and connect, and therefore influence decision-making, this could be very useful information with direct implications for negotiations, marketing, and group discussions. In discussion groups, when we want to reach the best solution and hear other opinions that might challenge our own, we do not want others to easily conform and to automatically agree with us. In this case, a comfortably cool room is better. If, on the other hand, we want to convince others to agree with us and make similar decisions, then a comfortably warm room would be a more conducive environment. A moderately warmer temperature could also lead to more purchases, so the next time you go shopping, you might want to keep in mind that if you're feeling a bit warm, you might end up making more purchases than you expected!

As you can see, environmental factors such as temperature and light in the office and the office layout (whether it is a closed or open space, etc.) influence productivity and happiness at the workplace, which is a key factor in the success of an organization. Dissatisfied employees are less productive. Moreover, the physical environment has an influence on various behaviors that are seemingly unrelated to these factors, such as conformity or ethical behavior.

Organizations should put a great deal of thought into designing the physical environment and in decisions regarding ambient temperatures and light. Attention to these factors in the workspace will benefit both the orga-nization and its employees, maximizing not only employee satisfaction but also their performance.

As for you, the individual worker, be more aware of how your environment may affect you and, as much as is possible, try to implement changes in it. If you can have them, keeping a small heater or fan at your workstation may help you to work better, even when the office isn't set up ideally. Also be more aware of the influence of the physical environment on your behavior, negotiations, and judgments. Use it for your own benefit.

Attention to these work-space factors will benefit both the organization and its employees.

4

Take a Walk in Nature

The Influence of Green
and Blue Spaces

Flowers are restful to look at. They have neither
emotions nor conflicts.
—SIGMUND FREUD

I often take walks along the beach early in the morning or in the late after-noon after work. I am not the only one. I see many people walking along the beach, enjoying the blue water and the sounds of white-crested waves crashing toward shore. And to view the sun setting on the horizon, above the distant glimmering water—what a blessing to be able to do that! I remember meeting one of my neighbors walking along the beach who pointed at the water and said, "This is my psychiatrist." Over the years I've heard this and similar remarks from other people, in different places and at different times and in different natural settings. "It keeps me sane," or "It's the best medicine," or "It helps me cope." As a psychologist and a researcher, that made me think.

Most of us know that natural settings are agreeable and good for us. But in what way? Well, now the science is in.

Many studies have examined the effects of nature on stress, mood, positivity, and cognitive performance as well as nature's restorative effects and whatever other benefits might be found.

The results are quite clear. We can now say with confidence that nature is good for all of the above, and that we can tap into its benefits in different (and surprising) ways that are easy, accessible, and virtually cost free. Pretty much anyone can instantly improve the quality of their life at work (and at home) through exposure to nature.

Discover Your Better Nature

Stress is a widespread phenomenon in Western society and work is one—if not the leading—source of stress for adults. Study after study confirms the detrimental effects of stress on our lives—on our bodies, on our minds, on our behaviors, even our looks; short-term stress can cause headaches, chest pains, tense muscles, upset stomachs, insomnia, negative moods, angry outbursts, overeating, substance abuse, and more. The World Health Organization has called stress "the health epidemic of the 21st century," and implicated stress in a host of serious ailments including cardiovascular disease (high blood pressure, heart disease, arrhythmia, heart attack, stroke), depression, anxiety, eating disorders, skin and hair problems, gastrointestinal problems, and sexual dysfunction.

Work-related stress can be caused by a number of factors including pressure and high demands, lack of control, tense relationships with colleagues and bosses, worries over job security, and fears of being fired—these and others are unfortunately too common for workers these days. On the job, stress is the culprit for absenteeism, lack of focus, mental and physical fatigue, decreased productivity, and burnout. Moreover, the World Health Organization estimates that depression and anxiety disorders cost the economy $1 trillion a year in lost productivity.[1] This estimate is based on missed workdays as a result of stress, direct compensations, and insurance costs (health-care costs are higher for workers who report that they are stressed), and on the fact that stressed employees do not function at their optimal ability when they do come to work.

I hope the above is enough to convince you that if you have excessive stress in your life, you absolutely need to do something about it. Commonly recommended techniques for managing stress include meditation, mindfulness, exercising, getting enough sleep, deep-breathing exercises, yoga, and seeking professional help. All are no doubt effective and highly worthwhile; we will discuss some of them in other chapters of this book. What's less often recommended? A healthy dose of exposure to nature. Studies show that being in nature is not only an aesthetically satisfying experience, it is scientifically proven to reduce stress, and in a number of surprising ways that make it available to pretty much every person.

A number of studies sought to test the effects, psychological and physiological, of taking a walk in nature as compared to being in an urban environment. In several studies conducted in Japan,[2] researchers compared the influence of forest and urban environments on stress. The studies examined the effects of *Shinrin-Yoku,* or the practice of "forest bathing." This term was coined in 1982 by the Japanese Ministry of Agriculture, Forestry and Fisheries to describe making contact with the forest, taking in the forest atmosphere. Participants were brought to either a forest area or city area. Researchers took several physiological measures from the participants before and after they spent time in either the forest or in the urban environment, including heart rate, blood pressure, and concentration levels of salivary cortisol (the "stress hormone"—a higher level indicates more stress). In a particularly unique study,[3] researchers went to twenty-four different forests and to a city environment to examine 280 participants. In each round of the study, twelve participants were divided into two groups of six and brought to either a forest or city environment, where they spent one day before swapping environments for the second day. Before arriving at a particular site, participants were measured for stress levels (cortisol, heart rate, blood pressure). After they spent fifteen minutes at the site, researchers measured these stress levels again, and once more after the participants took a sixteen-minute walk in the surroundings. They found that the forest environment reduced stress. Those who spent time in the forest had lower levels of cortisol, lower pulse rates, and lower blood pressure than those who spent time in the city environment. Similar stress-reducing effects were found from just viewing or walking in the forest.

In a study published in 2018,[4] researchers from Sichuan Agricultural University in China asked sixty participants to walk for fifteen minutes in either a bamboo forest or in a city area. Here, the researchers took before and after measurements of blood pressure and electrical brain activity (EEG) and administered a psychological test measuring participants' attention. Similarly to previous studies, blood pressure significantly decreased for those who walked in the bamboo forest. There were also changes in the brain waves as shown in the EEG, which indicated mental relaxation during the forest walk. In addition, there was an increase in attention for those who walked in the forest but not for those who walked in the city—we'll take a look at these effects later on in this chapter.

A study conducted on the West Coast led by researchers from Stanford University replicated and extended previous studies.[5] Participants were asked to take a fifty-minute walk in either a natural or downtown environment near Stanford, California. Before and after the walk, each subject completed several cognitive tasks and then filled out questionnaires that assessed positive and negative feelings and emotions including anxiety and rumination. The results clearly showed the benefits of a nature walk as compared to walking in an urban environment. Those who took a stroll in nature exhibited lessened anxiety and a decrease in negative emotions, including rumination, as compared with those who walked downtown. As for cognitive performance, a number of cognitive tasks improved after the nature walk while none improved after the downtown walk.

But must it be a forest that we go to for stress relief? Does it matter to which natural environment we are exposed? Natural environments come in different shapes and degrees of "naturalness"—there are also beaches, lakes, mountains, and even city parks. Do they all have similar effects on stress?

In a study published in the *International Journal of Environmental Research and Public Health*,[6] researchers compared the effects of nature and city areas on stress, but unlike previous studies in this area, they varied the nature settings and city settings. Participants were asked to visit four different locations. Two were natural settings that included trees and plants—one virtually untouched by humans and the other with evident signs of human influence, for example, with distant buildings in view. The two other destinations were urban environments, one somewhat built up and the other highly developed. Participants' stress levels were determined via saliva samples that measured cortisol level, as well as a questionnaire that tabulated self-report of different facets of stress. Similar to what previous studies found, exposure to nature reduced stress (as measured both subjectively by self-reporting and objectively by concentration of cortisol). No significant differences were found among the varying degrees of "naturalness" of the nature settings. In other words, a walk in a park near your office can help you combat stress just as a walk in a remote forest would.

Power Up with Some Green Energy

Nature offers so much more than beauty. Work and life are often stressful. Taking breaks during work and taking walks in nature are great ways to recover from mental fatigue and to improve performance. Even when you are busy at work, try to find the time to take a walk outside, preferably in a natural setting. It doesn't have to be in a forest or near a lake or a beach, a simple stroll in a park or any other spot that has trees, grass, or flowers will do. If you are able to hear the birds chirping or see a pond, that's a bonus. You'll be amazed how relaxed you feel upon returning to the office, with renewed forces and energy. A respite in nature, even a short one, does wonders to clear your mind and recharge your batteries, thus setting you up for increased productivity and a better mood.

Sometimes You Gotta Have the Blues

Nature is not only green space such as parks, forests, and woodlands. It is also blue space: oceans, lakes, rivers, and waterfalls. Most of us love to be near water, to listen to the waves and gaze at the sea. People are willing to pay between 8 percent to 12 percent more for a house with water views,[7] and hotels charge more for a room with an ocean view. Many people like to go to the beach and just watch the waves, claiming that this is their therapy. Most of the studies that investigated the influence of nature on our well-being focused on green spaces, but growing numbers of studies have examined the influence of blue spaces.

A group of researchers from the United Kingdom presented participants with 120 photos that depicted natural and built areas.[8] Half of the photos contained elements of water. They found that photographs of green nature or built environments that also contained water were perceived as having more restorative value, were preferred more, and aroused a more positive effect than those without water. Photographs of built environments with water were rated similar to photographs of nature. In other words, green spaces and blue spaces have similar positive effects.

Several studies conducted in different countries found that proximity to blue space reduced stress and was positively related to well-being. For example, a study conducted in two German cities, Cologne and Dusseldorf, both located along the Rhine River, found that people who walk along the promenade reported emotional attachment to the place and said that it helped them reduce their stress.[9] Two other studies, a recent one conducted in 2019 in Hong Kong and another one conducted in New Zealand, found similar results. Living in a neighborhood in proximity to and with views of blue space and intentionally visiting blue spaces were related to better subjective well-being.[10]

To reach a more general conclusion, a group of Spanish scholars conducted systematic research and reviewed thirty studies that examined the influence of blue space. Indeed, they also found a positive association between exposure to blue space and mental health and well-being.[11]

A study by two British researchers addressed the question of the association between blue space and well-being in a different and unique way.[12] They developed a smartphone app that recorded people's location by GPS. They approached the participants at various random moments and presented them with a subjective well-being questionnaire, while recording their location. The questionnaire included inquiries about satisfaction with their life and their mood and emotions at that moment. The researchers collected one million responses from more than twenty thousand participants. The results showed that when people were in natural settings they were happier than when they were in an urban environment, and the happiest locations were marine and coastal areas.

It seems then that both green and blue spaces contribute to well-being and mental health. Both are therapeutic, induce calmness, and help to reduce stress and anxiety.

Try the Blue One

If you feel stressed and anxious, try to go to an outdoor blue space such as the ocean, a river, or a lake. Take a walk along the sea or the river, or just sit and view the water. You will be amazed how restorative it will be and how calmer and happier you will feel.

An Office with a View

What about simply *viewing* nature? A study conducted in South Korea investigated the association between having a window view of nature (in this case, a forested area), job satisfaction, and job stress.[13] The participants were 931 office workers, both management and clerical, 481 of whom sat near a window with a view of the forest, while the other 450 could not see the forest or any other natural setting from their windows. The employees were given several questionnaires measuring job satisfaction and job-related stress based on factors including their relationships with colleagues and supervisors, uncomfortable job demands (working late, job overload, etc.), and role issues such as unclear responsibilities. The results clearly showed correlations: Those who sat in an office with a window view of the forest were less stressed and more satisfied with their jobs compared to those who could not see a forest from their window.

Still, there is hope for those who can't see nature from their workspaces. Another study headed by Agnes Van den Berg, a pioneer and leading researcher in the field of environmental psychology, compared the effects of a walk through four different environments on reducing stress, inducing restoration (from depleted emotional and cognitive resources), and elevating one's mood.[14] However, the walks were *imaginary*—a succession of PowerPoint slides shown to participants who were asked to vividly visualize their particular walk by focusing on the photos in the slides.

The experiment began with the researchers showing the participants a particularly terrifying film clip to induce stress. Next, the researchers showed each participant one of four PowerPoint presentations, each taking the viewer on a simulated walk through a different environment: a city street with no vegetation; a well-tended park; a woodland park; and a wild, wooded environment. Before and after the simulated walk, participants answered questions that measured their moods and restorative states, responding to statements such as "My mind is not invaded by stressful thoughts"; "I can make space to think about my problems"; "I'm able to take time out from a busy life"; or "I can leave all my problems behind me."

Similarly to previous studies of actual walks, participants on *imaginary* walks in natural environments recovered more from stress, were in better moods, and reported increased restoration as compared with those who "walked" in the urban environments. Interestingly, there was no difference in the effects of the three nature settings, despite their varying degrees of naturalness. These results suggest that nature, no matter the specific setting, positively contributes to stress relief, restoration, and a better mood. What is also exciting in my mind is that one doesn't need to physically visit a natural setting in order to find stress relief; it is enough to simply view or imagine walking through the setting.

So, if you were thinking, *But what if I don't have the time to go out?* or *What if I work smack in the middle of a concrete jungle with no nature in sight?*—not to worry. If you can't take a break to walk in nature, either because you do not have enough time or there is no natural setting nearby, simply view photos of nature or imagine taking a walk. You simply need to enter the search term "virtual hike" on the internet to instantly "get away from it all" and relieve stress and recover.

Sounds of Nature

Not only does viewing, walking in, or imagining nature reduce stress and aid restoration, but just *listening* to nature sounds helps. In one study conducted in Sweden,[15] researchers investigated the effects of various sounds on recovery from stress. Participants were given a stressful arithmetic task while researchers measured their skin conductance level (SCL) and heart rate variability (HRV), which are indicators of psychological recovery from stress. When recovering from stress, a subject's SCL decreases and HRV increases. After being subjected to the stressful task, participants were given a recovery period during which they listened to one of four recordings created by the researchers: a nature sound featuring tweeting birds and sounds from a fountain, road traffic at high volume, road traffic at low volume, and ambient noise from a quiet backyard—however, with the soft whirring of a home-ventilation system in the background. The results showed that the skin conductance level was lower when participants heard the nature sounds than when they heard the other three urban sounds, meaning that stress recovery was fastest when accompanied by nature sounds. (Heart rate variability did not differ significantly under all conditions.) These results suggest that after a stressful situation, physiological recovery is faster when individuals are exposed to the sounds of nature.

In a later study,[16] a group of researchers from Pennsylvania State University examined the effect of sound on stress recovery and mood enhancement, but this time in a more nuanced way. Participants were exposed to close-up footage of a surgery to cause discomfort and negative mood. Before watching the video, the participants completed a scale called the Brief Mood Introspection Scale (BMIS), which measured their affective state.[17] Participants rated sixteen different emotional words, such as *lively, tired, happy, calm, energetic,* and *sad,* on a four-point scale, where 1 meant "do not feel" and 4 meant "definitely feel." After viewing the disturbing video, participants were asked to listen to one of the four audio scenarios: natural sounds consisting of birdsong and rustling leaves, natural sounds with motorized noises in the background, natural sounds with human voices in the background, and a control group that heard no sound. Then they were once again given the BMIS questionnaire to assess their moods and affective states. Those who listened to the pure nature sounds experienced the greatest mood and stress recovery of all the groups.

In today's world, one merely needs to have a pair of earphones and a cell phone to instantly reap the benefits of nature sounds. There are plenty of online podcasts and clips that play nonstop sounds of beaches, rain forests, babbling brooks, jungles, and the like. So after a stressful or negative situation, you can plug yourself into the sounds of nature for effective stress relief and mood enhancement.

It turns out that nature is a scientifically proven stress reducer. You can walk in it, look at it, listen to it, or even take an imaginary hike in it in order to reap the benefits. It costs nothing and is accessible to each person in one form or another. Given the pervasiveness and destructiveness of stress, it would be wise to incorporate the benefits of nature into your life in one way or another.

Cognitive Overload, Mental Fatigue, and Recovery

When you are performing long and effortful mental tasks, whether at work or while studying, or writing an essay or a thesis, at a certain point you realize that your efforts become more grueling and your effectiveness plummets. You reach a point where you are just treading water and all effort is futile. You've become mentally fatigued and need to recover in order to return to your task in due time and at a satisfactory level.

In a perfect world, you could take all the time you need to recover your powers. However, in the real world, mental fatigue and lack of attention can cost you dearly—at work, serious errors and falling productivity could end up costing you your job. You need to recover your powers or else. You don't have the luxury of time.

All of us suffer from mental fatigue at times, particularly on the job or when working on an important project. For some, mental fatigue is a daily affair, particularly in jobs that demand concentration. Once you are mentally fatigued, concentration, attention, and performance suffer, and you need to recover. Here, nature is a readily available and effective remedy. As the below studies bear out, nature, in one form or another, can help us recover faster from mental fatigue and restore our productive powers.

Before we move on, a few words about Attention Restoration Theory (ART). This theory explains how natural environments can have a restorative effect on attention, and how exposure to nature helps us recover from mental fatigue.[18]

According to ART, we have two types ("subsystems") of attention based on different brain functions: *directed* attention, which is voluntary and willful, and *undirected* attention, which is passive and requires no volition. Directed attention, due to its effortful nature, has a limited capacity. When working on a cognitive task that demands directed attention, at some point mental fatigue sets in and attentive resources are depleted. You feel exhausted and you need a break.

On the other hand, there is undirected attention—our ability to effortlessly absorb incoming stimuli in our waking hours. Here is where nature is absolutely the best. Nature offers captivating scenes such as sunsets, mountains, and lakes that invite us to lose ourselves in effortless, undirected attention, permitting our overchurned mental machines a much-needed respite.

In contrast, urban environments include stimuli that, whether we like it or not, commandeer our direct attention (we have to avoid cars, notice traffic lights, look at or ignore aggressive advertisements, hear sirens and industrial noise, etc.).

The following studies provide fascinating insights as to nature's versatility in restoring our mental fatigue and improving our cognitive and recuperative powers.

In one study, a group of researchers from the University of Michigan and Stanford University conducted a pair of experiments to investigate how exposure to nature influences cognitive performance.[19] In the first experiment, they asked thirty-two college students to read aloud a series of numbers and repeat them backward—a task requiring intense directed attention. Participants were then given an additional task to cause further mental fatigue. Next, the researchers asked them to take a fifty-minute walk, either in a park near the campus or in downtown Ann Arbor. After the walk, participants were again given the backward digit task. Students' performance improved after walking in nature, but not after taking a walk in the city.

Then the researchers conducted a second similar experiment. Only this time, instead of taking a walk, the students were presented with *pictures* of either nature or urban scenes and asked to view them. Before and after they viewed the pictures, participants were given several cognitive tasks, some of them requiring directed attention. Those students who viewed nature scenes improved their performance, while those who viewed urban scenes did not. The conclusion from these two experiments: Interacting with nature in one way or another improves performance in cognitive tasks that demand directed attention.

In a similar study, Rita Berto, a known researcher on environmental psychology, gave participants the Sustained Attention to Response Task (SART), in which a series of numbers appears rapidly on a computer screen and participants have to press a button when they see any number *except* for a particular target (e.g., hit the space bar when you see any number except for 3).[20] This task demands directed attention and causes mental fatigue. After performing the SART, participants were asked to look at twenty-five pictures. Half the participants viewed pictures of nature scenery such as lakes and forests, and the other half viewed pictures with no nature scenery in them. After viewing the pictures, they again were given the SART. The results were clear: Only those who were exposed to pictures of nature scenes performed well on the SART in the second round. In other words, only those who viewed nature photos restored their attention and overcame their mental fatigue, thus demonstrating the restorative power of nature to induce recovery from mental fatigue.

Just Look at the Green Garden . . . but for How Long?

How long does our "nature break" need to be to have an effect? A group of Australian researchers gave 150 students the same boring task we just discussed, the SART.[21] In the middle of the task they were told to take a very short break, only forty seconds, to view a city scene; half of the participants viewed a scene featuring a concrete roof, and the other half saw a flowering green roof. Those who viewed the flowering green roof performed significantly better on the second half of the task than those who viewed the concrete roof for the same time. Even a brief view restored their mental fatigue.

These results show that attention can improve after simply viewing nature scenes, even for a very short time in a microbreak of less than a minute. Truly amazing when you think about it.

Give Your Thoughts the Green Light

If you can't take long breaks during work, take short breaks of only a few minutes and find a green surface to look at. It can be something you see from your window (grass, trees, etc.), a plant in the office, or a picture. You'll find that you are more attentive and perform better when you return to your task.

Plants

Many offices have indoor plants on tables or on the floor for decorative purposes; occasionally, plants serve as a partition. But might they be doing more than looking pleasant and dividing a space? Several studies have examined whether indoor plants have similar effects on workers as being exposed to nature scenes.

In one study, a team of researchers from Norway and Sweden divided participants into two groups, one sitting in an office setting with four indoor plants, and the other seated in the same office setting but with no plants.[22] To start, participants were given a task called the Reading Span Test, in which ninety-six sentences appear on the computer screen in batches of four or six sentences, and participants are asked to remember the last word of each sentence. The test is a way for researchers to measure attention capacity. There was no difference between the two groups the first time the test was taken, which means there were no preexperimental differences between the plant and no-plant groups. Thus, the first measurement served as a common baseline. Then the researchers gave participants a difficult proofreading task to increase mental fatigue, and then they administered the Reading Span Test once again. Those who sat in the room with the indoor plants improved their performance in the second round, whereas those who sat in the room with no plants did not improve. The only variable that was shifted in the experiment was the presence of plants. These results suggest that the presence of plants in one's physical space improves attention recovery after performing a mentally fatiguing cognitive task.

Another study conducted in Norway sought to examine the effect of indoor plants on work-related stress, productivity, and sick leave.[23] The researchers approached employees in three office workplaces in which workers were free to personalize their areas, with or without plants, if they chose. The employees were asked questions regarding the plants in their office such as the number of plants they could see while working and the proximity of the plants to their workstations. They were also asked about their perceived stress at work, sick leave, and perceived productivity:

1. Are you satisfied with the quality of your work?
2. Are you satisfied with the amount of work you are doing?
3. Do you show responsibility for your work?
4. Do you feel creative and problem-oriented at work?

The results showed that the number of plants that were in the proximity of workers had a small but significant association with fewer sick days and higher productivity (but no such association with perceived stress). Norwegian researchers also found that employees who worked in an office without windows brought in many more indoor plants to their workspaces than those who worked in an office with windows. In addition, the windowless employees decorated their walls with three times as many pictures of nature as their windowed counterparts—more solid proof of our affinity with nature.[24]

In a study conducted in Taiwan,[25] the researchers systematically examined the influence of different views (urban or nature) and of indoor plants on physiological and psychological reactions. They showed participants six different photos of workplaces, each with a different combination of window views and plants: (1) no window, no plants; (2) no window, with plants; (3) window view of city, no plants; (4) window view of city, with plants; (5) window view of nature, no plants; and (6) window view of nature, with plants. Each image was viewed for only fifteen seconds. While the participants viewed the photos, the researchers measured their physiological reactions with various tests: EEG, which measures brain waves; EMG, which, in this case, monitored the facial muscles of the forehead; and blood volume pulse, a measure of sympathetic arousal and cardiovascular responsiveness to stress. In addition, participants completed a State Anxiety Inventory, used to measure anxiety during a certain period of time.

The results clearly showed that the different photos elicited different physiological reactions and states of anxiety. A window with a view of nature *and* indoor plants had the greatest beneficial effect. All views of nature proved more beneficial than urban views. Anxiety and stress were highest for the photos showing an office with no view and with no indoor plants.

The findings concerning the influence of indoor plants are mixed and not as decisive as the influence of outdoor nature. They do show, in many cases, the positive effects of plants in the office. Further research is needed in order to arrive at more robust conclusions. Still, if you have a mentally taxing job and your workspace has no plants, do yourself a favor. Bring in some plants. Not only might they improve your job performance and help lower stress, but they will beautify your workspace.

Make It Your Second Nature

As much as possible, bring nature into your workspace. Plants are terrific, and photos of nature scenes are great too. You might also put on earphones with ambient nature sounds. This is a wonderful technique for easing stress, relaxing your mind, and freeing it for truly productive and clear-headed thinking. All of the above will benefit you without your even feeling it. We cannot help but be at our best when exposed to nature because, evolutionarily speaking, it is where we come from and is our "home base."

The implications of these findings are significant. The work that you do can be stressful and tax your resources significantly, and science has proven that nature is a reliable stress reducer. As we've seen, a walk in nature can be greatly beneficial. Even a window view of nature can have a restorative effect and enhance cognitive performance and well-being.

Taking time for nature walks and working in an office with scenic windows would be optimal. While this isn't practical for all of us, even populating your space with plants, peaceful pictures, and listening to recordings is effective and will benefit you day after day.

These suggestions are important on a personal and organizational level. Employers would also benefit from considering the positive effects of allowing workers to take breaks for walking outdoors and placing plants in the workplace wherever possible. As the above studies show, doing so would go a long way to reducing sick days and increasing worker productivity, job satisfaction, and well-being. Once a company's workers become more productive, more satisfied with their jobs, show up to work more often, and are in better moods, the benefits for organizations can only snowball from there.

Part II

Whatever Works for Your Team

Surprising Factors That Change How We Work Together

5

Wordless Interactions

How Our Subtle Gestures Speak Volumes to Our Colleagues

The handshake of the host affects the
taste of the roast.

—BENJAMIN FRANKLIN

We often form immediate impressions when we interact with others. When sitting opposite a stranger, in a job interview or negotiation, we evaluate that person based on multiple factors, only one of which is verbal communication. Indeed, even before a word is uttered, we make an instant assessment of the person facing us. Studies show that people will gain an impression of who you are within the first seven seconds of meeting. Crucially, the research suggests that a person's trustworthiness is assessed within *a tenth of a second*.[1] This makes total evolutionary sense. After all, if you encounter an enemy who has bad intentions for you, only those who quickly read the "tells" of his potential aggression and leave the scene will survive. Others who wait around for verbal or other messages to evaluate the safeness of the encounter will be harmed or killed.

We've known for a long time that verbal utterances represent only a small piece of the pie in human communication. Other nonverbal factors exert their influence to a great extent. These include facial expressions, body language, eye contact, voice quality, attire, attractiveness, height, and more. We will discuss some of these factors later in this book. In this chapter, we will examine the factors we tend to neglect but that are extremely consequential: how people communicate with one another without speaking.

The Handshake

Many studies show that early impressions are crucial and influence employment interviews. Interviewers often make their decision a few minutes into the meeting.[2] The handshake is often the first impression of a job candidate, a client, or a person we are negotiating with.

Searching the internet for information on the importance of a handshake delivers almost one million hits, including advice on how to properly shake hands in an interview situation. Many sites give suggestions on the proper handshake, one that will help in job interviews, negotiations, or even introductions to new people and potential new friends. Suggestions include that your handshake should be firm but not crushing, and the handshake should last about two to five seconds.[3]

Some interviewers initiate a handshake with the candidate while others do not; sometimes it is the candidate who initiates the handshake. A firm handshake is generally considered to have a critical influence in job interviews and social interactions. Just recently I served on a committee that was interviewing candidates for the CEO position in a certain company. We interviewed several candidates and not one of us initiated a handshake; rather, we just presented ourselves. Two of the candidates initiated a handshake with all of us while the others did not.

Did that act influence us? Did the fact that a candidate initiated a handshake influence my judgment? And did the manner in which he shook my hand influence me?

It seems that there is almost universal agreement that a good handshake is crucial for interview success. However, empirical research examining the handshake in the context of the job interview is scarce. Still, let's take a look at what the science tells us.

A group of researchers from the University of Iowa, Texas A&M University, and Creighton University in Nebraska investigated the association between a candidate's handshake and the interviewer's assessment.[4] Students participated in a mock interview with human resources professionals. Several independent raters shook hands with the students before and after the interview and assessed their handshake firmness. In addition, the students completed a personality questionnaire. At the end of the interview, the interviewers completed a hiring recommendation. A positive association was found between the firmness of the handshake and the interviewer evaluation. Those who had a firm grip and looked the other person in the eye received better hiring recommendations. The researchers concluded that: "Individuals who follow common prescriptions for shaking hands, such as having a firm grip and looking the other person in the eye, receive higher ratings of employment suitability from interviewers."

Does a handclasp convey valid information about a person's characteristics? Two studies found that a firm handshake was associated with extroversion and dominance, and a weak handshake was associated with introversion, neuroticism, and shyness.[5] In one study, 112 participants were invited to complete four personality questionnaires. Each questionnaire was administered by another experimenter in a different room, and each time the experimenter shook the participant's hand at the beginning of the meeting. The handshake was rated by the experimenter on various dimensions such as grip, strength, duration, vigor, completeness of the grip, and eye contact. These dimensions were highly correlated and together composed what was called a "firm handshake." Participants with a firmer, longer handshake were more extroverted and open to experience and were less shy and neurotic as measured by the personality questionnaires.

But handshakes can influence more than just an interview. In an interesting study,[6] the researchers conducted a series of tests to examine the influence of a handshake on dealmaking. They found that a handshake in the beginning of the negotiation increased cooperative behaviors and influenced the outcomes of the negotiations. In one study from the Midwestern United States Business School, students from two classes on negotiation at the university were paired with randomly assigned partners and were asked to negotiate on the details of the job offer. One participant was given the role of the boss and the other one the role of the candidate. The boss and the candidate had to decide about three things: salary, start date, and office location for the candidate, and they had to reach an agreement. At the end, the participants were asked whether they shook hands in the beginning of the negotiation. Pairs who shook hands came to a better joint outcome.

In an additional study, pairs of participants were similarly negotiating, only this time it was not the participants' choice whether or not to shake hands. Half of the pairs were asked to shake hands before the negotiation and the other half did not shake hands. Again, pairs who shook hands agreed more than those who did not shake hands and were more open during the negotiation. It seems that a handshake signals cooperation and thus influences the negotiation process and its outcome.

In another interesting study called "The Power of a Hand-shake in Human-Robot Interactions," the researchers designed a robot that can shake hands.[7] Each participant was introduced to the robot, which either shook the participant's hand or not, and then the participant and the robot were given a joint task. At a certain stage the robot needed help navigating through an obstacle. Participants who shook hands with the robot helped and removed the obstacle more often than those who did not shake hands with the robot.

Two studies investigated the influence of a handshake between two people, as perceived and judged by a third-party observer. In one study,[8] the researchers asked participants to observe videos with a pair of animated human figures meeting for the first time in a business setting, one a "host" and the other a "guest." In some of the interactions, the host displayed encouraging and inviting behavior (approach behavior). Specifically, the host approached the guest with open arms and smiled. In the remaining interactions, the host displayed discouraging behavior (avoidance behavior), stepped away, crossed her arms, and did not smile. Half the time the host initiated a handshake, while in the other half there was no handshake. The participants rated the host on trustworthiness and interest in doing business. The researchers found that a simple handshake at the beginning of the interaction enhanced the evaluations of trust and willingness to continue business. In cases of avoidance behavior, a handshake decreased its negative effect. Manipulating just the single variable, the handshake, was enough to confirm the symbolic effect of shaking hands.

In a later study,[9] the researchers used the same type of simulation, but this time they manipulated the ethnicity and the gender of the figures in the animated video and took into consideration the gender and ethnicity of the participants. They found that the effect of the handshake in evaluating the interaction was more positive in Caucasian than East Asian participants. This result can be explained by the fact that a handshake is a more common and recognized practice in North America than in East Asia. They also found that for male participants, the effect of a handshake was more positive when the host was a man than when the host was a woman. This difference was not found for female participants.

The above findings suggest that a handshake influences first impressions and can influence interview evaluations as well as the outcome of other interactions.

Sometimes a handshake makes all the difference in our perception of someone's personality. One famous example is from the 2004 Australian elections. Mark Latham, leader of the Labor Party, was the party's great hope to win over then prime minister, John Howard. However, the day before the election, Latham and Howard were filmed shaking hands outside a broadcasting studio in Sydney. It appeared as if Latham was pulling Howard toward him, placing Latham in a position to tower over his shorter opponent. The footage reached the media and received wide coverage. Latham's handshake was reported as being "aggressive," "bullying," and "intimidating." Brian Loughnane, the campaign director of the Liberal Party, said this incident generated more feedback than anything else during the campaign, and that it "brought together all the doubts and hesitations that people had about Mark Latham." Latham dismissed the impact of the incident, saying, "We got close to each other, sure, but otherwise it was a regulation man's handshake. It's silly to say it cost us votes—my numbers spiked in the last night of our polling."

A more recent and entertaining example of the symbolism of the handshake can be seen in President Donald Trump, who seems to have invented his own "Art of the Handshake." Co-opting the friendly handshake into a tool of dominance, especially with heads of state, Trump's handshakes can be unpredictable.

Japanese prime minister Shinzo Abe got the full treatment during his White House visit, when in a marathon nineteen-second handshake, he was shaken by the president four times, patted thrice, and held captive in the agonizingly prolonged grip of his host. Amusingly, it attracted so much attention that one martial arts academy even released a tongue-in-cheek tutorial on how to defend against President Trump's handshake.[10] Several handshakes between President Trump and Emmanuel Macron, the president of France, attracted a lot of attention. In one meeting held in France, President Macron, who was escorting his American guest, was pitted with Trump in a twenty-nine-second epic battle for dominance. Both leaders were in positions of implicit power—Macron, the host and leader of France on his home turf, and Trump, the leader of the world's most powerful country. It was a sight to see as the two men maintained their machismo throughout, shaking and patting each other repeatedly and not letting go, refusing to back off, all the while with smiles on their faces.

Clearly, a handshake signifies so much more than two people holding hands!

Shake It

Before going for a job interview, practice your handshake with a friend. Try to make it firm, but not too firm. Best is to reciprocate the exact firmness of the hand that is shaking yours, which psychologically generates a sympathetic bond. Listen carefully to your friend's feedback. Studies show that your handshake affects how people judge and evaluate you. Although there's not much you can do about the shape of your face or the pitch of our voice, your handshaking technique is totally under your control and therefore can be used to start the interview on a sympathetic footing.

Belonging, Connecting, and the Chameleon Effect: Mirroring Others to Fit In

Have you ever noticed that the person you are talking to is mirroring you? When you crossed your legs, did she also cross her legs? When you touched your face, did he do the same? Unless that person did it very overtly, you probably didn't notice it. However, studies show that people often, and unconsciously, mimic postures, gestures, facial expressions, and other mannerisms of the people they are interacting with, to the point of actually mirroring those behaviors. Mimicry occurs naturally, automatically, and unconsciously in social situations for various reasons, and it's evident in approximately 30 percent of all interactions. This is called the *chameleon effect*—the tendency to mimic or mirror others without intent or awareness.

Like most of us, I've probably mirrored and imitated other people's behavior at times without noticing. But once I became aware of this phenomenon and its consequences, I realized that I was in fact mimicking people in some interactions, and that sometimes people would mimic me. I also noticed the chameleon effect in other people's interactions in real life, as well as in television interviews. People often mirrored each other and imitated each other's gestures, like crossing their legs, touching their face, or repeating what the person they were interacting with was saying.

About twenty years ago, two prominent researchers were among the first to investigate this phenomenon. John Bargh, now a distinguished professor of social psychology at Yale University, together with Tanya Chartrand, now a professor at Duke University, conducted a study when they were both at NYU.[11] They examined the reactions of two participants who were given a joint task and had to interact with each other. However, one of the "participants" was actually a research assistant, part of the research team, who was directed to demonstrate certain behaviors and mannerisms, such as nodding his head or rubbing his face. The participants were recorded, and the results clearly showed that they unconsciously mimicked their partner; when the research assistant touched his face or shook his foot, they did the same.

This automatic, unconscious behavior has been found to influence our judgments and behaviors more than you probably think. Studies show that mimicry enhances affinity and empathy[12] and trust.[13] For example, in Bargh and Chartrand's study, half of the participants were mimicked by the research assistant while the other half was not. The participants who were mimicked reported liking the other "participant" more and perceived their interaction as smoother than those who were not mimicked.[14] Another study found similar results when participants interacted with computer avatars in virtual reality. They liked the avatar that mimicked them more than the avatar that did not.[15]

Mimicry enhances affinity, which in some circumstances is translated into tangible rewards. Waitresses who mimic their customers by verbally repeating their order receive better tips.[16]

Mimicry is related to belonging and connecting; when people want to fit in and build a relationship with someone, they unconsciously mimic that person.[17] One study divided the participants into pairs, where one participant was instructed to role-play a job candidate and the other a recruiter. In one-third of the pairings, the candidate was instructed to mimic the recruiter (without the recruiter's knowledge). In another third, it was the other way around, with the recruiter being instructed to mimic the candidate. In the remaining pairings (the control group), no instructions were given to mimic. In the two groups in which mimicking occurred, the recorded level of rapport was significantly higher, and the candidate was perceived as better. These results have direct implications on interviews. The interviewer often arrives at a judgment quite early on and develops a gut feeling whether the job candidate will be pleasant and trustworthy, or not.

Sometimes we don't want to enhance bonding and affinity, since it might endanger other existing relationships. Men and women involved in romantic relationships are less likely to mimic an attractive person of the opposite gender than single people are.[18] It seems that people who are romantically involved want to shield those romantic relationships and unconsciously mimic attractive people less to maintain some distance from them.

If indeed mimicry enhances belonging and connection, it should occur more when we feel excluded and have a stronger need to connect and belong. But how do we create an exclusion situation in the lab? Researchers often use an online game developed by Kip Williams, a social psychologist who focuses particularly on the effects of ostracism.[19]

Williams was sitting in the park one day when a Frisbee hit him in the back. He saw two guys looking at him, expecting him to throw the Frisbee back to them. After throwing the Frisbee back to them, to his surprise, they threw the Frisbee back to *him*. He approached them, and they formed a triangle and began to play a game. After a few minutes of playing together, the two stopped throwing the Frisbee to him. Williams says that he was amazed at how bad that exclusion made him feel.[20] It gave him the idea to create a similar situation in the lab. First, he created a face-to-face tossing ball game, but he later developed Cyberball, a virtual ball-tossing game.

In this game the participants believe that they are playing virtual catch with two other players, but in fact there are no other players; a computer program controls the tossing. The experimenter decides how many times the ball will be tossed to the participant and consequently creates a condition of exclusion or inclusion. Studies show that when the ball is tossed to the participants only a few times in the beginning and then they are left out of the game, they feel bad and their sense of belonging is threatened. Cyberball has been used in more than one hundred studies on ostracism.

A group of researchers took Cyberball further and wanted to examine whether people who are excluded will exhibit more mimicry behaviors as a result of their need to belong.[21] In this study, men and women played Cyberball, believing they were playing with two other players. In the *inclusion condition*, they received the ball as often as the "other participants" did. In the *exclusion condition*, they received the ball only a few times at the beginning of the game and then waited in vain for the "other participants" to toss them the ball. Then, in what they believed to be another unrelated experiment, they were asked to describe several photographs to another participant, who was actually a member of the research team. The research assistant was instructed to move her foot throughout the interaction. Those who had been excluded in Cyberball mimicked the behavior of the research assistant and moved their foot more, compared to those who had been included. These findings suggest that when people feel excluded, they want to connect and to belong with the subsequent person they interact with, and they exhibit this automatic and unconscious behavior of mimicry.

In a second experiment, the researchers wanted to examine whether mimicry is selective, and whether being excluded from our own social group has an effect on our tendency to mimic. To address this question, they created a situation where women were excluded—either by other women (members of their own group) or by men (not members of their own group). Similar to the first experiment, the researchers created exclusion and inclusion conditions with Cyberball—but this time, the participants (all women) were told the gender of the other two "participants." After the Cyberball game, the women interacted with either a male or female research assistant. Women who were excluded by other women and who then interacted with a female research assistant showed the greatest mimicry behavior. In other words, when people are excluded by members of their own group, they feel an increased threat to their sense of belonging. Consequently, they mimic other people from their own group, driven by the need to feel like they belong again.

In addition to helping us connect, mimicry reduces the sense of threat. A study by researchers in the Netherlands found that the level of the stress hormone cortisol increased in a group of participants who were not mimicked, and it did not increase in a group of participants who were mimicked.[22] In other words, those who were not mimicked felt more stressed.

Mirror, Mirror

When being interviewed or negotiating with your boss for a promotion or raise, try to gently and very subtly mirror the other person's motor behavior, such as touching your face, stretching your legs, etc. Mirroring inconspicuously will have a positive effect on how much the other person likes you. But don't overdo it! As we will see, in a nonfriendly situation, mirroring actually results in feelings of coldness and alienation.

Mimicry and Persuasion

Mimicry does not only increase liking and bonding and connecting, it also influences customers' decisions and behaviors and increases persuasive abilities. We all know that the behavior of salespeople, the way they speak, smile, listen to us, etc. influences our decisions. But would you believe that just the fact that the salesperson imitates your nonverbal and verbal behavior influences your purchase decisions? Several studies found just that. A group of marketing researchers from the United States and the Netherlands asked students to participate in a marketing study introducing them to a new sports drink.[23] In one group, the experimenter mimicked the participants' verbal and nonverbal behavior, whereas in the control group the experimenter did not mimic the participants. Those who were mimicked liked the drink, said they would buy it, and thought it would be successful more than those who were not mimicked.

Another study was conducted at an actual store.[24] The researchers focused on customers who were interested in buying an MP3 player and asked four salespersons in that department to either mimic or not mimic the customers' verbal and nonverbal behavior. Customers who were mimicked by the salesperson were more likely to buy the MP3 player, and they evaluated the salesperson and the store more positively than those who were not mimicked.

Mimicry and Helping Behavior

A series of studies showed that mimicry also increases the willingness to help other people. In one study,[25] a researcher asked participants their opinions on several advertisements. The participants didn't know that this was not really the point of the experiment. While the participants were being spoken to, the researcher mimicked half of them, including mirroring their gestures and body postures. The researcher then "accidentally" dropped six pens on the floor. Participants who had been mimicked helped out more frequently by bending down and picking up the pens. In a similar interesting experiment, the participants who were mimicked helped to pick up the pens of another researcher conducting the experiment, not the one who mimicked them.

In yet another experiment, participants were asked their opinions on various advertisements, much like in the pen-dropping study; the researcher mimicked half of the participants by copying the position of their legs, arms, and body (if they were leaning forward or sitting up straight). They were then given the opportunity to donate to a certain charity. The results were astonishing: 76 percent of those who were mimicked donated money compared to only 43 percent of those who were not mimicked.

Taken together, these findings strongly show that, without our awareness, mimicry influences our decisions and judgments, and it has a beneficial effect on how others judge us. It seems then that mimicry is relevant for a variety of interactions in which you need to establish a good rapport with others, such as job interviews, discussion groups, collaborating on solving a problem, deciding whether to embark on a new project or investment, and more. People like, feel more connected to, and give more positive evaluations to those who mimic them. Keep this in mind in your next interaction with your colleagues or supervisors discussing your ideas, promotion, or salary. Try to mimic the person you are interacting with, but *in a very subtle way*. For example, if that person sits up straight, try to do the same; if that person crosses his or her hands or legs, do that too. When asked a question, you can repeat some of the words in your answer. But do not exaggerate and be careful not to go overboard—in some situations, mimicry can backfire.

When the Chameleon Effect Goes Wrong

One might ask: If mimicry builds rapport, doesn't it make sense to consciously exploit the power of mimicry in social situations? The answer is complicated. Mimicry is a double-edged sword—effective in certain contexts and detrimental in others.

The influence of mimicry depends on the context, particularly whether it is done in a friendly or a formal situation. To explore this, researchers instructed a female experimenter, who was blind to their hypothesis, to greet subjects in either a friendly and informal manner or a polite but highly professional manner.[26] Through subtle cues, she signaled either a desire to bond with the subject or a narrow focus on conducting the study properly. She maintained that demeanor throughout her interactions with each subject. In both conditions, the experimenter either mimicked subjects' postures, gestures, and non-verbal mannerisms, or she did not. The experimenter's mimicry was subtle and deliberately inexact (delayed by two to four seconds) so as to prevent conscious detection on the part of the subjects.

Later, participants rated how they felt and were also asked how physically cold or warm they felt. Participants who interacted with the friendly, informal experimenter reported feeling colder when they were *not* mimicked as compared to when they were mimicked. In contrast, participants who interacted with the formal, focused experimenter exhibited the reverse pattern—feeling colder when mimicked and warmer when not mimicked. So, people actually feel colder when exposed to inappropriate amounts of mimicry in a given interaction, depending on whether the interaction style is affiliative or nonaffiliative. The conclusion: If mimicry occurs in a clearly nonaffiliative context, it might raise suspicions and evoke awkward feelings. Therefore, if you want to consciously mimic someone in the workplace to try to establish rapport, you must distinguish when it is a good time to do so—namely, in a less formal situation.

Studies also found that third-party observers watching an interview made judgments about the interviewee that were based on mimicry. People who mimicked an unfriendly interviewer were rated as less competent than those who did not mimic that interviewer.[27] This was not found to be true when the interviewer was friendly.

Researchers from the United States and the Netherlands, including Tanya Chartrand and John Bargh, have demonstrated that when mimicry is inappropriate, it signals that something is "off."[28] A person may feel a sudden chill down his or her spine or goose bumps when a person or situation makes them feel uneasy or uncomfortable. Even so, the person may not consciously know why the other person makes them feel that way, for the interaction itself may be perfectly polite, mundane, or even pleasant. It's just that there is something incongruent that gives them the chills.

When it happens in the wrong social context, mimicry can also have a negative effect on our performance. For example, in one study,[29] participants were randomly assigned to be mimicked or not to be mimicked by a research confederate (a research assistant who pretended to be another participant). Each pair was given a joint task and told they would be randomly assigned to be the leader or worker; this was done to manipulate the power dynamic between the two. Following that, they were given a task that demanded attention. The findings are interesting. Those who were assigned to be leaders performed better on the attention task when they had been mimicked than when they were not mimicked. In contrast, those who were assigned to be workers performed better when they were *not* mimicked than when they were mimicked.

In order to understand these results, try to think of the social norm: typically a worker mimics a leader, but a leader does not mimic a worker. It seems that mimicry is beneficial when it adheres to social norms, and it has a negative effect when it violates them.

Likability is very important in success at the workplace, especially for young people who still have junior roles but are aspiring to climb the corporate ladder. Try to detect mimicry in your interactions. If you notice that the other person is mimicking some of your gestures or repeating your words, it might be an indication that he or she likes you and wants to connect. This might be a good sign and a cue for your behavior. Additionally, a firm handshake has long been regarded as a key to career success—and the research has certainly backed that up.

It seems that, especially for individuals, nonverbal communication can be just as important as what we say to our colleagues and bosses. Be aware of the messages you are sending and receiving.

6

We Need to Talk

Expressing Emotions, Negotiating, and Giving Gifts

Let us never negotiate out of fear.
But let us never fear to negotiate.
—John F. Kennedy

We have seen in the previous chapter how our interactions are affected by subtle and nonverbal communication such as handshakes and mirroring. Some of our interactions seem more straightforward, but even here, subtle cues are at work! In this chapter we will focus on negotiations and gifts. We negotiate about terms, pay raises, major business deals, and so forth. It is at such moments that we need to use all the tools at our disposal, even the seemingly trivial ones. For when all things are equal, the tiniest differences assume big proportions in their ability to tip the scales in your favor. You will see how the subtle cues, like your tone as a negotiator or the timely expression of a particular emotion, have the power to put you at an advantage. It is at such times that you've got to use "whatever works."

We will also discuss a fairly common employer-employee interaction (i.e., gifts to mark holidays or other such forms of recognition). Here, too, there are subtle cues at play that, through a simple manipulation, can boost worker satisfaction and productivity to the maximum extent in return for a thoughtfully proffered gift.

Negotiations

In our personal lives, we negotiate all the time—with our romantic partners, our children, our parents, our friends. We negotiate with our children about their curfew time, with members of the family about household chores, and more. We also negotiate when we are buying or selling, especially big-ticket items like homes or cars. Very often, we find ourselves in negotiations in our work environment for salary, contracts, promotions, loan terms, mergers, and other crucial business transactions.

It is only natural, then, that we'd want to understand the factors that maximize our chances in negotiations. Books and articles on how to negotiate successfully offer excellent strategies to employ, including showing how the other side's needs will be met, not succumbing to time pressure, being prepared to walk away, doing your homework, and more. And various scientific studies have shed light on novel strategies and tactics to use in order to achieve the best possible result in your next crucial negotiation.

Over the past decade, researchers have focused not only on certain actions in negotiations, but also on emotions. Once, the standard notion was to avoid showing emotion and to maintain a poker face; however, a growing body of empirical evidence demonstrates that, in certain circumstances, expressing emotions (particularly anger, but also disappointment, sadness, envy, happiness, and excitement) is an effective negotiating strategy.

It seems intuitive that we'll get better results from negotiating with positive emotions and expression than with a negative affect. But is that always true? A group of researchers led by Shirli Kopelman, a leading expert in the field of negotiations, conducted three experiments to examine the effect of strategically exhibiting emotions on negotiation outcomes.[1] In their first experiment, the researchers split up a group of students into three emotional conditions: positive, negative, and neutral. Those in the *positive condition* were coached to display positive emotions while bargaining, avoid hostility, and try to make the other party feel good. Those in the *negative condition* were coached to be zealous and persistent in their bargaining and to be tough. Those assigned to the *neutral condition* were coached to think logically, be rational, and control their emotions.

Duly coached, each participant was then paired with another and given a role in a simulation of a dispute between a developer and a contractor over the cost of the contractor's work. They were both told that if they settled the dispute, they would be able to work together in the future on other projects. Otherwise, if the dispute remained unsettled, the contractor would go bankrupt, and there would be no future opportunities for them to work together. The participants were introduced to each other and given one hour to negotiate. The findings clearly showed that those who employed the strategy of displaying a positive emotion had the best chances of assuring a long-term business relationship compared to those in the other two groups. No surprises there.

The researchers then tested the effectiveness of displaying positive emotions in a different sort of negotiating situation: the ultimatum—when one negotiator says something to the effect of "that's my final offer, take it or leave it."

To start, participants were asked to play the role of someone planning to get married who is meeting with the caterer of the wedding. The participants were told that the caterer had previously quoted them a price of $14,000 for the catering service. Then, they were shown a video clip in which the caterer proceeds to raise the price from $14,000 to $16,995 in a "take it or leave it" proposition. He claims that another couple is interested in hiring his catering service on the exact same time and date. The caterer shoves the contract forward and says that the participant needs to decide immediately whether to sign or not. Three separate clips were filmed by the researchers for viewing by different groups of participants. In each, the proposition was identical but was delivered by the manager using different tones of voice and facial expressions to express either a positive, negative, or neutral emotion. In the *positive condition*, the business manager spoke in a friendly and pleasant tone and smiled often. In the *negative condition*, the manager was intimidating and antagonistic. In the *neutral condition*, the manager spoke in monotone and did not display emotion.

After viewing the clip, participants were handed a contract with the figure of $16,995 and told to decide whether to sign it or reject it. Participants accepted the caterer's offer less often when it was accompanied by a negative affect rather than positive or neutral. Once again—and not totally surprisingly—a display of negative emotion is not recommended in a "take it or leave it" situation.

In a third experiment, participants watched the same clips as in the previous experiment. This time, the participants were allowed to make a counteroffer rather than immediately accepting or rejecting the caterer's proposal. Once again, the manager's negative display of emotion led to a worse result: The negative emotion was so angering that it provoked participants to shoot back with counteroffers that were even *lower* than the initial offer.

Taken together, these results suggest that what you'd expect is true: Displaying positive emotions, conveying friendliness, and smiling is most effective in reaching agreements in a negotiating dispute or ultimatum situation. This all seems logical and suggests the benefit of establishing a positive atmosphere.

However, negative emotions such as anger and disappointment often arise at particular moments in negotiations and can cause them to go sour. Your negotiating partner makes an annoying offer or demand, refuses outright your "reasonable" offer, or says something that provokes you. The person on the other side of the table is being pigheaded, won't budge, and won't be persuaded. You feel the anger and frustration mounting inside you. The question is: Should you show it or hide it? Looked at dispassionately, which course of action will contribute most to your desired outcome?

The answer according to studies: It all depends. Surprisingly (and refreshingly, for the hotheads among us), in certain circumstances, displays of negative emotions are more effective in negotiations and lead to concessions and getting a better deal.

Anger: Who Has the Power?

As Aristotle said more than two thousand years ago, "Anybody can become angry, that is easy; but to be angry with the right person, and to the right degree, and at the right time, and for the right purpose, and in the right way, that is not within everybody's power and is not easy."

So what happens when one person exhibits anger in a negotiation? Studies show that emotions displayed by one person elicit either a similar emotion or a complementary emotion in the other person. For example, if one person gets angry, then the other person might get angry too. This is called emotional reciprocity. On the other hand, emotions may elicit complementary emotions—such as anger being responded to with fear.

Whether anger elicits a reciprocal or complementary response could decide the fate of a negotiation. If anger is countered by anger from the other side, tensions mount, the temperature rises, and the heat might be too much to allow for a conciliatory atmosphere. If, on the other hand, anger arouses fear in the other party, there is a good chance it will lead to concessions. A crucial factor determining whether a show of anger will evoke fear and gain more concessions, or whether it will draw an angry return of fire, is how *powerful* each of the negotiators is. "Power" in a negotiation is based on the availability of alternatives to getting what you want. For instance, if a salesperson desperately needs to close a sale (for lack of other offers or for meeting a quota), he or she is not powerful. That salesperson has a built-in susceptibility to anger and is prone to make concessions. If that salesperson dares to become angry during the negotiation, it will more often than not be met by anger from the other side (who picks up on the salesperson's weakness from his body language, verbal nuances, and other cues). If, on the other hand, a salesperson trying to sell a product knows that he or she has enough offers from other companies, he/she feels powerful and is virtually immune from angry displays. In such a case, displays of anger will only elicit hostile reactions and high resistance to concessions.

Marwan Sinaceur from ESSEC Business School in Paris and Larissa Tiedens from Stanford University conducted several experiments to examine this aspect of negotiating.[2] They asked 157 students to imagine they were employed by a company that sells technical equipment and were negotiating with a potential client over warranty terms. The participants were divided into two conditions: those having many alternatives at their disposal and those with only a few alternatives. In the *few alternatives* condition, they were told that it was not a good period for the company and that if this deal falls through, it will be difficult to find another opportunity. In the *many alternatives* condition, they were told that it was a good period for the company and that other deals were possible. All of the participants were presented with a dialogue between the negotiators and asked to indicate their agreement to the various terms discussed. Half of the *many alternatives group* and half of the *few alternatives group* received a dialogue in which the negotiator exhibited an angry tone; the other half of each group received the same dialogue, however with a tone that lacked anger.

The study showed that the participants with few alternatives made more concessions to an angry negotiator than to a neutral one who did not display anger. When the participants had many alternatives (i.e., when they were high-powered negotiators), there was a Teflon effect—neither anger nor lack of anger made any difference in concessions. Thus high-powered negotiators with many alternatives are virtually immune to displays of anger and are far less prone to make concessions. In contrast, low-powered negotiators who fear a deal falling through will naturally be vulnerable to anger and make concessions.

When Anger Is Good

The next time you are in a negotiation, ask yourself who sits in the position of power (typically, the party who is less in need of the other party). If it is you who enjoys the higher power position, and a particular negotiating point or behavior gets you angry, express your anger. This might help you reach a better result. If, on the other hand, you are in a low-powered position, you have no choice but to swallow the frog and conceal your anger. A show of anger on your part will sabotage your prospects.

The Target of My Anger: The Person or the Offer?

If anger erupts during the course of a negotiation, it can be directed either at the opposing negotiating partner or the offer itself. A study conducted by a group of Dutch researchers from Leiden and Tilburg Universities sought to answer the question of whether the *target* of anger makes a difference in extracting concessions from the other side.[3] In this experiment, the researchers asked participants to play the role of a cell phone salesman and hold several rounds of negotiations with a potential buyer over the phone's price and warranty period. The participants believed there was a buyer in another room, but in fact it was a computer programmed to propose different offers in order to eliminate any confounding biases due to body language, tone of voice, etc. At certain points during the negotiations, the participants were informed of the "buyer's" thoughts and emotional reactions. Two negative emotions were presented: anger and disappointment. Half of the participants received an emotion directed toward the offer (e.g., "This *offer* makes me really angry," or "This *offer* really disappoints me") and half received an emotion directed at the person (e.g., "This *person* makes me really angry," or "This *person* really disappoints me").

The experiment showed that anger, when it was directed toward the *offer* and not the person, increased agreement from the other party for fear of losing the deal. However, when anger was directed at the person, it only hardened their hearts and made them loath to accept an offer. In contrast, when disappointment was expressed, it was far more effective when directed at the *person* rather than the *offer*. The researchers inferred that this expression of personal disappointment arouses feelings of guilt for not satisfying "reasonable" expectations, resulting in a softened stance and more concessions.

Talk It Over or Game Over?

When negotiating, if you begin to feel genuinely angry, don't take it out on the other person! Express your anger toward the offer itself. It will bring much better results. Say you are disappointed or angry that such an offer was made, but do not say you are angry at the person.

Have a Plan

Sometimes the shoe is on the other foot, and we become the object of anger or disappointment. What's worse, we begin from a low-powered bargaining position (with only few if any alternatives). What to do?

An interesting study conducted by a group of researchers from Saarland University in Germany found that if you go into a negotiation with a goal and an *if-then* plan, you will concede less when facing an opponent who expresses anger.[4] Having a goal is important, but it is often not enough; you have to know how to achieve it, and if-then plans show us how to advance and reach our goals.

For example, you might enter a negotiation with the general goal of remaining calm and unperturbed by your opponent. But being human, when our buttons are pushed, especially unkindly, well, it's surprising how fast our unflappability crumbles; instantly, we react to anger with fear and agitation, or we return fire and retaliate in anger. In other words, we lose our cool and are derailed from our logical selves. The if-then plan provides a valuable buffer by telling you exactly what to do in a specific scenario in order to achieve your goal.

In the Saarland University researchers' study, ninety-four students were told they were the buyers of a smartphone and were negotiating with the seller over the price, the warranty period, and download credit. Again, the participants' negotiating partner was actually a computer program. Six rounds of negotiation were held in which the buyer (the participant) and the "seller" (the computer) made offers and counteroffers via text messages. There were three anger conditions and one control group. In all three anger conditions, the "opponent" sent messages such as "Your offers make me angry! Either you seriously start making better offers or we both end this without any profit." In the first anger condition, participants were told nothing beforehand; in the second, *anger with a goal*, they were asked to go into the negotiation with a general goal, specifically, "I will negotiate persistently and in a composed manner without being influenced by my opponent"; in the third anger condition, *anger, goal and a plan*, they were given the same goal, but with an *if-then plan* to implement the goal. In this case, the goal was, "If my opponent starts making demands or gets angry, I will remind myself that s/he depends on me as much as I depend on her/him, and I will stick to my offer." In other words, the if-then plan provided participants with a simple approach to attain their goal: to remain focused on the fact that the opponent needs you as much as you need him.

As expected, and similar to other studies, those who faced an angry and threatening opponent without being prepared were the biggest losers, making more concessions and agreeing more to the seller's terms. Next came the participants who were given only a general goal to guide them. In contrast, the effectiveness of the if-then plan in facing anger was undeniable; as a matter of fact, the if-then plan achieved similar outcomes to those of the control group (no anger expressed) in achieving the best result. The key is that the if-then participants were able to regulate their emotions and move calmly toward their goal.

An if-then plan is an important tool when entering a negotiation in general, even if anger is never expressed. In particular, an if-then plan mitigates your vulnerability in a low-powered position situation.

The same researchers conducted more experiments to examine the influence of an if-then plan on low-powered negotiators.[5] As we have seen, when you are in a low-powered position, there is a greater chance you will make more concessions. This is true in salary negotiations as well as transactions with a buyer or a seller. If, for example, you negotiate your salary and you know you have something valuable that you contribute to your company, you are in a higher power situation than if both you and your employer know that there are other people who can replace you, which places you in a low-powered position. The researchers found that low-powered negotiators who had an if-then plan or a goal achieved more in the negotiation than the control group who had no plan or goal.

The researchers continued their inquiry by asking whether a goal or a plan can improve the inferior situation of a low-powered negotiator as compared to the situation of a high-powered negotiator. Subjects were asked to play the role of a job candidate negotiating with an employer over salary, vacation days, and working hours. The participants were seated in front of a computer screen and told that the "employer" in the experiment was in another room. Again, the other person was in fact a computer in order to eliminate confounding biases. This time, the participants were divided into four groups: (1) high power, (2) low power, (3) low power with a goal, and (4) low power with a plan.

Low-power and high-power status were achieved by several things. Participants chosen to be low power were asked to imagine they were job candidates who had only few alternatives. Moreover, they were asked to negotiate while sitting with their hands under their thighs and their legs close together.

This posture has been shown by previous studies to decrease the perception of power.[6] In contrast, in the high-power condition, participants were asked to imagine they had many alternatives and, while doing so, stretch their legs and cross their hands behind their head, a posture associated with high power. In order to cement the low status of the low-power negotiators, participants in the lower power condition were reminded by the "employer" that the market was competitive and received text messages during the negotiation saying that there are other candidates for the job.

The findings were clear. The low-power participants received offers that were lower than those of the high-power participants. This is not surprising, given that when we know we have few or no alternatives, we accept less ambitious offers. On the other hand, the low-power participants who entered the negotiation with a goal or a plan received significantly higher offers than low-power participants without a goal or a plan. What is surprising is that the low-power negotiators who had a plan ended up with similar final offers as the high-power negotiators.

Be Prepared

Before entering a negotiation, make sure to have an if-then plan for better results. Think in advance how you will respond to a certain offer by the other person, what to do if the other person expresses anger, and other potential scenarios. By doing so you will feel more prepared and more secure—an excellent mindset for a negotiation and a strategy that will make a positive difference in your demeanor and perceived power.

Is Anger Always Authentic?

Several years ago I served on a committee at the university where I teach. Our meetings were typically stormy, with divisions of opinions and even arguments. I recall how one professor on the committee would express his anger and irritation in a very loud and animated way, including banging his fist on the table.

Rumor was that before he became a professor, he was an aspiring actor. That knowledge primed members of the committee to perceive his anger as unauthentic and, as a result, it defanged him. We didn't feel a bit intimidated by his displays of fury since the professor's anger was felt to be feigned.

Sometimes, people pretend to be angry in order to achieve a better deal. The question is: Does feigned anger achieve what genuine anger can? Or do we see through it as the ruse that it is? A group of researchers led by Stéphane Côté, a well-known researcher on emotions from the University of Toronto, together with professors from the University of Amsterdam, conducted several experiments in which they examined the effect of a negotiator displaying false anger.[7] They wanted to compare acting angry on the surface, without actually feeling such anger internally, to expressions of neutral emotions or authentic anger.

In one of the experiments, 140 undergraduates were shown a ninety-second video clip of a "student" responding to an ad for a used car. After articulating his concerns about the automobile, the student negotiator said he would not pay the asking price of $3,500 and countered with an offer of $2,400. One-third of the participants viewed a version of the clip in which the actor playing the student displayed no emotion. Another third saw him pretend to be angry in a somewhat exaggerated manner, with eyes wide open, glaring, and with jaw clenched. The final third saw yet another version in which the actor was feeling genuine anger (by being coached in method acting where he was asked to recall a real-life event that made him feel angry and channel that intense emotion into the scene). After viewing the video clip, participants assessed the student-buyer's toughness and authenticity and were told to make him a counteroffer on the car.

The findings conclusively showed that feigned anger is counterproductive. Those who viewed the clip in which the actor pretended to be angry responded to the attempted deception by demanding a *higher* price than other participants who viewed the emotionally neutral clip. Apparently, negotiators were able to see through feigned emotion and, as a result, *lose their trust in the good faith and sincerity* of the negotiating partner. In response, they came back with greater rather than reduced demands. In contrast, participants who viewed the scene in which the potential buyer was feeling genuine anger rated him as a tougher negotiator—and responded by offering the car at the lowest price from among the three groups. Anger that seemed authentic had an intimidating effect; anger that smelled of fakery was off-putting and counterproductive.

Anger Intensity: Express Anger, Not Rage

If you express anger in a negotiation, how high should you turn up the heat? How intense the anger? Should you display your anger moderately? Or is it better to be vociferous, perhaps shouting and banging your fist on the table or exhibiting other shows of anger? Are the two modes different in their effectiveness? Researchers put this question to the test in an experiment that concluded: All other things being equal, mild anger expressed in a negotiation is more effective than no anger.[8] High-intensity anger is not effective and elicits smaller concessions than moderate anger. The researchers suggest that displays of extreme anger in a business negotiation is considered less normative and less appropriate, thus reducing the irate negotiator's perceived status and his effectiveness in the negotiation.

Don't Lose It or You'll Lose It

As we have seen, if you become genuinely angry during a negotiation, expressing the anger can be advantageous in certain situations. But never yell, shout, or "lose it"! Doing so will only reduce your status and hurt your bargaining position. Always express anger verbally and toward the *offer* rather than the person.

What About Threats?

Anger communicates an implied threat, however it doesn't go all the way. While you can express anger by openly saying you are angry or through nonverbal communication, you express a threat by simply stating what you intend to do if your offer is not accepted. A group of researchers conducted several experiments to examine which of the two is more effective in negotiation: an expression of anger or a threat.[9] They compared negotiations that included angry statements such as "I am really angry, and this is getting on my nerves" to negotiations that issued threatening statements such as "If you don't seriously modify your offer, there will be consequences. It's up to you." Threats, when calmly delivered, were found to be more effective than anger. In other words, a negotiator who plays it cool and shows no extreme emotions, but instead communicates threats calmly, will be more effective and achieve better results than an angry negotiator.

Women, Men, and Emotion

It might be hard to believe for some readers, and it is truly unfortunate, but the effectiveness of anger depends also on whether a man or a woman is expressing it. According to the social-role theory, men and women have different gender roles and are expected to behave accordingly.[10] Any violation of conventional roles is frequently met with sanctions. Although women are perceived as more emotional than men, they are nevertheless expected to be agreeable and refrain from displays of anger. Actually, anger is one of the few emotions that people believe men express more often than women. A number of studies show that women who deviate from gender role expectations evoke negative reactions and evaluations, and that anger is perceived differently if expressed by a male or a female.

A series of studies conducted by researchers from Yale and Northwestern Universities examined the relation between the expression of anger by men and women and the conferral of status, salary, and perceived competence.[11] Male and female participants watched videos in which professional men or women actors played the part of an interviewee who was either a low-ranking assistant trainee or a high-ranking CEO. In the *anger condition,* the actors portraying interviewees expressed moderate anger in reply to a certain question. In the *no emotion condition,* the "interviewees" were instructed not to express emotion. Each participant watched one interviewee and then answered questions about the status and salary the candidate should be given and rated the interviewee's competence. The findings were quite disturbing. Women were accorded lower status when they expressed anger, regardless of their rank. In contrast, the status accorded to males was based solely on their rank and not influenced by expressions of anger. As for salary, participants were willing to pay the unemotional female interviewee more than the angry female regardless of her rank. Again, expression of anger did not influence the salary they were willing to give to the male interviewee. In addition, participants rated the angry female CEO as significantly less competent than all the other interviewees.

The researchers suggest that when people view a woman displaying anger (i.e., not behaving as expected), they attribute that expression of anger to internal causes, to her personality. In contrast, anger in men is viewed as situation related, the result of an external cause. Therefore, when a woman expresses anger in an interaction, this might imply a lack of self-control and that she is not suitable for a high-level position.

Two studies headed by Jessica Salerno from Arizona State University produced similar results. One study found that women who expressed anger in a group discussion (mock jury) lost influence over others, while men who expressed anger gained influence.[12] In the other, Salerno's team examined how anger expressed by male and female attorneys in court influences evaluators.[13] Participants viewed a male or a female attorney who presented his or her closing argument in either an angry or a neutral tone. Participants were asked whether they would hire that attorney and to provide their impressions of him or her. Participants reacted *less* favorably to women who expressed anger compared to women who did not. In contrast, they reacted *more* favorably to men who expressed anger compared to those who did not. They used positive aspects of anger, such as power and conviction, to justify hiring an angry male attorney and used the negative aspects of anger, such as obnoxiousness, to justify their unwillingness to hire angry women. Remember, all participants heard the same closing arguments; nevertheless, women lost and men gained for expressing the same emotion.

Thus it seems that when women express anger, a perceived violation of gender roles and expectations, they are penalized in various ways. Men who express anger are perceived as comporting with their gender role and thus are not penalized and are sometimes even praised. This is something to keep in mind when considering whether to express anger in a negotiation.

Gender in Negotiations

Of course, gender roles are not limited to expressions of anger. The female gender role includes characteristics such as being accommodating, concerned for the welfare of others, supportive, warm, and interpersonally oriented. The male gender role includes characteristics such as ambition, assertiveness, competitiveness, and task-oriented behavior. The fact is that success in financial negotiations is often reliant on being assertive, ambitious, and competitive, exactly the characteristics that are congruent with the male role. In other words, the negotiator role is inconsistent with the female gender role but consistent with the male gender role. True, gender beliefs and expectations have changed since the 1980s, when role theory was first introduced, and more women today work at jobs once considered the domain of males and hold managerial positions. Unfortunately, many people still hold on to these outdated values and believe that a woman should not display assertiveness and ambition. It is reasonable to assume, then, that women have a systematic and built-in disadvantage in negotiations. Indeed, numerous studies have found exactly that and suggest this stereotype as a contributing factor to the gender pay gap.[14]

A group of researchers from Germany conducted a meta-analysis that examined gender differences in the outcomes of economic negotiations.[15] They reviewed fifty-one studies involving a total of 10,888 participants and found that men have an undeniable advantage over women in negotiations. This meta-analysis, however, found that the gender differences in negotiations are influenced by the context and situation in which the negotiation takes place. For example, in negotiations that are more congruent with the female role—when the woman is negotiating on behalf of another person—the male advantage is reduced or even disappears. The researchers also found that gender differences were reduced when negotiators had real-life negotiation experience and suggested that women, to a greater extent than men, ought to be trained to negotiate.

Several studies examined a specific question: Are women penalized merely for being the initiator of a negotiation over salary, compensation, or other resources for improving their work situation and environment (e.g., more space, research funds, or secretarial support)? A group of researchers from Harvard University and Carnegie Mellon University conducted several experiments that examined the differential evaluations of men and women who initiate negotiations.[16] In one experiment, participants adopted the role of senior manager in a company and were asked to evaluate candidates based on a written résumé and interview notes. All participants received the same résumé and notes, but some were told that their candidate was a woman and some that their candidate was a man. Some were told that the candidate initiated negotiations about compensation and some were not told that the candidate initiated negotiations. The candidates who initiated negotiations were evaluated less favorably than those who did not, but the effect was twice greater for women than for men. In other words, women candidates who initiated negotiations about compensation were penalized more than men who did the exact same thing. The researchers also found that a participant's willingness to work with a candidate who initiated negotiations was lower than with the one who did not initiate—only if that candidate was a woman.

In a third study, participants saw videotapes of candidates (rather than a transcript) who either accepted the compensation offers or initiated negotiations. They found that female participants penalized both male and female candidates who initiated negotiations. In contrast, male participants penalized female candidates who initiated negotiations more than they penalized male candidates who did the same thing. So, women are penalized more often than men for initiating negotiations. Are they also less likely than men to initiate negotiations at work? A 2018 meta-analysis examined this question.[17] The researchers reviewed studies from 1977 to 2016 and found that indeed, compared to men, women were less likely to initiate negotiations. However, similar to the meta-analyses I mentioned previously, they found that gender differences depended on the context. When the situation was more ambiguous and not clearly defined as a negotiation, women did not feel they had to fit neatly into their gender role, and they were more likely to initiate negotiations. Also, when the situation was more consistent with the stereotyped female gender role, for example, when it was more cooperative than competitive, the gender differences were smaller. These studies suggest that, overall, women have a disadvantage in economic negotiations and are less likely to initiate negotiations on compensation and salary. This disadvantage weighs down upon women's prospects for receiving higher salaries and job promotions.

All this is certainly not to say you shouldn't negotiate—failing to do so can seriously affect how much you earn, and most recruiters do expect it. However, these scientific findings about employer reactions to people who negotiate are important to keep in mind.

The only finding we can draw on for encouragement is that the researchers found that gender differences have decreased from year to year (from 1977 to 2016). Hopefully such differences will eventually evaporate and become a thing of the past.

Disappointment

The palette of emotions in a negotiation is not limited to anger or positive emotions; earlier, I mentioned that negotiators can also express disappointment. Professor Gert-Jan Lelieveld from Leiden University led a study on expressing disappointment in negotiations.[18] Lelieveld and his colleagues hypothesized that the key factor in the effectiveness of expressing disappointment in a negotiation is whether it evokes guilt. If it succeeds in doing so, then it leads to higher concessions and more generous offers. If, on the other hand, the expressed disappointment conveys weakness, then the other party might exploit this weakness and make lower offers.

Two of the factors that determine whether or not disappointment will evoke guilt are our relationship with the other negotiator and the extent to which we can identify with him or her. When two people share commonalities (they have a good relationship, similar affiliations and interests, etc.) there is a tacit "kinship" that is at stake. Suppose, for example, that an employee asks for a raise from her boss, and the boss suggests a much lower figure than what was requested. If the two have a good relationship and the employee communicates genuine disappointment, there is a greater probability it will evoke guilt in the employer and lead to a better offer.

Lelieveld and his colleagues set up a negotiation between student pairs. Half of the students were partnered with another student from the same university they were attending, while the other half were told they would be paired with a student from another university. In both conditions, the participants were given the identity of the other student without meeting them; they were told their partner was seated in the next room. In actuality, there was no other student. To spark the "interaction," the participants were asked to indicate their agreement with six statements about bargaining behavior, for example, "During negotiations my own outcomes are important," which they were told were delivered to the other "student." Shortly after, the experimenters presented the participants with the typed reactions of the "other student," expressing either anger or disappointment.

The findings were clear. Participants who conveyed disappointment were not as generous to students from another university than to students studying at the same university. Bear in mind that the sole variable manipulated here was a common affiliation (i.e., whether the negotiating pair attended the same or a different school). The researchers generalized this finding to conclude that when an in-group member, in this case a student from the same university, communicates disappointment, it arouses feelings of guilt and consequently leads to higher offers. In contrast, when an out-group member communicates disappointment, participants feel less guilty and therefore make lower offers.

We have seen how the expression of emotions can influence negotiations between workers and employers, with a client, and among team members. However, there is another way that employers and employees interact—giving gifts to show appreciation and to enhance job satisfaction and productivity. The question is what is the best type of gift and the manner of delivering it, including subtle cues (aside from value) for sustaining employee satisfaction, motivation, and appreciation?

It Really Is the Thought That Counts: The Motivating Value of Gifts

When workers believe that their managers care about them, they become more committed to the organization and work more effectively.[19] A mega survey of

Gallup Polls conducted worldwide among a large population of workers and managers shows that workers who believe that their manager cares about them as a person report higher job satisfaction, are less likely to quit, and are more motivated to work hard. One powerful way managers can show they care is by giving appropriate gifts to their workers. So the logical question is: What type of gift should an organization give to its employees?

Should it be a material gift, an object that the employee can keep, such as a coffee cup or a nifty gadget? Or should it be an experiential gift, such as a trip or tickets to a concert or a show? Digging deeper, if it's a material gift the employer finally decides upon, should it be a monetary or nonmonetary gift? Of all the possible types of gifts, which is the most effective for making employees feel more appreciative and motivated to reciprocate by working harder?

A fascinating study conducted in Germany in a natural work environment examined the association between different types of gifts (monetary and nonmonetary) and worker productivity.[20] To begin with, they recruited workers to catalog books from a library. The workers, sitting at different tables and in front of a computer, were given a pile of books and asked to enter each book's title, author, publisher, and year of publication into an electronic database. Before the participants began working, they were told they would receive their usual salary plus an additional gift (money or a thermos bottle). One group of workers was told they would receive a monetary gift of seven euros. Another group was told they would receive an attractively wrapped thermos bottle (also valued at seven euros). A third group did not receive any gift. In order to get a quantitative indicator of productivity, the total number of characters entered into the database was counted.

So which type of gift do you suppose increased productivity? If you could choose between a certain sum of money or a gift that costs the same, which would you choose? The rational and sound choice, from a theory of economics perspective, would be to choose the cash, since with cash you can buy the exact same gift or something that's totally different and more to your liking. And yet, the results of this study were quite clear. Those who received money increased their productivity by only 5 percent while those who received the thermos bottle produced a full 25 percent (!) more characters than in the baseline condition. But before jumping to conclusions, one immediate objection comes to mind:

Perhaps the workers thought the thermos bottle was worth more than seven euros? In order to avoid that pitfall, the researchers added another condition in a subsequent trial by affixing a price tag to the bottle reading "7 Euro," precisely the same value as the monetary gift received by other subjects. Yet still, even with this added condition, the workers entered 21 percent more characters in response to receiving the thermos bottle, thus demonstrating a similar effect.

Next, the researchers examined whether the workers preferred nonmonetary gifts (of a known value) over receiving the cash equivalent—despite the fact that money affords them multiple opportunities to purchase one of literally thousands of other products (including the same gift). In order to examine that, they added another condition: They gave the workers a *choice*—of receiving seven euros in cash or receiving a thermos bottle valued at seven euros. Given that choice, logic set in and more than 80 percent of the workers chose the cash! But this time, amazingly, productivity leaped to 25 percent higher than baseline in the cash condition—much higher than when they received the exact same sum of money, *but without being given a choice* of gift. So what's going on here?

Winnowing the kernel of truth from the above results leads to this key insight: What was important to the workers was the *effort* the employers made to find the right gift. Even though most of the workers wanted the money, they were appreciative of the fact their employers devoted thought to a product that might come in handy for them. Infused with genuine appreciation, the employees worked harder.

To further investigate whether it is really the time and effort invested in a gift that matters, the researchers added another group, the "origami" group. Workers were given an origami shirt folded out of a five-euro bill and two euro coins glued on a postcard. In other words, the workers received seven euros, the exact same amount as in all the previous monetary conditions. Here, however, touched by the creative origami gift in which the employer obviously invested more time and effort, employees exhibited their appreciation and responded by working harder. This time there was an almost 30 percent increase in productivity!

It is said that old clichés survive because they contain true wisdom. These remarkable results, taken together, indeed suggest that "it's the thought that counts." When workers believe that their employers have put in the time and effort to tangibly show their appreciation, they reciprocate and productivity increases. Caring, or at least the expression of caring, really matters.

Give a Gift, Get Much More

It's hard to imagine someone who does not love receiving money as a gift. But here's something that might sound counterintuitive: The gifts that will motivate your employees or team members to the greatest extent are not necessarily monetary. Generally speaking, employees are happier and more motivated by a nonmonetary gift that shows you have invested thought, time, and effort in them. It communicates that you care about and appreciate your employee as a person. If you want to motivate your colleagues, employees, or team members, and at the same time do something for society, give them a monetary bonus that they can donate to a charity of their choice. This will motivate them no less than receiving a bonus for themselves, with the added value of giving to others. Everybody wins—you, the employees, and society. Rest assured that the thought and effort you invest will invariably pay top dividends in terms of loyalty, job satisfaction, and productivity.

The Gift That Keeps On Giving: Charity

Is it possible that giving workers money to donate to others also increases performance? A study conducted by two British researchers showed that it does. They examined the effect of financial versus social incentives on performance.[21] In their study, participants were asked to enter computer bibliographic records of academic publications, including names of the authors, title, page number, and year of publication. One group of participants received a conventional incentive in the form of a monetary bonus while the other group received a social incentive—donating money to the charity of their choice. Interestingly, both monetary bonuses and donations increased performance, with the difference between the two remaining insignificant. The fact that bonuses increase productivity is of course unsurprising. It is, however, morally refreshing and encouraging that a prosocial bonus (i.e., money given to a valued charity), increases performance. Employers should consider this type of gift. Donating to a valued charity in the employee's name seems to strike a noble chord in the minds of both employer and employee.

A Wineglass or a Wine-Tasting Event?: Giving a Material or Experiential Gift

Several years ago my daughter organized a birthday party for me. It was a great celebration, and I received very nice presents such as bags, jewelry, and clothes that I still enjoy today. Such gifts are called "material gifts." I also received two gifts that were different: One friend treated me to a day at a spa, including lunch, and we had a great time. Another friend gave me a pair of concert tickets for the philharmonic, which I used with pleasure. Such gifts are called "experiential gifts."

So what makes us happier, wineglasses or a wine-tasting event? Tickets to see a particular band or their latest recording? Since 2005, numerous studies have sought to answer the question of what makes people happier—gifts that are material or experiential? Many of the studies were led by Thomas Gilovich, a well-known social psychologist and Cornell University professor. The majority of studies concluded that experiential gifts lead to greater satisfaction and happiness.[22] For instance, in one study participants were asked to choose between two types of purchases—a material object or a social experience. Significantly more often they chose the social experience, saying that it would make them happier.[23] Another study asked participants to think of either experiential or material purchases made recently costing more than $100 and the level of enjoyment received from them.[24] They reported deriving greater enjoyment from the experiential purchase. The same researchers conducted another study in which participants were asked to recall a specific material purchase or experiential purchase and were given a questionnaire to assess their mood. They were in a better mood when they recalled an experiential rather than a material purchase. In a similar study, Carter and Gilovich asked participants to recall either an experiential or material purchase that cost at least fifty dollars.[25] At the time of the purchase, there was no difference in satisfaction between the material and the experiential purchase. However, later on they were more satisfied with the experiential purchase. Professor Gilovich, together with his colleagues, concluded that experiential purchases or gifts bring more lasting happiness compared to material purchases such as jewelry or gadgets.[26] We often experience buyer's remorse, but we regret missing experiences, such as a trip we did not go on or a performance we did not buy tickets to. Anticipation of experiences makes people happier and more excited than waiting for a delivery of material goods.

Studies also show that experiential gifts with multiple participants improve social relationships. Since social relations are highly important to a smooth-running organization, employers ought to occasionally reward their employees with experiential gifts such as a fun outing for company employees. These findings suggest that employers would be well advised to opt for experiential gifts that can take the form of tickets to a major show or a weekend at a nice resort, depending on the available gift budget.

It is clear that expressing emotions plays a major role in negotiations, beyond dry statements of offers and counteroffers. Emotions typically aroused during the course of a negotiation can play a big part in the final outcome. In this chapter we've reviewed studies that show when and how to express emotions in a way that maximizes your chances of achieving the best possible result.

As we've seen, it is okay to express such anger appropriately when it serves you. However, if you enter a negotiation in a low-powered position, make sure to prepare yourself in advance with an if-then plan. This will put you on firmer footing, ease anxiety, and supply you with smart, well-reasoned counteroffers or proposals to have at the ready rather than falling into the trap of blurting out rash or unconsidered reactions in the heat of the moment.

Emotions also play a part in gifts or bonuses to employees. Although it is known that monetary bonuses increase performance, and that most of us love receiving cash, we see that the thought behind the gift actually does count. Nothing touches us more on the job than the feeling that we are valued as an individual for our contribution. From the employer's standpoint, the absolute best and most cost-efficient (free!) way to do this is through a short, personal handwritten note to accompany the gift, expressing authentic praise for the employee. There is no better asset for an organization than happy and motivated workers who feel appreciated.

In this chapter, we've explored some challenging but normal workplace interactions. Next we'll look at the subtle forces at play in stickier situations—when workers are behaving badly.

7

Sticky Fingers

Ethical and Unethical Behavior in the Office

In looking for people to hire, you look for three
qualities: integrity, intelligence, and energy. And, if
they don't have the first, the other two will kill you.
—Warren Buffett

Cases of unethical behavior in the workplace can end up as major news items. Recall the Enron financial statement fraud, the Wells Fargo scandal where fake accounts were created on behalf of the bank's clients without their consent, and others. These stories reach the news and capture our attention since they are major scandals occurring in prominent corporations. The consequences can be seismic, as when Enron shareholders filed a $40 billion lawsuit after the stock plummeted. In the Wells Fargo scandal, numerous regular bank clients (as most of us are) were stolen from, without knowing it. These cases of fraud frighten us and remind us of our vulnerability to sophisticated forms of theft. But not only consumers suffer, because it can work both ways. Companies and organizations can also be the victims of dishonesty on the part of their employees. Admittedly, not on a scale of major headline-grabbing cases, but nevertheless, in a way that erodes their bottom lines and pollutes the corporate culture—by employees stealing, cutting corners irresponsibly, taking illegitimate absences, performing under par, etc.

There are many everyday occurrences of managers and employees behaving badly at work that will never reach the news. Maybe you have a coworker who sneaks out early several days a week or consistently comes in late when the boss does not see, takes credit for work done by others, lies to other employees, misuses company time by surfing the internet instead of working, pads the expense account by including personal expenses, takes home company supplies such as pens and notebooks, or calls in "sick" but goes to the movies or the beach instead. (A friend of mine who was a manager of a big division told me that whenever she walked into the office, she saw her secretary playing computer games, instead of working on her assignments.) These types of unethical behavior are common incidents in the workplace and cost organizations billions of dollars each year.

Of course, some people are more honest than others and have higher personal moral values and standards. Some are less selfish, and some people just have more self-control. The ethical climate and culture of the organization is also very important; emphasizing ethics, and not just success, as one of the most important principles of the company can also influence employees' behavior. Coworkers also influence and establish a standard. Even so, lesser-known situational factors can impact our behavior, and this chapter will explore them. Identifying these controllable situational factors that affect behavior can help managers, supervisors, companies, and organizations to save money and cultivate a better atmosphere.

Anxiety

John was recently hired at a big advertising agency, where he was expected to come up with new and creative ideas. He often felt stressed and worried that his ideas wouldn't be good enough and that he would lose his job. His colleague David was much more relaxed. He did not feel the same pressure as John. Both had the opportunity for unethical behavior: for example, to take credit for someone else's ideas, or to call in sick. Do you think the fact that John was more stressed and anxious might lead him to act unethically?

Well, we don't know about John, but studies show that anxiety is in fact related to unethical behavior.

Is it possible that the more anxious you are, the less ethical your behavior will be? Two professors specializing in ethical behavior, Maryam Kouchaki from Northwestern University and Sreedhari Desai from the University of North Carolina, examined this question.[1] They conducted several experiments to determine whether people who feel threatened and anxious will behave less ethically. In the first experiment, they asked participants to listen to music while answering several questions. Half of the participants listened to the *Psycho* soundtrack, which was found to raise anxiety, and the other half listened to classical music: *Air* by Handel. While listening to the music, they were asked to read various scenarios depicting unethical behavior. Then, they were asked to rate on a scale of 1 to 7 the likelihood that they would engage in such behavior. For example, one scenario described a situation in which an employee was alone at the office and remembered that he was out of copy paper at home. Participants were asked whether they would have taken paper home. The findings indicated that the participants who had listened to the anxiety-causing music were more likely to engage in unethical activities than those listening to calm, classical music.

In a second experiment, the researchers examined whether being in a state of anxiety would increase not just the *likelihood* of behaving unethically but would also influence actual behavior. Two groups of participants were shown a video clip. One group was shown an anxiety-raising video of a mountain-climbing accident, and the other group saw a neutral video about fish. They were then given a simple task—to detect whether there were more dots on the right or left side of the screen—and they were given money for each correct answer. Without their knowledge, they had the opportunity to cheat, believing nobody could detect them. Participants in a state of anxiety cheated more often than those who saw the neutral video.

In a third experiment, the participants were again divided into two groups, one in an *anxiety-raising condition* and one in a *neutral condition*. In the anxiety condition, they were told about a study that found that many commonly used brands of toothpaste have high levels of nicotine. In the neutral condition, they were told about a park that was expected to help the development of the district. They were then asked to imagine that they were Sam, who had just started to work for a well-known media firm, and that after a nine-week probationary period, management would decide whether Sam's job would be permanent. Then they were told that Sam's boss asked him to write a report that the boss had to present to the chairman of the company. The boss asked Sam to include a meeting with another company that never actually happened. In other words, the boss asked Sam to cheat. Those in the anxiety-inducing group said that they were more likely to include the fabricated meeting in the report than those in the neutral group.

The researchers also conducted a field study at the workplace, rather than in the laboratory, in which they asked employees to indicate how nervous and anxious they are at work, and they asked their supervisors to rate their subordinates' unethical behavior on a scale of 1 to 7. They were asked about behavior such as lying to clients or employees and misreporting actual hours at work. They found a correlation between feeling anxious and threatened and unethical behavior. However, we have to remember that correlation does not mean causality, and people who display unethical behavior might be more anxious. Yet the three laboratory experiments clearly suggest that anxious people engage in unethical behavior more often.

These results have direct implications for companies and organizations. In previous chapters we've shown that anxious and stressed workers are less productive, and their performance is affected. But most employers and employees probably don't realize that anxiety is also related to unethical behavior. Companies should therefore invest effort and money to reduce anxiety and stress.

Time of Day

Does the time of the day have an effect on moral behavior?

Ethical behavior is related to personal values, and we've established that some people are less honest than others. However, ethical behavior is also related to self-control and resisting temptation. That is, even knowing that no one will

Give Them a Break:
Every Mission Needs an Intermission

Many studies found that physical exercise improves not only our physical condition, it also effectively reduces stress and anxiety and improves alertness and concentration. Even five or ten minutes of exercise is enough to reduce anxiety. Companies should encourage their employees to work out. They might want to pay for a gym membership if they don't have a gym in the company building and give the employees an hour during the workday to exercise. Another option could be to bring an aerobics, Pilates, or yoga instructor to the workplace and organize a class at some point during the day. Yoga is a mind-body practice that is proven to help reduce stress and anxiety. Paying for these classes and gym memberships is a good investment of the company's money, not only because anxiety and stress are related to poor performance and productivity, but because, as these studies suggest, anxiety is related to unethical behavior such as cheating and stealing.

Another source of anxiety is worrying about our children while we are at work. On-site day care may help to reduce anxiety. (When my children were small, there was no day care at the university; I was always worried and dashed home at the end of the day. Now the university offers day care; you can even stop by during the day just to peep through the window and see your children playing. I can't help but be a bit envious of my students!)

Companies' financial investment in anxiety-reducing resources will ultimately pay for itself—with interest—in the form of higher productivity and more ethical behavior. Every mission needs an intermission.

find out if you took some paper from the office, you won't do it if you can resist temptation. The question is whether there are times of day that we have weaker self-control. For example, when we're watching our weight, we know that we're not supposed to eat another piece of cake, and if we have self-control we can resist the temptation. Sometimes, our self-control is not that strong; we do take that second piece. Studies show that self-control has a certain capacity. When we're tired, we have less self-control to resist temptation and to listen to our moral compass.

Maryam Kouchaki investigated this question when she was a fellow at the Safra Center for Ethics at Harvard University.[2] Kouchaki's team conducted several experiments comparing morning ethical behavior to evening ethical behavior. In one experiment, participants were given a certain task in which they could easily cheat and believed nobody would find out: They were shown two triangles with twenty dots, and they had to press a button to indicate whether there were more dots on the left or on the right side. One group came to the experiment in the morning and another group in the afternoon. Afternoon participants cheated more than morning participants. The researchers suggested that people are more tired and depleted at the end of the day, and this depletion of self-regulatory resources can lead to unethical behavior. When people are tired and drained after a long workday, they have less control of their behavior, and therefore are more easily tempted to behave unethically. These results suggest that we should be more aware at the end of the day that our resources may be depleted, and try to avoid putting ourselves in tempting situations.

To make it more complicated, another study found that morality is indeed related to the time of day, but it depends on whether the person is a morning or an evening person.[3] Researchers divided the participants into groups of morning, intermediate, and evening people, based on their answers to questions such as "How alert do you feel during the first half-hour after waking up?" Participants were then given opportunities to cheat in the morning and in the evening. Evening people cheated more in the morning, and morning people cheated more in the evening.

Self-Control

I was the chair of the psychology department and was going through a tough personal loss. I tried to run the department as usual, although it was very difficult for me to attend to people and be focused on various subjects and meetings. I had to use all my resources not to show my true emotions. I remember that one of my colleagues came to my office and really upset me. In other circumstances, I would have been angry but would have had the self-control to answer quietly. I'd never shouted at anyone at work before, even when I was upset. But at that time, I did not have resources. They were depleted since I had been trying to suppress my emotions and grief all day and to be attentive to other issues. I did not have self-control; so, I shouted at that person and told him what I had thought about him for years but had never said before.

When we have self-control, there is a better chance we will not yield to temptation and will not behave unethically, not report more working hours, or use unacceptable language. However, people do not have indefinite resources; we can have less restraint and feel tired at any time during the day. When we use all our efforts to regulate our behavior or our emotions, or to work on a cognitive task, then we might have less patience for other things that might seem unrelated. We might snap at people, or not pay attention, or we might not resist temptation and engage in unethical behavior. Our self-control can be weakened by certain situations, and that can lead to less ethical behavior.

A group of researchers led by award-winning professor Francesca Gino from Harvard University, who was honored as one of the world's fifty most influential management thinkers by Thinkers50, conducted several experiments.[4] They examined whether people would cheat more when they put effort into a certain task and used their resources of self-control. For example, in one experiment, the researchers asked participants to watch a video on the computer. Various unrelated words ran across the bottom of the screen as they watched. In the *non-depleted condition*, the participants were not given any instruction regarding these words, while in the *depleted condition*, participants were told not to look at or read these words, which demanded a special effort. Then the participants were given the opportunity to cheat by overstating their performance on a problem-solving test (they believed nobody could find out that they cheated). More people cheated in the depleted condition than in the non-depleted condition. That is, when they had to pay special attention not to look at the words, they used their resources and had less self-control to resist the temptation.

Overload and depletion were found to be related not only to cheating, but to less compliance with rules. Over three years, a group of researchers observed the hand-washing habits of 4,157 caregivers in thirty-five hospitals in the United States.[5] Most of the caregivers were nurses, and the rest were care technicians, physicians, and therapists. They found that the caregivers washed their hands less often as the day progressed, not following standard procedures, and it decreased at a greater rate when work intensity was higher. This is another example showing that when we are tired and depleted, there is a decline in our self-regulatory capacity, and, as a result, we see reduced self-control and less compliance with rules. These results might not surprise you, but they are very important and alarming. Washing hands is proven to reduce infection, and not complying with this important rule may increase the rate of infections.

Sleep and Unethical Behavior

Ruth, a midlevel manager in a big company, is very nice and polite; she is never rude and is usually attentive. Lately, however, people have noticed that she is less polite and tends to shout at colleagues. They thought that something bad happened to her, or that she was upset about something. To their surprise, they found out that she was not upset at all, but she had started going out every night until 2 AM, and therefore had been sleeping much less than she was used to. This lack of sleep affected her behavior. We know that sleep deprivation affects performance and mood, but here we are talking about self-control. Employees who work longer shifts and are tired do not have sufficient cognitive resources and consequently have less self-control. Indeed, lack of sleep was related to unethical behavior.[6] In one study, the researchers showed that the more time participants slept the night before, the less they cheated on a test. In another study, participants rated their sleep over the prior three months, and their supervisors rated their ethical behavior using items such as "claiming credit for someone else's work." Findings showed that insufficient sleep was negatively correlated with unethical behavior.

The implications of these results are significant. Individuals should take into consideration that reduced self-control caused by the factors previously discussed may lead to unethical behavior. One of the things we can do is to take breaks in order to charge our batteries. Employees should be given the opportunity to rest, to be given a little downtime, and not to be asked, if possible, to work on shifts that interfere with their sleep. We know that being overtired and depleted influences our performance. However, these studies show that an overworked employee has the potential risk of breaking some often crucial rules.

Ethical behavior is extremely important to an organization's functioning and to ensuring good relationships among colleagues. These values ought to come from the top: management sets the tone followed by employees. As mentioned in the beginning of the chapter, companies lose a lot of money due to the unethical behavior of their employees. Organizations that uphold an ethical culture will reduce such damage to a minimum.

Of course, there's more to ethics than refraining from bad behavior; it's also about actively cultivating good practices. According to a study conducted at Bentley University,[7] 86 percent of millennials said that it is a priority for them to work in ethical and socially responsible companies. An article in *The Guardian* entitled "Millennials want to work for employers committed to values and ethics" discussed a survey conducted in the United Kingdom of two thousand people.[8] A hefty 44 percent thought that a job that helped others was even more important than getting a high salary; 36 percent said they would work harder for a company that benefited society. Clearly, social values and ethics are important to today's younger generations. Working for a company that donates to worthy causes and that maintains fairness resonates with them and sparks their enthusiasm to be part of such an outfit.

Moreover, ethical values cover more than the obvious transgressions of stealing, lies, and fraud. Such values also relate to social issues such as respect, fairness to workers, and diversity (of different ethnicities, genders, and backgrounds). The importance of diversity will be discussed in the next chapter.

8

Diversity in the Workplace
Different Is the New Efficient

Diversity: the art of thinking independently together.
—MALCOLM FORBES

Today there is more awareness of the need for diversity in the workplace. Diversity is the degree to which a group is composed of different people, especially of different races, genders, ethnicities, cultural backgrounds, and other characteristics.

While many companies strive for a wide range of employees, there is still a lot to be done. Take, for example, the top management of my university. Over the last ten years, the president, the provost, and the general manager were men, with only one or two women deans (depending on the year). I'm sure you'll agree that this is far from gender diversity. However, many companies *are* undergoing a process of change, and there are now more women and people of color in top management positions and on the boards of directors.

Studies show that ethnic and gender diversity in the workplace is not just a moral or a politically correct issue; it also has a practical benefit. Diversity has a positive influence on company performance. Numerous studies found that organizations and businesses with gender diversity perform better. For example:

- A 2008 report found that Fortune 500 companies with more women directors showed significantly better financial performance.[1]
- Researchers from Australia, the United Kingdom, and Malaysia found that companies with more women in top management positions or on the board of directors showed better financial success.[2]
- Researchers from the Credit Suisse Research Institute reviewed 2,360 companies and found that those with at least one woman on the board performed better than companies that did not have any women on the board. They concluded that companies with a higher percentage of women in senior management or on the board of directors exhibited better financial performance.[3]
- A study conducted in 2019 in Vietnam examined the influence of women board members on the performance of 170 nonfinancial corporations listed on the Vietnamese stock exchange. It found that the number of women on the boards of directors was positively related to the firms' performances.[4]
- Another study found that companies with more women in top management performed better, but only if the company focused on innovation.[5]

Of course, diversity is not only about gender; racial diversity has similar effects. For example, researchers from Texas and California surveyed 177 national banks.[6] They received data on the financial performance of the banks, their racial diversity, and the emphasis the banks made on innovation. The findings showed that in banks that emphasized innovation, racial diversity was positively related to performance; the more diversity, the better performance.

Another study investigated the influence of racial diversity on the performance of juries.[7] Participants were involved as juries in a mock trial of sexual assault. They were assigned to six-person groups of jurors that were either all white or composed of four white and two black jurors. When deliberating on the case, the diverse groups were found to make fewer inaccurate statements and exchanged a wider range of information than all-white groups.

The benefit of diverse groups is also evident in science. Richard Freeman, a professor of economics at Harvard, together with his PhD student Wei Huang, analyzed 2.5 *million* research papers in scientific journals and examined the ethnic identity of the authors.[8] Their findings, published in the prestigious journal *Nature*, showed that papers with authors from different ethnicities were more cited than those that were written by authors of the same ethnicity. Typically, the more a paper is cited, the stronger and more influential it is.

A McKinsey report examined the influence of gender and international diversity on a company's financial performance.[9] Researchers examined the board composition of 180 companies in France, Germany, the United Kingdom, and the United States from 2008 to 2010. The results were clear: The financial success of the diverse companies was significantly higher than those that were less diverse. These studies clearly show that diversity has great benefits for companies and enhances their performance. The reasons are quite obvious. People from different backgrounds have different perspectives, knowledge, and points of view that lead to more innovation and creativity. When you bring to the room people with different opinions, the decision-making process is more complex, and people consider more information. The more points of view and perspectives that are heard, the more chance of a better solution and more innovation and creativity.

In the article "How Diversity Makes Us Smarter," published in *Scientific American*, Katherine Phillips from Columbia Business School, one of the leading researchers on diversity at work, suggests an additional reason that diverse groups perform better: members of homogenous groups believe that they will easily come to an agreement because they have similar perspectives. In contrast, when individuals work in diverse groups, they anticipate that there will be disagreements due to their differences. As a result, the group members work harder and prepare themselves better since they believe it will be more difficult to reach a consensus. This hard work often leads to better results.[10]

If this is true, is it possible that just the inclusion of one group member of a different race than the others could influence the group performance, without them even being aware of that person's opinions or thoughts? The results of the following fascinating study say yes.

Researchers examined the influence of racial diversity on the decision-making and performance of financial traders.[11] They trained people with a background in finance to calculate the true value of shares of stock. Participants were then assigned either to homogenous groups or to diverse groups (i.e., a group that included at least one person of a different race or ethnicity than the other members). The researchers conducted their study in two markets: North America and Southeast Asia. In North America, the nondiverse group was composed exclusively of white traders, whereas the diverse group included one African American and one Latino trader. In Asia, the nondiverse group was composed exclusively of Chinese, and the diverse group included Malays and Indians.

The results were almost unbelievable. Participants in diverse groups were significantly more accurate in pricing stocks than participants in homogenous groups. In fact, they were 58 percent better at pricing the assets to their true value. The homogenous groups tended to pay irrational and too-high prices that were further from the true value of the stocks as compared with the heterogeneous groups. In other words, there were greater chances of creating a dangerous bubble when a homogenous group was trading than when the traders were of differing ethnicities. That is an astonishing finding that can have a very significant impact. It's also interesting to note that the beneficial effect of diversity was retained even when no unique information was received from the minorities, and even when they did not possess special skills. The researchers concluded that "their mere presence [the minorities] changed the tenor of decision-making among all traders."[12]

It seems that just the presence of an individual from a different ethnic group causes group members to be more analytical and critical and behave more logically, rather than trading at unreasonable prices. This study has significant implications, not just for financial markets, but for the workplace in general; including various ethnicities in a group or organization would seem to enhance prospects for arriving at a better decision. And this holds true for members of both the majority and minority ethnicities within the group.

The findings of these studies suggest that diversity should be a goal for companies and organizations for both moral and practical reasons.

How Diverse Is Your Team?

The studies in this chapter indicate that having a diverse team will help us to make better decisions. So the next time you're collaborating on a project at work, look around you. Are your team members all the same race or gender as you? If so, be careful to consider all your options and avoid making decisions too quickly. You could probably benefit from getting an outsider's perspective. When assembling a working team, task force, or committee, make an effort to include as many people as possible from different ethnicities, genders, and backgrounds.

The studies presented here demonstrate the importance of choosing the right combination of group members for a specific task and how factors we are not aware of affect our behavior and decisions.

The Influence of Native and Foreign Language

We live in a globalized world in which companies often employ workers from other countries, and we engage in frequent communication with businesses around the globe. Millions of people hold important conversations and negotiations in which at least one side, and often both sides, chooses English as the most convenient medium for communication, despite English not being their mother tongue.

Findings show that decision-making in a foreign language differs from decision-making in your native tongue. And surprising as it may sound, not only decisions, but also moral judgments are affected by using a nonnative language. The influential psychologist and economist Daniel Kahneman received the Nobel Memorial Prize in Economic Sciences for his research on decision-making and judgments. Kahneman's book, *Thinking, Fast and Slow*, summarizes decades of his research, much of which was conducted with his friend and fellow researcher Amos Tversky (they collaborated by conversing with each other in English and Hebrew); unfortunately, Tversky died before the

Nobel committee awarded the prize. As Kahneman says, decisions and reasoning involve two main types of processes: analytic and systematic, and intuitive and heuristic.[13] Intuitive decisions rely more on emotions and are more prone to biases, which can result in faulty and sometimes illogical decisions. These cognitive biases do not happen by chance. They are the outcome of the human tendency to employ "heuristics" in day-to-day life. Heuristics are simple and efficient rules that people use to form judgments and make decisions as they go about their daily lives. They can be likened to "mental shortcuts," "rules of thumb," or simply "common sense." Typically, heuristics focus on *one aspect of a complex problem and ignore others.*

Indeed, our decisions are often biased and not rational. One such bias is the *framing bias.* People make decisions based on whether the options are presented as a loss or as a gain. Take this problem, for example, which is often used in studies:

> Recently, a dangerous new disease has been going around. Without medicine, 600,000 people will die from it. In order to save these people, two types of medicine are being made.

The problem framed in terms of gains says:

> If you choose Medicine A, 200,000 people will be saved. If you choose Medicine B, there is a 33.3 percent chance that 600,000 people will be saved and a 66.6 percent chance that no one will be saved.

The problem framed in terms of losses says:

> If you choose Medicine A, 400,000 people will die. If you choose Medicine B, there is a 33.3 percent chance that no one will die and a 66.6 percent chance that 600,000 will die.

As you can see, the numbers are exactly the same. However, in the first case, the problem is framed in terms of positive gain, showing how many people will live. In the second case, when it is presented in terms of loss, it shows how many people will die. Medicine A is presented as a sure option, while Medicine B is more risky. Studies show that we have an aversion to loss, which is the tendency to give more weight to negative outcomes. Therefore, people make different decisions depending on how the problem is presented. They are more willing to choose the riskier option and select Medicine B if the problem is presented in terms of losses and also mentions death. They are more conservative and choose the less risky Medicine A when the problem is presented in terms of gain and positive outcomes.

A group of researchers led by professor Boaz Keysar from the University of Chicago, who conducted many studies on negotiation and decision-making, investigated what happens if this problem is presented in a foreign language, compared to one's native language.[14] In several experiments, they presented the problem to three groups of participants: a group of native English speakers who spoke Japanese as a foreign language, a group of Korean native speakers who knew English as a foreign language, and a group of native English speakers who spoke French as a foreign language. All the participants were presented with the same problem, some in their native language and some in the foreign language, some framed in terms of gain and some framed in terms of loss.

The results clearly showed the effect of framing when the problem was presented in the participants' native language. Participants were more likely to choose the sure option when presented in terms of gain (how many will live), and the riskier option when presented in terms of loss (how many will die). And yet this effect *disappeared* when participants made the decision in a foreign language; the framing did not influence their decision. It seems that a nonnative language increases systematic processes and reduces biases.

Let's take another example of bias:

Imagine you are in a store and you want to buy a jacket for $125 and a calculator for $15. The salesperson tells you that you can buy this calculator for $10 in their other store, which is located twenty minutes' drive away. Would you make this trip?

Now, read this problem:

Imagine you are in a store and want to buy a jacket for $15 and a calculator for $125. The salesperson tells you that in their other store, the same calculator costs $120 and that the store is a twenty-minute drive away. Would you make the trip to that store?

When a Forked Tongue Is a Good Thing

Try this: If you are fluent in another language, try thinking through your next decision using that language. Assess that decision compared to your decision-making powers in your mother tongue. You might be pleasantly surprised by a decision made in a foreign language, because the chances are that it will be more rational and less biased! When you work in a team, try to include a person who speaks a foreign language, and if possible, conduct the discussion in that language. There is a better chance you will reach more rational and less biased decisions.

If most of the team members are not fluent in another language, ask that person to reach the decision in her or his language and see if there are points you did not think of.

If you think that in both cases the discount is exactly the same, five dollars, then you are right. In the first case, the discount is 5 out of 15, and in the second case, it is 5 out of 125, but in both cases you save exactly the same amount. Therefore, whatever you decide should not be influenced by the fact that the discount is on the expensive item or on the cheap item. However, most people choose to make the trip to save the five dollars out of the fifteen than to save the five dollars out of the $125. They think that it is worth taking the trip for saving one-third of the price and not for saving only 4 percent. This is another example of the framing effect. A group of researchers examined whether a foreign language will influence these decisions.[15] They presented these two problems to two groups of Spanish-speaking participants. Some of the participants were presented with the problem in their native language, and some in English. They found that the framing effect was much stronger when participants were presented with the problem in their native language. In other words, when the problem was presented in Spanish, the participants were more likely to respond that they would make the trip when the discount was out of 15 euros than when it was out of 125 euros. For the participants who read the problem in English, the framing effect was reduced, and the difference between those who said they would make the trip to save 5 out of 15 euros and those who said they would take the trip to save 5 out of 125 euros was much smaller.

These experiments strongly suggest that decision-making in a foreign language reduces the incidence of biases. When making choices in a foreign language, people rely more on systematic processes that follow normative rules as compared to decision-making in one's native tongue, which is more intuitive and biased. The reason for this, researchers suggest, is that using a foreign language reduces and weakens emotional response and increases distance.

Foreign Language and Moral Decisions

Studies show that foreign language also influences moral decisions.

Consider this dilemma:

> A small incoming train is about to kill five people, and the only way to stop it is to switch the train to another track. However, doing so will kill one person who stands on the other track but will save the lives of the other five.

This is a difficult dilemma. In order to save five people, we have to actively do something that will kill one person. A utilitarian response considers the outcome and the consequences for overall well-being. According to this view, if an action increases the well-being in a situation, it is considered morally right. Thus, a utilitarian response will be to sacrifice one person to save five, since it supports the greater good. On the other hand, this would violate the moral prohibition against killing, and it is difficult to imagine ourselves taking an action that kills someone. Therefore, people routinely avoid that option and choose not to do anything—even though it means five people would die.

Three studies have investigated the influence of foreign language on the answers to this moral dilemma.[16] The researchers presented this dilemma to participants either in their native language or in a foreign language. In all three studies, those who read the dilemma in a foreign language made utilitarian decisions significantly more often, choosing to divert the train and kill one person to avoid killing the five, compared to those who read the dilemma in their native language. The researchers suggest that the increased psychological distance resulting from the use of a foreign language leads to moral judgments that are untainted by extraneous emotional considerations.

Taken together, the studies presented in this chapter show that ethnic and gender diversity in the workplace is very important, not only from the moral point of view, but also in light of its practical benefit. Many studies have shown that companies with greater diversity are more financially successful than those with less diversity, and that the mere presence of a group member of different ethnicity positively affects the group's performance. More women and ethnic diversity in managerial positions and on boards of directors will increase the financial performance of a company and make it more successful. Indeed, upholding diversity as an ideal produces a situation in which everybody—employers, workers, and society—wins.

Foreign language also influences the workplace. Studies show that a foreign language activates more systematic and rational thinking. These findings have implications for negotiations, business decisions, and moral decisions in organizations. Frequently, business negotiations in Western countries are held in English, even though it might not be the mother tongue of the people doing the negotiating, and English is enlisted to serve as common ground. These experiments suggest that business negotiations and decisions made in a foreign language rely more on systematic processes and clearly reduce the incidence of biases compared to decisions made in a native language. In terms of profitability, less biased decisions are more desirable. It is therefore recommended that, if possible, teams should include a participant whose mother tongue is different from the language being used. This is true not only for teamwork. Individuals who make savings, investments, and personal decisions in a foreign language rather than in their native tongue may be less biased in their thinking.

9

Will This Tie Get Me Hired or Fired?

How the Clothes We Wear Affect Us and Our Team

> What you wear is how you present yourself to the world, especially today, when human contacts are so quick. Fashion is instant language.
> —MIUCCIA PRADA

When I gave a talk at Google headquarters about my first book, I invited several friends who were employees of more conservative workplaces and who had never been exposed to a high-tech company. They were amazed and a bit shocked when they saw Google employees wearing jeans, T-shirts, and sneakers, clothes they thought were nonprofessional and overly casual. What was appropriate in one organization was clearly inappropriate in another and was received differently, at least at first glance!

Over the past decades, there has been a change in what is considered acceptable workplace attire. It is typically less strict, but some workplaces and organizations have dress codes or guidelines, and what is acceptable in one organization may not be okay in another. It depends on the nature of the job and type of organization; some require a more formal style, others allow casual dress, and many have casual dress days at least once a week. Employees usually adhere to the dress code of their organization. Banks or law firms, for example, have a strict dress code. Men are expected to wear dress pants or suits, and women are expected to wear tailored pants or knee-length skirts and a matching blazer. They know that they can't come to work wearing a T-shirt or plastic sandals, or with the top shirt buttons open. There are many career services websites that suggest what to wear for work and define what is considered business professional. However, sometimes it is not that clear. This is true especially for women who can't decide the length of their skirt even when wearing professional suits. Some workplaces may require businesslike attire, but no longer insist on a tie. In other workplaces, such as many high-tech companies, employees wear whatever they choose, and most of them come to work in T-shirts and jeans.

Additionally, several cases that drew attention to this issue helped to change certain requirements, especially for women. In December 2015, a London receptionist, Nicola Thorp, was sent home for not wearing high heels. She collected signatures and launched a parliamentary petition calling for a law prohibiting firms to force women to wear high heels. In 2010, the Swiss bank UBS issued a forty-four-page dress code. It included details not only about suits, jackets, and blouses, but also about ties, pockets, and types of glasses, and instructions about open and closed buttons. This code made headlines, was criticized and ridiculed, and was consequently revised the following year. Japan's Nippon TV and Business Insider Japan reported in late 2019 that women at several workplaces were not allowed to wear glasses. (Men, to be clear, were allowed to do so.) Women in Japan started the hashtag "glasses are forbidden," which led to many angry reactions on social media. Many people saw a direct link between the ban on glasses and the requirements of many workplaces in Japan that women wear high heels to work, regardless of the difficulty and inconvenience. Consequently, Japanese women started a social media campaign, the #KuToo movement, protesting this requirement.[1]

Why do we pay so much attention to dressing for the job? Well, there is a set of cultural expectations and norms—all of which change over time—that have been conditioned in our minds. When one's attire does not comport with the norms or expectations that are appropriate for the role, it instantly generates a dissonance that is often judged unfavorably, or at least gives us pause (like my friends who were shocked to see Google employees in casual dress). Different roles can run the gamut of job interviewees, parents, children, professionals (of both collars), government workers, clergy, teachers and other functionaries and, most commonly, everyday people doing everyday things. So while physical cues such as clothing and color are visible to the eye, those same cues must pass through the filter of cultural expectations, norms, and perceptions—which are invisible—before final judgment is passed.

Around 1995, when I taught psychology at Harvard, I noticed that almost all the male professors put on a tie before they entered the classroom, and many of them took it off as soon as they were back in their office. I asked the young professors if they were told to wear a tie when they were teaching, and the answer was that they felt it was expected of them. Today, professors in many universities don't wear a tie or a suit, but I believe there is an unspoken dress code. Most of the professors won't enter the classroom wearing shorts or flip-flops. However, they might dress like that if they are working in their lab or their office. Nobody ever told me what to wear when I gave a lecture, either in the university or to various audiences, such as to employees of big companies. However, I want to convey professionalism, and therefore I dress accordingly.

But beyond dressing to be viewed as a professional, there's more to the question of attire than meets the eye. I recently watched a lecture in social psychology by Matthew Lieberman, a professor of social sciences at UCLA. Professor Lieberman came to his undergraduate class dressed in a white shirt, tie, and a black jacket. He opened the class by giving his students several simple commands such as "stretch right" and "stretch left"; the students gladly complied. After several neutral commands he asked the students to give him the finger. Most of the students did not do that.

Lieberman said that he has taught this course about fifteen times, and each time he has started with this exercise. He said that at each lecture, most of the students complied and gave him the finger. The only difference was that in the previous sessions he was dressed casually and not with a tie and a jacket. The fact that he was wearing a suit made him appear to be an authority figure, and it was hard for the students to disrespect him and give him the finger.[2] This is an example of how a person's attire could, practically speaking, dictate the behavior and attitudes of others without their being aware of it. In this case, Professor Lieberman was dressed in an imposing and authoritative black suit and tie, which subdued the vast majority of intelligent students into deferent behavior.

So clothes do indeed exert a tangible influence on others. Does this mean that any time you dress in formal attire you will inspire deference and respect in others? Well, clothes psychology is not as one-dimensional or as straightforward as that. We need to dig deeper. Back in the day, when the book *Dress for Success* came out,[3] it was followed by studies on the effects of different types and colors of clothes; everything seemed simple. Want to excite your date? Wear something red. Looking to sell a luxury product to a high-end client? Wear a tie. Want to command respect and exude status? Don a black suit and tie, and so forth. But reality is more complex.

How Perceptions and Judgments Are Altered by Attire

We are all conditioned by our culture to behave, speak, and dress within an "acceptable" domain. When we encounter a transgression of such norms, we briefly stop to assess the contradiction and typically pass some sort of judgment. This holds especially true in our assessments of professionals—doctors, teachers, technicians, dentists, clergy—who occupy a narrower sliver of norms and expectations.

In a survey conducted in 2009 by medical students in the United Kingdom,[4] 586 adult patients were asked to rate photographs of male and female medical doctors wearing different attire including scrubs, professional-formal, professional-informal, smart casual, casual, and the traditional white suit. In each photograph, the doctor had a stethoscope around his or her neck. Patients preferred and had the most confidence in the doctors wearing the white coat—you know, the same white coat we've been conditioned to see on scientists and doctors in movies, TV shows, and commercials. The white coat has become an established stereotype that has been repeatedly reinforced by advertisers, who are expert in pressing our psychological buttons. Similar results were found in another study conducted by researchers from the Ochsner Health System in

New Orleans, Louisiana.[5] They showed patients four images of the same doctor, each one with different attire. In one image, the doctor wore a traditional white coat; in the other image, a white coat with scrubs; in the third image, he wore scrubs with no coat; and in the fourth image, he wore a shirt and a tie without a coat. The patients were shown the images and were asked to state their preference. The results clearly showed that most patients (69.9 percent) preferred doctors wearing a white coat.

Style of clothing has been shown to be a marker of professionalism in specific professions. For example, students perceived teachers who were dressed casually as more approachable but less knowledgeable than those who dressed more formally.[6] A study conducted by researchers from the University College London led by Adrian Furnham, one of the most cited researchers in the United Kingdom,[7] showed that dentists and lawyers who were dressed formally were perceived as more capable, and potential clients preferred them over those wearing casual attire such as a T-shirt and jeans.

Many studies prove that the way we dress influences the way we are perceived and judged, to the point of warping objective perceptions. Would you believe that performances of classical soloists were assessed differently by music professionals solely according to the kind of dress the musicians wore? A remarkable study by Noola Griffiths from Teesside University in the United Kingdom found just that.[8] Griffiths filmed several female violinists playing three pieces. The women were dressed in different styles: one wore jeans and a T-shirt, one wore a club dress, and one wore a concert dress. The violinists were similar in height, eye color, and hair length. The video clips were shown to elite music students and to members of the Sheffield Philharmonic, who were asked to rate the violinists' performances. In reality, all three video clips were dubbed with the exact same soundtrack. However, although the music was the same, the observers were swayed, and in fact prejudiced, by the violinists' style of dress. Those who were dressed in concert attire were rated higher on technical proficiency than violinists wearing a club dress or jeans and T-shirt. These results are particularly interesting since the evaluators were musicians themselves, who ostensibly were focused purely on the music quality rather than extraneous details. Take heed of this study, particularly in your work, because it confirms an all too human reality you should pay attention to. Clothes actually do color how we are perceived, including our objective performance.

Indeed, professionals at different levels are subject to certain expectations and stereotypes, and this is especially true for women. Peter Glick, a social sciences professor at Lawrence University,[9] is well known for his studies on sex stereotyping. Glick and Susan Fiske, from Princeton University, coined the term *benevolent sexism*. It means that women are perceived as delicate, sensitive, and weak, and need to be protected and provided for.[10] Studies show that benevolent sexism is no less oppressive than direct hostile sexism, where a woman is perceived as a threat to the male authority at the workplace. In one of Glick's studies, male and female participants were presented with videotapes of women wearing either sexy clothes (heavy makeup, high heels, and a low-cut top) or business-professional attire (little makeup, black slacks, flat shoes, and a turtleneck top with a jacket). Each woman was presented as either a manager or a receptionist. The participants were asked to rate how competent, intelligent, skillful, and responsible each woman was and also asked to define how they'd feel emotionally if that woman were a coworker (relaxed, happy, fond, irritated, disgusted, or frustrated were among the options). The results are quite disturbing. When a woman was presented as a manager and dressed more provocatively than the more neutral option, participants rated her as less competent and felt more negatively toward her. In contrast, the receptionist's attire—whether provocative or neutral—did not influence their judgment of her competency.

Another group of researchers replicated this study with different stimuli and found similar results.[11] Here, the participants were shown an image rather than a video of a woman who was presented either as an office assistant or as the CEO of an advertising firm. The same woman was pictured in each image, dressed one way in half the images (wearing a business suit) and another way in the other half (wearing a low-cut blouse without a jacket). When the woman was presented as a CEO and dressed professionally, she was perceived as more competent than CEOs dressed more provocatively. Similar to the previous study, no difference in perception of professionalism was found when the woman was presented as an office assistant. So it is not clothing per se that generates judgments, but the cluster of cultural expectations and status markers that color our perceptions.

Dressed for the Part or Best for the Part?

The next time you interview someone or judge the performance of a colleague, ask yourself if you were influenced by the way that person was dressed. Once you're aware of that possibility, there is a better chance you will judge others more objectively and based on merit.

A more nuanced study makes the same point and stresses the importance of small details on first impressions. While many studies assess the effects of different styles of dress, a study conducted in the United Kingdom found that even minor adjustments such as a skirt below or above the knee or a single undone button influences the way women are perceived and judged at work.[12] Female participants were presented with four images of women, differentiated by their clothing (somewhat provocative or not provocative) and by their job (higher-level senior manager or lower-level receptionist). Two of the four women wore a shorter dress (just above the knee) and two buttons unfastened on the blouse. The other two women were dressed somewhat more conservatively, with only one button unfastened and a slightly longer skirt. In each pair that was dressed somewhat more provocatively, one woman was presented as a senior manager and one as a receptionist. The same division of roles was applied to the less provocative style of dress. Here again, only the women with the higher-level position were perceived and judged according to style of dress. When a woman manager was dressed more provocatively, she was perceived less favorably and as less competent than when she was dressed less provocatively. Remember, the differences between the women were relatively minor: only a single undone button and a slightly shorter skirt. In contrast, the women who were presented as receptionists were judged no differently based on dress style.

Other studies, rather than focusing on provocative or non-provocative dress, compared the influence of professional-looking and unprofessional-looking clothes. Unsurprisingly, they show that professional dress conveys competence and affects people's perceptions of professional qualities. Regan Gurung, a professor of psychology and human development from the University of Wisconsin, currently investigates ways to diffuse prejudice and sexism. In 2017, he conducted an interesting study with his colleagues.[13] They presented participants with ten photos of women; five of them were wearing dress pants and a classic sweater as per the dress code of many workplaces. The other five women wore leggings and various tops such as a sheer blouse or casual flannel shirt. Participants rated the women who were dressed by the rules as more intelligent, powerful, organized, and competent compared to the women who did not follow convention.

"Big Mistake. Big. Huge."

Many will recall a scene from the hit movie *Pretty Woman*. Julia Roberts enters a prestigious boutique dressed cheaply in a provocative minidress and thigh-high boots and asks about prices. The shop employees snub her and refuse to tell her the price; they just say condescendingly, "Oh it's *very* expensive!" When she says she actually has money to spend, the shop assistant, not wanting any undesirables tarnishing her store's image, says, "I don't think we have anything for you. You are obviously in the wrong place. Please leave." The next day Julia Roberts enters the same boutique, dressed in the expensive new clothes she has bought—elegant white dress, white gloves, and a hat. The woman who works in the boutique doesn't recognize her. Julia Roberts turns to her and says, "I was in here yesterday; you wouldn't wait on me. You work on commission right?" Then she shows her all her shopping bags from the expensive stores on Rodeo Drive and says, "Big mistake. Big. Huge."

Well, that movie was made in 1990. In the meantime, culture, with its norms and expectations, has continued to evolve. So in the context of high-end stores and the attire of prospective customers, salespeople know better and are aware that millionaires don't necessarily look the part. There is even a fashion trend, actually a state of mind, called "normcore" (the combination of "normal" and "hardcore")—wearing unpretentious and simple clothing like sneakers, hoodies, and so forth. For the wealthy, and even famous, such attire is apparently liberating. Conceivably, normcore could evolve to actually become a "reverse" symbol of status.

A 2014 study conducted in Italy by researchers from Harvard University, including Francesca Gino, a well-known marketing researcher, bears this out.[14]

Two groups of women were recruited for the study. One group consisted of shop assistants who worked in expensive, high-end boutiques selling luxury brands like Dior and Valentino. The second group was composed of pedestrians who were recruited at Milan's central station. All of the participants were asked to imagine a thirty-five-year-old woman entering a luxury boutique. One group was told that the woman is wearing a dress and a fur coat, and the other group was told she is wearing gym clothes and a jacket. They were then asked to rate on a seven-point scale how likely she was to buy something in the store, and whether she'd spend more or less than the average store client. They were also asked if she could afford to purchase the most expensive item in the store. The shop assistants from expensive boutiques who were familiar with upscale trends thought that the woman who wore gym clothes had greater purchasing potential. In contrast, those who were unfamiliar with such an environment thought just the opposite. Here again, participants' reactions were determined by cultural norms and expectations, but this time the norms and expectations of a *subculture*—the exclusive high-end shopping environment—which the average pedestrian is not intimately familiar with. Again, context is key. Similar results were found when, rather than asking participants to imagine a woman shopper wearing either a fur coat or gym clothes, they were told to picture one woman wearing flip-flops and a Swatch on her wrist, and the other woman wearing high-heeled sandals and a Rolex.

In another experiment, Harvard students were divided into two groups and asked to evaluate the teaching and research abilities of a fictitious professor who either normally wore a tie and was clean-shaven, or wore a T-shirt and had a beard. One group was told he taught at a prestigious university while the other received no information concerning the school. They found that when the professor was thought to be teaching at a prestigious university (context), the casually dressed, bearded professor (i.e., the nonconformer), received higher evaluations regarding his status and competence. Opposite results were found when no information was given about the university. Apparently, people believe that a person who flouts convention in a high-status institution is probably more self-assured and is thus attributed with higher qualities.

The previous studies all suggest that choosing how to dress for a certain role is a dynamic concept that changes as societal norms and expectations change.

A Stylist for Court

Anna Sorokin, or Anna Delvey, as she presented herself to the Manhattan society, pretended to be a German heiress with a $50 million trust fund. The Russian-born young woman was a Manhattan socialite who managed to trick businesses, banks, and people. She wore expensive, high-end clothes, was always seen in celebrity circles, and gave generous tips, creating the impression that she was indeed a millionaire. Anna frequented the most expensive hotels and clubs in New York City and did not pay. She took loans from the bank that she never paid back and promised a friend to pay for a trip to Morocco with her, but left the friend to foot the $60,000 bill. She was arrested in 2017, convicted of theft and larceny, and sentenced to four years in prison. Vanessa Friedman, fashion director and chief fashion critic for the *New York Times*, wrote an article in April 2019 entitled, "Does This Dress Make Me Look Guilty?"[15] Friedman says that during the trial, Sorokin often wore short white baby-doll dresses and white lace dresses chosen for her by a professional stylist whom she had hired to guide her on what to wear in court. (By the way, other celebrities, for example, Paris Hilton, have also hired stylists to help them choose their outfits for court.) I'm sure the choice of dress was not just because her stylist wanted her to look pretty. White symbolizes purity and innocence.

Friedman brings up another interesting example: the trial of Elizabeth Holmes. Elizabeth Holmes founded a billion-dollar company claiming to have developed revolutionary blood tests that only required a very small amount of blood to produce results. These claims were found to be false, and Holmes was charged with "massive fraud." As a successful businesswoman, Holmes was known to always wear a black turtleneck and pants, similar to Steve Jobs. When she came to court, she wore a light-gray suit. According to Friedman, her dress choice was meant to symbolize going "from the dark side toward the light."

I totally agree with Friedman, and her opinion is backed by scientific proof.

The Role of Color

We have seen that the clothes we wear have an impact on the way we are perceived. It is not only the clothing style, but also the color of our clothes, that strongly influences the way we are perceived. Different colors are associated with different emotions, cognitions, and behaviors.

The Color White and the Color Black

White and brightness symbolize goodness, purity, and virtue, whereas black and darkness typically symbolize evil. We often use metaphors. For example, *pure as snow* or *the light at the end of the tunnel,* which relate the color white and brightness to positive things, and metaphors such as *dark ages, dark side, blacklist,* and *dark secret,* which relate the color black and darkness to negative things. You'll often see the same perceptions of black and white in movies: good characters wear white or light colors, whereas villains wear black or dark colors.

The question is: How strong and instinctive are these associations between white and good and black and evil, and might these associations influence our judgments and behaviors? Do dark or black stimuli evoke negative emotions, while bright and white stimuli evoke positive emotions? Is it really possible that a person wearing white will be perceived more positively than a person wearing black?

Studies show that we automatically and instinctively associate white and brightness with positive things and black and darkness with negative things. Researchers conducted several studies in which participants were presented with positive words such as *generous, brave,* or *gentle* and negative words such as *cruel, bitter,* and *liar,* and were asked to indicate whether each word was positive or negative.[16] This is an easy task. However, the researchers manipulated the font color of the words. Some of the words were displayed in white, while others were displayed in black, and they were all presented on a light-gray background. The researchers measured how long it took participants to categorize each word as positive or negative. The faster the participants answered, the easier the task was assumed to have been. If it is indeed true that positivity is automatically and instinctively associated with brightness and negativity with darkness, then the task should be more difficult and time-consuming when a positive word is dark and a negative word is bright. The reasoning is that white, which symbolizes good, is incongruent with negative words, and black, which symbolizes bad, is incongruent with positive words. Indeed, they found that it took the participants longer to categorize the words when they were white but negative, or dark but positive. These findings suggest that there is an instinctive association between brightness and positivity. We tend to associate dark and black with bad and evil, and white and bright with good.

If associating black/evil and white/good is automatic and instinctive, does it affect the way we perceive people who wear white or black clothes? Two researchers from Cornell University, Mark Frank and Thomas Gilovich,[17] conducted several experiments to examine this question. In one study, they examined the penalty records of professional teams from the National Football League and the National Hockey League in the United States over a period of fifteen years. They found that teams wearing black uniforms were penalized more than teams wearing other colors. There are several explanations to this finding. The teams wearing the black uniforms might have simply behaved more aggressively and deserved to be penalized more often. However, it's also possible that referees punish those who wear black uniforms more because they perceive them as more aggressive. In another study by the same researchers, football fans, students, and professional referees watched two nearly identical videos of football plays. In one video, the players wore a black uniform, and in the other, a white uniform. The participants were more inclined to penalize the team wearing black and rated them as more aggressive compared to the team wearing white.

These results clearly demonstrate that the black uniform color influenced the referees, leading them to perceive those who wear black uniforms as more aggressive.

So, should we wear white more often than black? In order to answer this, you have to remember the rule: Context matters. A black suit and a little black dress are considered classic evening wear. But your choice of dress should depend on where you're going—a night out or a job interview. It also depends on whether you are the interviewer or the person being interviewed. Remember that white is associated with innocence and purity, and it influences the way you are perceived. Think about all the associations and the metaphors related to black and white, think about the context, and then decide what image you want to present and how you want to be perceived. More importantly, wear what makes you feel comfortable.

The Color Red

When I give lectures about the influence of colors, I always ask my audience about their associations with red. I get many answers, such as danger, dominance, aggression, and energy. But there is one association that the audience never misses; red is associated with passion and sexuality.

I'm sure you want to know if there is scientific proof that wearing red influences the way we are perceived. There is—though the specific effect depends on the wearer's gender.

To examine this question, psychology professor Andrew Elliot and postdoctoral researcher Daniela Niesta conducted a series of experiments in which they showed male participants a black-and-white photo of the head and upper torso of a young adult woman.[18] For each experiment they chose a different photo: there were images of blonde women and brunette women, women who wore turtleneck sweaters and women who wore striped button-down shirts, women who were smiling and women who had a neutral expression. Within each experiment, the male participants saw the same woman—but on different background colors. Some saw the photo on a red background, others on white, green, or blue. The researchers asked the participants to rate how sexy she was and their level of attraction. In the final study, the woman's shirt was digitally colored red or blue, and the participants were asked to rate the likelihood they would ask this woman out, and how much money they would spend on her on a date. In all the experiments, the men who saw the woman on a red background rated her as more attractive and sexier than those who saw the same photo on a different color background. Participants also said they would spend more money on the woman who wore red. The effect of red was present across the board with all types of women, wearing turtlenecks or jackets, smiling or not, blonde or brunette. It's interesting to note that when asked what influenced their decision, the men were sure that the color of the background did not affect their judgments.

What about the influence of the color red on perceptions about men? A group of researchers headed by Andrew Elliot, the same researcher who conducted the experiments on men's perception of women, conducted a series of similar experiments. This time, women were presented with photos of men on either a red background, a white background, or a gray background. They asked the women participants to rate how attractive they perceived that man to be and their level of sexual attraction toward him. In two additional experiments, instead of the color of the background, the researchers varied the color of the man's shirt. Women perceived the man who was depicted on a red background or wore a red shirt as more attractive and more sexually desirable. The researchers suggest that red is associated with male dominance and power, just like in the animal world. Women are often attracted to dominant or powerful men and find them sexy. Therefore, when they see the man on a red background, it brings the association of dominance and power, and they find him more attractive.

These findings suggest that red might indicate assertiveness, power, dominance, and authority in men, while it conveys attractiveness and sexuality in women.

I've been asked many times by women what they should wear for different situations: job interviews, everyday work, delivering a lecture, etc. True, studies demonstrated that the way we are dressed influences the way we are perceived, and that women (more than men) are sometimes misperceived because of their clothes. However, the only advice I give is that a woman should dress the way she likes and wear what makes her feel comfortable. It has always been more complicated to be a woman in a traditionally male-dominated world, but we have "grown up" as a society (although there's still a ways to go) and it is morally and legally wrong to discriminate against women in any way, including penalizing her for her choice of attire.

For men who want to show confidence and power, my advice is to wear a red tie. If, on the other hand, you are going to a social gathering, or you are in a situation at work when you do not want to appear too powerful but rather friendly and a team member, a blue tie will do the job.

Again, the important thing is that you know what the color red conveys. In the end, it is your decision to make.

We Are What We Wear: The Influence of Clothes on Our Own Performance and Emotions

One of my students told me that when she goes to take exams, she chooses a shirt with an image of a child reading a book. She says that wearing that shirt makes her feel smarter. Is it possible that the way we dress influences our feelings and behavior and even our cognitive performance? According to studies, this is not pure fancy. The clothes we wear do in fact influence the way we feel, behave, and perform, including how we perceive ourselves. For instance, one study revealed that employees subjectively felt more competent and authoritative when wearing business attire, both formal and casual, than when wearing casual clothes. Interestingly, they felt less friendly when dressed in business attire.[19]

Even more interesting and less intuitive are the findings that the clothes we wear influence our own cognitive performance. Hajo Adam, a professor at the Jones Graduate School of Business at Rice University, and Adam Galinsky, an award-winning researcher and professor at the Columbia Business School, conducted an extremely interesting study.[20] Adam and Galinsky presented several experiments on the effect of a specific piece of clothing, a doctor's white lab coat, on cognitive performance. In one experiment they asked half of the participants to wear a white lab coat, while the other half did not. Participants were then given a cognitive task that demands selective attention, the Stroop Task; named after the psychologist John Ridley Stroop, this test was developed in the 1930s and is still widely used in cognitive psychology labs. In this task, the participants are presented with color words such as *green* or *blue*. The color of the ink and the word meaning are either congruent (e.g., the word *red* appears in *red* ink) or incongruent (the word *red* appears in *blue* ink). Participants have to name the ink color, rather than saying the word itself, as fast as possible. It is of course more difficult to do so when the font is blue, for example, but the word says *red*. Participants who wore the white coat performed significantly better than those who didn't wear the white coat. But there's more.

As I mentioned previously, the influence clothes have on us is mediated by cultural expectations and norms, all of which are unseen. A further crucial element that also exerts an invisible influence is "context," a person's internal representation of a particular situation. To probe the effect of context and whether it affects performance, the two researchers refined their experiment and found something interesting.

This time the participants were assigned to three groups. Two of the groups were asked to wear a white lab coat. However, one group was told that the coat was a *doctor's* coat and the other group was told that the coat—totally identical—was a *painter's* coat. Participants in the third group did not wear a coat; however, the experimenter placed a coat that they verbally described to them as a doctor's coat on a table in clear view. All of the participants were then given a task that demanded attention (spotting small differences between two very similar pictures as fast as possible). Amazingly, those who wore the "doctor's coat" performed significantly better than those who wore the "painter's coat," even though the coats were totally identical. They also significantly outperformed those who merely viewed the coat described as a doctor's suit. Did wearing the doctor's coat make people "smarter"? More reasonably, it gave them a boosted feeling of competence, which oiled their cognitive machinery. Again, participants were affected by an invisible force, that of context. Another study led by Professor Michael Slepian from Columbia University found that people wearing formal clothing evidenced more abstract thinking.[21]

But the clothes we wear influence not only our cognitive performance, but also our physical performance. A group of researchers from Germany took fourteen pairs of male athletes who were matched for age and size.[22] They competed against one another, once wearing a red jersey and once a blue jersey. When wearing the red jersey, participants had significantly higher heart rates and were able to lift heavier weight before the fight compared to those wearing a blue jersey.

Clothes and Negotiations

The clothes we wear influence our perceived power and feelings of dominance, which has implications for negotiations. Michael Kraus from the University of Illinois and Wendy Berry Mendes from the University of California, San Francisco, conducted a very enlightening study.[23] They invited adult men from the San Francisco Bay Area to a lab. The men were asked to wear a black suit with a long-sleeved dress shirt, black socks, and a pair of black leather dress shoes, or a white T-shirt, blue sweatpants, and plastic sandals. They were then asked to engage in a negotiation game with another participant who was not aware of the clothing requirements. In addition, the participants' testosterone levels were measured before and after the negotiation game.

Similar to the previous experiment in which participants wore a "doctor's coat" and thereby performed more intelligently, participants dressed in business attire performed better in the negotiation, making fewer concessions and greater profits compared to those who wore the T-shirt and sweatpants. In other words, just wearing professional clothes influenced negotiating behavior, feelings of confidence and dominance, and, most importantly, the outcome of negotiations.

Furthermore—and more surprisingly—the type of clothes worn had a physiological effect on the participants' testosterone levels, which is a marker of dominance among other things. The men who wore the sweatpants evidenced lower testosterone than those who wore the business suit.

It seems then that in critical business negotiations, unless you are supremely confident of the outcome, stack the cards in your favor by wearing business clothes. They might boost your negotiating power before you speak your first word.

Naturally, you are free to choose what you wear. Totally your decision! Always bear in mind, however, that how you dress affects how you are judged by others and how you feel about yourself. This is true on both a personal level (social gatherings, friends, acquaintances, dates, and so forth) and in one's working life (interacting with customers, colleagues, bosses, negotiating partners, and in job interviews). Crucially, always observe social and cultural norms. Never show a lack of respect for a particular occasion or setting. What is appropriate for a date, for example, is often not appropriate for a funeral or a house of worship. However you choose to present yourself, always be guided by how comfortable you feel psychologically wearing your chosen apparel, because if it feels unnatural, it will show—projecting outwardly to others through your body language and mannerisms, and inwardly producing a somewhat counterfeit sense of self, as if to say "this is not the real me," and throwing you off your game.

10

Judging a Book by Its Cover

How Our Physical Attributes Shape Perceptions and Interactions

Do not trust alone to outward appearances.
—AESOP, "THE CAT, THE COCK, AND THE YOUNG MOUSE"

J udging and assessing individuals is part of the work environment. Workers are evaluated by personnel managers, colleagues, supervisors, and employees—in job interviews, when people are considered for promotion or for a new role in the company, and even when choosing whom to bring in on a project or invite to lunch.

Naturally, we would want these evaluations and judgments to be based solely on merit while ignoring other irrelevant factors. However, there are other variables that are liable to seep into our minds, undetected, that could sabotage the task of choosing the best teammate. Studies show that hiring decisions are often based on factors that might not be relevant to the job requirements. For example, Lauren Rivera found that hiring practices are not limited to finding the best candidate based on the skills required for the job.[1] Recruiters often look for people who are similar to themselves in characteristics such as lifestyle, leisure activities, experiences, and the way they present themselves. If indeed this is the case, it explains the fact that there are more men in banking positions and more women teachers. We also often make judgments based on our biases about people's physical characteristics. These include (but are not limited to) facial features, their physical attractiveness, whether they have a high- or a low-pitched voice, and talking rapidly, to name a few. We can also unwittingly be affected by stereotypes.

As a psychology professor and researcher, I am well aware of the potency of seemingly irrelevant factors in skewing human judgment. Nonetheless, I am not exempt from such forces affecting me, as well. As a member and chair of the clinical department at my university, every year I interviewed students who wanted to be accepted to the clinical program. There were always several candidates with similarly excellent grades, glowing letters of recommendation, who all made a good impression in the interview, but I could not choose all of them. I also served many times on a committee charged with selecting candidates for a particular job position or post to fill. I never felt at ease at the end of these processes. I kept asking myself if, even with my knowledge, I might not be influenced by these other factors. Because it was important to me to reach the best decision, I found that I needed to remain vigilant and on guard lest I fall into the trap of errant judgment.

This chapter will present studies that show how various factors link directly with final evaluations, whether for hiring employees or deciding on promotions, job assignments, and other interactions among colleagues. Being aware of these factors can help nullify their effect in making work-related decisions and in day-to-day judgments of other people.

Physical Appearance: Beauty Is Only Skin-Deep

There's a fable I used to read as a child, and it goes like this: One day a young mouse went out into the world for the very first time. When he came back to his family's hole, he told his mother about the strange animals he encountered. One was soft and furry with a long winding tail, looked very beautiful, and purred. Another animal looked very scary, with pieces of raw meat on his head, a chin that wiggled; it spread its feathers and made a frightening cry. The mouse's mother smiled at his story and explained that the scary animal was not so frightening, just a harmless bird, but the beautiful fluffy animal was a mouse-eating cat that could have eaten him for dinner.

This lovely fable illustrates how careful we should be not to judge people by their looks. Although the fable is about a young mouse who still has to learn, studies show that the decisions and judgments of not only children, but grown-ups, and even of professional interviewers and decision-makers, too often rely on physical appearance.

Alexander Todorov, a Princeton professor who is well known for his studies on first impressions, found that people make split-second judgments based on the shape of a person's face. People made voting decisions after being exposed to the candidates' faces for less than a second, and they made inferences and judgments about a person's competence after a very brief exposure to that person's face.[2] In the hiring process, appearance is often our first impression of the applicant. Many résumés include a photo, which is the first thing the decision-maker sees.

In a faculty meeting I attended many years ago, each department head had to deliver a brief report on the new students he or she accepted that year. It was and still is very difficult to be accepted into graduate studies in psychology, and many good candidates were rejected. When a particular professor's turn came up, he quipped that he had accepted a certain number of new female students, and they were all very pretty. He was immediately chastised by the other professors for his inappropriate remark, and they were right, of course. However, I asked myself right then: Was the professor's flippant remark actually a telling indication, a bubbling to the surface, of the power of physical appearance in the interview context?

In some cases and in some professions, there appears to be a clear preference for physically attractive people. For example, in some restaurants, all the servers, men and women, are good-looking. I once walked into a restaurant and the first thing I noticed was that all the servers were tall, blond, and had blue eyes. It was definitely not a coincidence. In an article in the *Telegraph* from 2016, reporter Soo Kim describes the requirements for airline cabin crew.[3] She cites as an example an advertisement in the *New York Times* from 1966: "A high school graduate, single (widows and divorcees with no children considered), 20 years of age (girls 19 1/2 may apply for future consideration), 5'2" but no more than 5'9", weight 105 to 135 in proportion to height and have at least 20/40 vision without glasses." According to Soo Kim, there are still many physical appearance requirements for cabin crew.

Interviewers and decision-makers who have to choose among applicants for a job for the most part say, and often believe, that looks and physical appearance don't matter and should not be considered. The question is: Is that really true? Are there biases against certain people just because of their physical appearance?

Many studies show that physical attractiveness is an advantage, and that there is a prejudice against unattractive people. Good-looking people are more likely to be hired, to be promoted, and to get a raise.[4] In 1972, three researchers, Karen Dion, Ellen Berscheid, and Elaine Walster, wrote an article entitled "What Is Beautiful Is Good."[5] They showed that people often associate being beautiful with being better, and they tend to attribute more positive characteristics such as warmth, trustworthiness, and kindness to physically attractive people. Years later, researchers still find that people who are considered more attractive have an advantage in many situations, including as job candidates, in interviews, and in advancement opportunities.[6]

However, the association between physical attractiveness and evaluating job candidates is more complicated than it seems. Although people often discriminate in favor of the more attractive candidates, studies have found that in some cases, attractive people are being discriminated against. This phenomenon is called *beauty is beastly*. Tracy Vaillancourt, a professor at the University of Ottawa in Canada, suggests that there is an intrasexual competition among women, and that women react negatively to attractive females.[7] So, what is one of the factors that might influence how a candidate's attractiveness affects the evaluator's decisions? Gender.[8] Several studies have found negative reactions to attractive people of the same gender. Maria Agthe, a professor of social psychology at Ludwig Maximilians University in Munich, studied this effect.[9] In several experiments, Agthe and her colleagues found that evaluations of job applicants were positively biased toward attractive candidates of the other gender and negatively biased toward attractive candidates of the same gender. A group of researchers from the University of Groningen and Tilburg University in the Netherlands concluded that sometimes a person of the same sex might be perceived as a rival.[10] For example, in one experiment they asked students to read a job description, gave them several photos of mock applicants, some attractive and some less attractive, and asked the students to rate the likelihood that they would hire each of them. The only difference between the applicants was their photos. Results showed that men gave a higher rating to attractive candidates (both male and female) than to unattractive candidates. Women, however, preferred less attractive female applicants over highly attractive female applicants.

In a second experiment, the researchers asked human resource management (HRM) professionals rather than students to rate the mock candidates. These male participants' results were similar to those of the students and showed that professionals also discriminate against unattractive candidates. However, unlike the students, the female HRM professionals did not give higher scores to unattractive females than to attractive females. The researchers suggested a tentative explanation that the female HRM professionals were older and in less competition for sexual partners than students. Further research is needed to try to explain these results.[11]

Another study showed the importance of the applicant's gender. Researchers submitted 2,656 pairs of CVs in response to advertised jobs.[12] Each pair contained the CV of a male or female candidate without a photo, and one almost identical CV with a photo of the candidate that was either attractive or plain looking. They set up a telephone number with a voice mailbox and a Gmail account for each beauty category. Attractive men (in the photo) received many more callbacks than plain-looking males or candidates who had no photo. The results were very different for female candidates. Women applicants who sent their CV with no photo received significantly more callbacks than those with a photo, whether it was plain or attractive.

Several studies found that facial marks, such as scars or birthmarks, can influence interviewers' decisions. Researchers from the University of Houston and Rice University conducted two experiments.[13] In the first one, they asked participants to watch an interview with applicants who either had a port-wine stain, a scar, or no facial marks at all. Those who viewed an applicant with a facial mark rated the candidate lower than those who saw an applicant with no facial marks. In the second study, they asked managers to interview applicants with or without facial marks. Again, they found that the applicant with the facial mark received a lower evaluation. A later study found that interviewers had more negative feelings and displayed more negative behavior toward a person with a facial mark.[14]

Several factors may affect the influence of physical appearance on decision-making, and whether it is an advantage, a disadvantage, or irrelevant.

One factor is the type of job. A group of researchers headed by Professor Stefanie Johnson from the University of Colorado presented participants with photos of attractive and unattractive women. They asked the participants to rate their suitability for several stereotypically masculine and feminine jobs, for example, director or secretary.[15] The researchers found that attractiveness was beneficial for both men and women. However, while for men attractiveness helped in jobs that were considered both masculine and feminine, for women, attractiveness helped more when they applied for jobs considered feminine. (Unlike previous studies, they did not find the *beauty is beastly* effect.) Being attractive helped women less when they applied for masculine jobs, but they were not discriminated against.

Another factor that might affect the influence of physical attractiveness in hiring decisions is the desirability of the job. Researchers presented participants with photos of attractive and unattractive candidates and asked them to choose the most appropriate candidate for the job.[16] The researchers did not specify the type of job but described one job as very tedious, uninteresting, and laborious, and the other as interesting and exciting. More participants selected the attractive candidate for the more desirable job. In contrast, the reverse was true when the job was undesirable; more participants chose unattractive candidates for the less desirable job. Those who made the hiring decision believed that attractive people are entitled to good jobs and therefore will be less satisfied in less desirable jobs.

Organizational policy might also play a role in determining the influence of attractiveness. Many organizations use outside professionals to interview and select job candidates. However, in some organizations, employees choose their future coworkers. In some cases, the employee who chooses the candidate might work in cooperation or compete with him or her.

From personal experience, I know that peer selection is not uncommon. In my psychology department at the university, we, the professors, are the ones who evaluate the candidates and choose our colleagues, and it is possible that some might ask themselves how a certain candidate will influence their life and career in the department. In some cases, they might believe that they can cooperate better with a certain candidate and therefore promote their own career. Some people may feel that a certain candidate might compete with them for the best PhD students or for research grants. Although academic life is mainly about professionalism and science, there is certainly an element of politics that can't be ignored—as Henry Kissinger, former US secretary of state, said: "Academic politics are so vicious because the stakes are so small." Don't get me wrong, from my thirty years of experience in hiring decisions, I believe that in the vast majority of the cases our only consideration was who was the best for the job. However, that is not to say that sometimes other considerations might have influenced the decision. These considerations are not unique to the university. The question is whether physical attractiveness plays a role in such situations.

A group of researchers from the United Kingdom, the United States, and Singapore examined this question.[17] They asked participants to evaluate candidates based on two conditions: cooperation and competition. In the *cooperation condition*, participants were told that the candidate will work with them on a joint task and they might both be promoted, but it will depend on their joint work. In the *competition condition*, they were told that they will work on separate tasks and only one of them will be promoted, while the other one will leave the company. Participants were given CVs with photos of attractive and unattractive male and female candidates. The findings are quite revealing. In the case where the participants were expected to cooperate with the candidate, they preferred attractive men. In contrast, when they were expected to compete with the candidate, they preferred unattractive men. There was no difference in the preferences for attractive and unattractive females. These findings suggest that attractive male candidates are perceived as more competent, and therefore they are preferred in situations that require cooperation, yet they are discriminated against in a competitive situation, where people are worried that they will be outperformed. In contrast, females were not perceived as more or less competent based on their appearance, and therefore it did not matter if it was a competitive or cooperative situation.

Baby Face

I was once a member of a committee that had to choose someone for a managerial position that required dominance and leadership. After interviewing several candidates, there were two that we liked the best. One of them was a young man with what you might call a "baby face"—a round face with a small nose, large eyes, small chin, and high forehead. Both candidates seemed intelligent and had similar experience and references. All the members of the committee gave higher evaluations to the candidate who had a more mature face. The committee said that both of them were good, but their gut feeling was to choose the more mature-looking candidate. In the end, neither of them was chosen for the job for different reasons, but I kept asking myself what caused us all to prefer one over the other. I could not remember anything really differentiating them besides the baby face, which might have made him look a bit submissive and naïve. Is it possible that was the only reason we all thought he was not dominant enough?

People make all kinds of inferences and judgments when they look at a baby-faced person, not just that the person is cute. Social psychologist Leslie Zebrowitz, a well-known expert on face perception and facial stereotypes, has conducted many studies that demonstrate that individuals with baby-faced features are judged as warmer and more honest, trustworthy, innocent, and naïve. (Findings from an enlightening study on social perceptions show that criminal defendants with baby faces received more lenient sentences than others with more mature faces.[18])

Zebrowitz and her colleagues show that in screening candidates for senior executive positions, baby-faced individuals were perceived as weaker and less competent than individuals who looked more mature.[19] For example, baby-faced individuals were less favored as congressional leaders and for occupations requiring leadership, dominant qualities, and shrewdness. On the other hand, they were favored for occupations requiring warmth and compassion, such as nursing.[20]

Other studies bear out Zebrowitz's findings. One group of researchers printed 584 identical résumés of white and black males and females with either a baby face or a mature face and put each one in stamped, unsealed envelopes addressed to the principal researcher. They attached a photograph to each résumé, with either a baby face or a more mature face. The résumés were then "lost" in all kinds of places such as phone booths, park benches, and public transit stops. The researchers wanted to examine how many of them would be sent to the address on the envelope in order to help the person who "lost" the résumé. Only 36 percent of the résumés were sent back to the address on the envelope; for white and black females and for white males, résumés with baby faces were returned more than those with mature faces. There was no difference between baby faces and mature faces for black males.[21] And, in another revealing study, three marketing and business researchers created fictitious news articles about a pharmaceutical company.[22] The company, according to their story, introduced a new product that had side effects, and the question was whether the company had prior knowledge about them. The article was titled "CEO Denies Knowledge of Side Effects," and included a photo of the CEO. To make the accompanying image, the researchers took a single photo and manipulated the eyes and the chin to create two variants, one with a baby face and one with a more mature face. In addition, they created three different severity situations, depending on the percentage of people who experienced the side effects (1 percent, 10 percent, and 20 percent). In total, they had six versions of the article to cover the possible combinations of CEO facial features (baby face or mature face) and the severity level (1 percent, 10 percent, and 20 percent). Each participant saw the article with either the baby-face or the mature-face photo, and with only one severity level. They were then asked about their attitude toward the company (negative or positive) and what they thought about the honesty and integrity of the CEO. People had more favorable opinions about the company and rated the CEO as more honest when the CEO had a baby face, but only in the low-severity case (where 1 percent of the users experienced side effects). That is, in a more severe crisis, it did not matter if the CEO had a baby face. However, when the severity of the damage was low, then the CEO's facial features did matter.

More Than Meets the Eye

When you interview someone, or have a conversation with a colleague to decide if you want to pursue collaboration, ask yourself if your decision was influenced by the way that person looked. As bad and unfair as it is, physical appearance influences judgment. If you are aware of this possibility, you will be less affected by it, and there is a better chance you will judge people based on their merit instead of on the way they look. Be aware of how appearances can sway you, and the truth will appear.

These findings clearly show that physical appearance matters. There is not much that the candidates can do about the shape of their face, for example, but these findings should be considered very carefully by those who evaluate candidates and make the hiring decisions. People in decision-making positions have to ask themselves whether they had any bias for or against an applicant based on attractiveness or any other physical characteristic. It would be wise to include both men and women on a hiring committee. If there is a big difference between the ratings of the two genders, members of the committee should ask themselves whether it has anything to do with the candidate's physical attractiveness.

The Sound of One's Voice

When I looked for an agent for my first book, I sent the proposal to a number of literary agencies. Some of them invited me to their offices to talk about my idea, others asked me to write them with more details. I felt that it would be better to deliver my ideas in person rather than in writing, and that proved to be true. My agent invited me to the office, our talk led to signing a contract, and the rest is history.

Some people believe that if an idea is expressed nicely, it doesn't matter if they write it or talk about it. A study published in 2015 examined this question. The researchers conducted several experiments in which they asked students to evaluate job candidates.[23] Some of the evaluators read what the candidate had to say, some listened to exactly the same thing, and some watched a video of the candidate delivering his or her pitch. Those who listened to the candidates evaluated them as more competent, thoughtful, and intelligent than those who just read what the candidate said. There was no difference between those who just listened to the candidates and those who listened and saw them in the video. Similar results were found when the evaluators were professional recruiters. So, although many people don't think so, evaluators who listened to candidates' job pitches were more interested in hiring them than those who just read the pitches with the exact same words.

Hear! Hear!

If you want to be hired for a position, aside from written correspondence (CV, email, text message), make a special effort to have your voice heard—whether through a recorded message or on the phone. Do this even if the written and verbal messages are exactly the same! This is a supereffective "one-two punch" that keeps your name and personality fresh in the mind of your prospective employer and provides a deeper, multilayered level. Furthermore, it communicates motivation, depth of character, and, perhaps even sneakily, an implicit "relationship." All other things being equal between candidates, this is a virtually effortless hack that will land you the job. However, it might be beneficial to make a script for the call, so you won't sound nervous or unfocused.

Voice Pitch

Our tone of voice is often indicative of our emotions and state of mind. The same answer in an angry, sad, or impatient tone is judged differently than when said in a pleasant or happy tone. But is the voice quality also a factor? Do we judge people not only by the tone of their voice but also by its pitch?

Animal vocalizations contain information. That is, certain types of vocal signals may indicate dominance or fighting abilities.[24] Voice pitch in humans (high or low) also has an influence on the listener. Voices carry cues regarding the person's age, gender, and mood. Furthermore, studies have found that people make judgments about attractiveness and personality traits, such as dominance and leadership, based on a person's voice.[25] Men with a lower voice were perceived as physically stronger,[26] as more attractive,[27] and as more dominant than men with a high-pitched voice.[28]

Examples from international politics help to illustrate just how strong this effect can be. Before the 1979 elections in the United Kingdom, Margaret Thatcher took lessons with a speech coach to help her lower the pitch of her voice. In the 2011 film *The Iron Lady*, Thatcher is told that the main problem with her voice is that "it's too high and has no authority." Indeed, researchers who analyzed her voice over time concluded that it became deeper and more authoritative. One of the Israeli candidates for prime minister in the 2015 elections, Isaac Herzog, has a high-pitched voice, unlike his opponent Benjamin Netanyahu, who has a deep, low-pitched voice. Herzog knew that his high-pitched voice might damage his image, and in a video message to potential voters, he talked while someone else dubbed him in a lower-pitched voice. At the end of the clip, he said that he knows his voice makes people hesitant to vote for him. Herzog did not win the elections, for reasons other than his voice, but he was right that it definitely did not help. Studies clearly show that voice pitch is related to voting intentions.

In one study, a group of Canadian researchers manipulated the voices of nine US presidents, creating higher- and lower-pitched versions for each president's voice.[29] Participants listened to the recording of both versions, not knowing it was the same person. They were then asked who would be a better leader; who seemed more honest, trustworthy, and more dominant; who could better handle the economic situation; who was more intelligent; and who was more likely to be involved in a scandal. They were asked to choose for whom they would vote in a national election. Participants were more likely to vote for individuals with the low-pitched voice and attributed to them more favorable personality traits than to the higher-pitched voices. They perceived individuals with the low-pitched voices as more dominant, more attractive, offering better leadership qualities, being better able to handle the current economic situation, having more intelligence, and being more honest and trustworthy than the people with higher-pitched voices. In a second experiment, the researchers examined the influence of voice pitch of a nonpolitical man who read a nonpolitical sentence. They created low- and high-pitched versions of the same voice. The participants heard both versions and were asked to choose for whom they would vote in a national election. Again, participants said they were more likely to vote for the candidate with the lower voice.

If we favor candidates with lower-pitched voices, what does that mean when it comes to women candidates? Do people perceive women with lower voices as more competent for leadership roles? Casey Klofstad, an associate professor at the University of Miami, has conducted several studies that examined the influence of the voice pitch of males and females on perception and voting behavior.[30] Klofstad and his colleagues asked men and women to record the sentence "I urge you to vote for me this November" and created high-pitched and low-pitched versions. Participants listened to pairs of the candidates' voices, one with a low pitch and one with a high pitch, and were asked for whom they would vote. Both men and women voted more often for the men and women with low-pitched voices. Klofstad also examined the results of the 2012 US House elections and found that more candidates with deeper voices won their races; he suggests that our bias for lower-pitched voices could potentially contribute to the underrepresentation of women in leadership positions and in government.

Is this also true when the leadership roles are stereotypically "feminine," such as presidents of school boards and Parent Teacher Organizations (PTO)? Apparently, yes. Similar to previous studies, Anderson and Klofstad presented male and female participants with recordings of high- and low-pitched male and female "candidates" for the president of the PTO.[31] Both men and women preferred female candidates with a low voice. The researchers suggest that women with lower voices are perceived as stronger, more competent, and more trustworthy. Therefore, it doesn't matter whether the position is stereotyped as "feminine" or "masculine"—we prefer lower voices for leadership roles.

What influences us more, face or voice? Klofstad examined this question and found that both voice pitch and facial characteristics influenced elections, but facial characteristics had almost three times more influence than voice pitch.

To make things more complicated, two groups of researchers from Canada and the United Kingdom found that although women trust men with low-pitched voices when they have to choose political leaders, they trust men with high-pitched voices more in other circumstances.[32] For example, a study published in the *British Journal of Psychology* found that women perceived men with a low-pitched voice as more attractive for short-term relationships but viewed them as less trustworthy.[33] Another study found that women trusted men with a low-pitched voice less in a game where money was involved.[34] So we trust men with low-pitched voices when it comes to leading the country—but not when it comes to our own money!

A group of researchers wanted to examine whether this association between voice pitch and perceived leadership found in the laboratory was also true in the real world.[35] They examined CEOs in public companies and measured their voice pitch, the size of the companies, and their salary. They found that male CEOs with a deeper voice managed larger companies and made more money. This is an interesting finding, but we have to remember that it shows an association, not causality. That is, we can say that there is an association between a deep voice in a male CEO and his status, but we cannot say that deep voice *caused* that status.

Bring Attention to the Obvious

Job candidates can't control certain elements of their physical appearance, the shape of their face, and the pitch of their voice. However, in some occasions, when they feel that their voice or looks might decrease their chances to be hired, it might help if they refer to their looks or voice. In one study, participants were presented with CVs and photos of attractive women who were candidates for a stereotypically masculine job in construction. In some of the CVs, the candidate said, "I know that I don't look like your typical construction worker, but . . ." and then described her qualities. In the control group, the applicant only described her qualities. Those who acknowledged that their looks were incongruent with the typical construction worker were rated higher and were perceived as more suitable for the job compared to the control group.

Just Bring It Up

If you know that something about your presentation, such as a high-pitched voice or a baby face, might negatively influence the way you are judged, mention it in the interview or conversation. You can say something like, "I know I have a young-looking face, but it has nothing to do with my qualities and qualifications for a managerial job." If you address it directly, people may be less affected by these irrelevant physical characteristics, and it will have less of an influence on the way you are judged.

People make constant judgments at work. Not only in job-related interviews, but almost every day. We make judgments about our colleagues, about our supervisors, and about our employees. We have an opinion about their dominance, intelligence, and leadership abilities.

The studies we've covered in this chapter are alarming—even disturbing. Interviewers and decision-makers should consider these findings very carefully. In a perfect world, we would judge each other in a totally objective manner, ignoring irrelevant details that might sidetrack a sober evaluation of a person's merits or shortcomings. And yet research suggests that there are numerous irrelevant factors at work, beneath the surface, such as physical attractiveness and voice pitch, that affect our judgments. Making hiring decisions on the basis of these physical characteristics, which are unrelated to the qualities demanded for the job, is not only an injustice toward the candidates, it also hurts the organization by not hiring the best people for the job. Armed with awareness of these factors, we will be able to arrive at better and less biased judgments and decisions.

Part III

Whatever Works for You

The Power of Our Personal Habits

11

Switching On and Off

How Our Technology Use Affects Us

Cell phones are so convenient that
they're an inconvenience.
—HARUKI MURAKAMI

What is the first thing you do when you wake up in the morning? Well, maybe the second, after you brush your teeth? Many people would answer that they check their phone. I know that the first thing I do when I wake up is check my email and messages. I often see messages related to work, questions from my students, requests and reading material from committees I am on, or assignments submitted by my students. Somehow, without noticing it, I start working at 6 AM, as soon as I wake up. After I get ready for the day, I check my email and messages again while I drink my morning coffee.

Recent technology has been a game-changer in the world and in the workplace: in manufacturing, communication, improved working conditions, and increased efficiency and productivity.

Since entering the new millennium, we have benefitted from technology in so many ways. Companies do their business with entirely new tools and methods that were unrecognizable only a couple of decades ago. Machines, computers, advanced communications, AI, robotics, and more. All these have resulted in streamlined costs, instant response times, higher output, improved productivity, and more.

Thanks to technology, more people today can work from home, keep flexible hours, and even avoid traffic. There is no doubt that technological advances have changed our lives and made our work more efficient and more convenient. However, there is also a negative impact. People tend to have less face-to-face communication, which has a detrimental effect on relationships. The literature in this regard grows from day to day, and the social effects are beyond the purview of this book.

Just the smartphone alone has been a planet changer. Most people in the world are reachable today at any moment, whereas in the past you needed to be lucky to catch a person at home or at work while conveniently located near a telephone. Not to mention the multiple capabilities at our fingertips. Some of these functions may be helpful in the workplace, but they can also be a significant distraction, as we shall see.

The Influence of Smartphones at Work

Wherever we go, we constantly see people looking at their smartphones. They may be busy with their email, listening to music, shopping online, scrolling through Instagram, checking the news, booking a table at a restaurant, reviewing their stock portfolio, or just communicating with their friends or family. We notice this behavior in classrooms, restaurants, movies, when we're with friends and family—and it certainly does not stop when we're at work. In 2007, 122.32 million smartphones were sold. In 2019, that number jumped to 1.56 billion. According to Pew Research Center in Washington, 96 percent of Americans own some kind of cell phone, and 81 percent of American adults owned smartphones in 2018.[1]

In a survey conducted by *Time* magazine, 84 percent of the respondents said that they could not go one day without their phones, and 50 percent said that they sleep with their phones next to them.[2] Most of us are familiar with that special sort of panic upon discovering that we have misplaced our phone and cannot find it. At a recent dinner party, we all sat and waited for the last guest to show up. Her excuse for being half an hour late was that she had almost arrived when she noticed that she forgot her phone, so she returned home to get it. I asked her if she was expecting an important call or if someone in her family was sick. She said no. She simply could not be two hours without her phone. This is called *nomophobia*, the fear of being without our mobile phone. This phenomenon encompasses four domains of anxiety: the fear of not being able to communicate, of losing connectedness, not being able to access information, and giving up convenience.

It's important to discuss the use of smartphones, since their existence and easy access to the internet has changed the way we work, where we work, and how many hours we work. Smartphones enable us to be more flexible at our jobs since we can answer and deal with problems at home or even while walking down the street, but on the other hand it makes it very difficult to detach and disconnect from work while not there. Recent studies have concluded that this has a negative influence on our well-being.

The constant use of smartphones for work-related issues increases stress. Employees feel the pressure to be available all the time and to respond immediately to work-related issues. A study conducted in Sweden, and funded by the Swedish Council for Working Life and Social Research, found that constant text messages (not necessarily related to work) were associated with stress and sleep disturbances.[3] In this study ten thousand men and ten thousand women between the ages of twenty and twenty-four answered questions about their smartphone use, including the number of phone calls and text messages received and sent each day. They were also asked about their habits, such as whether they woke up at night because of the phone. In addition, they were questioned on perceived stress and sleep disturbances. A year later they were asked the same questions. The results showed that around-the-clock availability was related to stress and other mental health symptoms such as depression.

Some researchers refer to overuse of the smartphone as smartphone addiction and suggest that, similar to other addictive behaviors, overuse of the smartphone can interfere with everyday life. In a study conducted in 2017 in

Germany, 262 participants were given a ten-item questionnaire that measured smartphone addiction. They rated items such as "I miss planned work due to smartphone use" and "Feeling tired and lacking adequate sleep due to excessive smartphone use" on a six-point scale (from strongly disagree to strongly agree). In addition, they answered several questions about their productivity at work that assessed the number of work hours they'd missed due to various reasons in the past seven days. The researchers found a moderate negative relationship between smartphone addiction and productivity at work.[4]

Some organizations try to keep the boundaries between home and work, while in others, the norm is constant availability, even at home. Many studies have found that detachment from work when you leave the workplace is positively related to health and well-being. Sabine Sonnentag, a professor of work and organizational psychology at the University of Mannheim, Germany, found that the more psychologically detached from their jobs people are after working hours, the less exhausted they are.[5]

Smartphones, Sleep, and Stress

Many people use their phones right up until they go to bed.[6] However, this has a cost. In a study conducted by researchers from Norway and the United States,[7] one group of participants read from an iPad for four hours before going to sleep, while the other group read for four hours from printed books. After five nights, the groups switched. Those who read from an iPad took longer to fall asleep and had less REM sleep. The researchers concluded that blue-enriched light from a tablet can have a negative effect on sleep. Another study found that longer screen time before bed was related not only to longer time to fall asleep but also to poor sleep quality.[8]

In another study, researchers led by Klodiana Lanaj from the University of Florida found that the use of smartphones at night was not only associated with less sleep, it was also related to morning depletion and reduced work engagement the next day.[9] The participants had to rate their agreement with certain statements such as "Right now, it would take a lot of effort for me to concentrate on something," and "Today while working, I forgot everything else around me." Those who used their smartphone for work late at night were less engaged with their work as a result of lack of sleep and depletion. In fact, these effects were found to be specific to the use of smartphones and greater than the effects of other devices with screens, such as computers, televisions, and tablets. These results suggest that we might consider the cost of using smartphones late at night. Sometimes it is essential to work at night and respond to various problems. But other times it is better not to engage with smartphones at night, since the price is next-day depletion.

Personal Psychology Lab

Conduct a small study with you as the only subject. For the next three days, avoid screens (phone, tablet, or computer) at least an hour before turning off the light and going to sleep. You can read or write, but not from a screen. So did you fall asleep faster after lights-out without your favorite device? See if you feel less depleted the next morning.

Now try this: When you work on a task that demands attention and cognitive functioning, turn off the phone for an hour and put it somewhere totally out of sight. You'll see an improvement in your performance.

Using smartphones at night is not the only cause for lack of sleep (you may not get enough sleep for other reasons). If you come to work tired, here is some practical advice. If you control your schedule, try to choose the tasks that require less effort and are more familiar when you are sleepy.[10] Another way is to avoid working for too long on one task if you are feeling fatigued. Take a break of about fifteen minutes. This will help you to perform better when you go back to work. Drink coffee or a beverage with caffeine. Try to work with other people when you are sleepy—that might also help.

On the other hand, some researchers suggest that smartphones can provide a recovery experience and relief from work-related stress. Studies show that media such as movies, TV, and computer games can be a positive thing. We have to take a break from work to "recharge our batteries" and recover our depleted resources, otherwise we will feel tired and stressed. When we rest we are detached from work, which is essential to recovery. Smartphones provide the opportunity to detach and relax, whether by listening to music, playing games, or other activities that help us recover from the workload.

Smartphones and Cognitive Performance

What about the influence of smartphones on our cognitive performance? People often check and answer messages and email while we are talking to them. It definitely affects their attention. (I'm sure you're familiar with that annoying habit. It's so common there's now an actual name for it: *phubbing*, as in phone-snubbing. You'd never do that, right?!) I know from my own experience that when I try to work on my computer and the phone is next to me, it is very difficult for me to ignore text messages; most of them are not related to work and definitely have a negative influence on my focus.

A group of Canadian researchers from the University of Waterloo conducted two studies in which they asked employees of various companies to estimate the amount of time they use their cell phone. The researchers gave the employees several cognitive tasks.[11] Those who reported high cell phone usage performed worse on various cognitive tasks. The researchers called their article "The brain in your pocket: Evidence that smartphones are used to supplant thinking."

I do not allow my students to use their smartphones during class, but I know that I can't totally control that. Two American researchers specializing in children's health and well-being found that about two-thirds of students said they used electronic media while sitting in class and while studying.[12] Several studies examined the influence of smartphone use on students' academic grades and anxiety. In one study, undergraduate students answered several questionnaires measuring satisfaction with life and their cell phone use, including an anxiety scale.[13] More specifically, they were asked to estimate the total amount of time they spend with their phones each day and to consider all uses except listening to music. They were also asked to estimate the time they spend sending and receiving text messages. The students who reported greater cell phone use, both total use and, specifically, texting, had lower academic grades and higher scores on the anxiety scale. These results are important and have implications on the work-related environment. The more people use their phones, the less focused they are, multitasking in a way that decreases their cognitive performance. Cell phone use was also related to anxiety. However, it could be the other way around; that is, the more people are anxious, the more they text and use their cell phones.

Other studies also found similar results on the negative association between self-reported use of cell phones and academic achievement.[14] Students who reported that they use their phones during class had lower grades than those who did not.

Smartphones definitely influence our cognitive functioning and behavior. However, studies that measure the influence of smartphone use on our cognitive functioning in the long run are still limited. We still need more studies to examine the influence of smartphones on our attention, memory, and delay of gratification. It's very likely that longitudinal studies will show a long-term effect of smartphone use. Studies examining changes in the brain in people who are addicted to the internet or to smartphones have suggested some changes,[15] but research is still in its infancy. So we know that texting and reading messages interferes with our performance. However, several eye-opening studies have shown that the mere presence of cell phones influences performance—even if we aren't actively using them.

In one study,[16] participants listened to a TED Talk for twenty minutes. They were divided into four groups. Participants in one group were allowed to use their cell phones during the lecture for educational purposes. Participants in the second group were instructed to put their phones in silent mode and not to use them during the lecture. Participants in the third group were instructed to turn in their cell phones before they entered the lecture. Participants in the fourth group were not given any instructions regarding their phones. During the lecture, the experimenter sent several text messages to cause a distraction. After the lecture, the participants were asked questions about the topic to see how much they had learned. Those whose phones were taken away performed better than the other groups.

In another study,[17] participants were given two cognitive tasks that measure attention and flexibility. Each task had two levels of difficulty. While the experimenter explained the tasks to the participants, she put her cell phone and her stopwatch on the table of one participant and a notebook on the table of another participant. Then she took the stopwatch and "accidentally" forgot the cell phone and the notebook on the table. For the more difficult tasks, participants who had the cell phone on their desks performed significantly worse than those who had the experimenter's notebook on their desks. (Here, it's interesting to note that the participants were affected by the presence of *someone else's* phone!)

Findings of a study published in 2017 by researchers from the University of California, San Diego (my favorite city), and the University of Texas clearly showed that the mere presence of a smartphone causes what they called a "brain drain."[18] In their experiment, 548 participants were assigned to one of three conditions: desk, pocket/bag, and other room. Participants in the *desk condition* were asked to leave their belongings out but to bring their cell phones since they will need them for a later study. They were asked to put their phones on their desks. Participants in the *pocket/bag condition* brought all their belongings to the lab and kept their phones where they usually keep them; about half kept them in their pockets and half in their bags. Participants in the *other room condition* were asked to leave all their belongings (including the phone) outside of the lab. The participants were then assigned several cognitive tasks. For example, they were given an incomplete pattern matrix and were asked to choose the missing element that completes it, or they were asked to solve several math problems while at the same time remembering a certain letter sequence. The results showed that the mere presence of a phone influenced their performance. Participants who left their phones in the other room performed better than those who had their phones on the desk and the performance of those whose phones were in their pockets or bags. The performance of participants who had phones in their pockets or bags fell between these two groups. It's noteworthy that when participants were asked how much the position of their cell phones influenced their performance, there was no difference between the groups. However, you could say that even though the participants did not do anything with their phones in this experiment, those who had them on their desk might have glanced at them to check their messages and were worried that they didn't answer messages and calls. Therefore, the researchers conducted a second experiment and added another condition: *power*. That is, in each condition, half of the participants had their phones on silent and half turned them off. The results showed that power did not have an effect; it did not matter if a phone was on or off, the mere presence of it influenced performance. Similar to the first experiment, participants in the other room condition performed better than those who had phones on their desks (regardless of whether a phone was on or off). The mere presence of a cell phone negatively influences performance, even when the phone is turned off. The researchers argue that we use mental resources to try to avoid automatic attention to the phone, which impairs our performance on the task we are working on. This is amazing! We know that using cell phones influences our attention, but these results suggest that just the fact that the smartphone is there is enough to impair our cognitive performance.

Email

Email is the most widespread method of communication in the workplace today. In 2013, most of the email sent was from business accounts; more than 100 billion email messages were sent and received per day.[19] In 2017, 290 billion email messages were sent and received each day. Using email has made office communication easier and less time-consuming. People can send a long manuscript, large images, and other big files to someone who works far away, and the material will reach that person in a second. A few moments later, the person might answer. An email can reach large numbers of people with a single click. There is no need for small talk, and unlike face-to-face communication, the message is not judged by extraneous factors such as physical appearance. Email is truly a quick and convenient means for conducting business and staying in touch with colleagues and customers. But it is not without its pitfalls—for communication and for our own productivity.

Did You Really Mean It?

A young intern in a law firm was working on a case with her boss. She was asked to review some material and write a report within a week. It took her a few days longer than that. The intern received an email from her boss saying, "Thank you for working so hard." Since she was late in handing in the document, she was not sure whether that message was sarcastic or not, and she was too shy to ask. Only a month later, when the boss complimented her again for her work, was she brave enough to ask and found out that the message was not sarcastic at all. Her boss really meant to compliment her.

Nonverbal communication such as body language and tone of voice provide important cues that are missing in email. It's easy to misinterpret a message without these clues. What is meant to be a humorous message, for example, might be interpreted as serious, and what is meant to be respectful might be interpreted as disrespectful.

At work, ambiguous messages can be misinterpreted, and unless the sender is aware of this, the misinterpretation will remain and may lead to serious problems. People can lose customers or business without realizing that it is because they were misunderstood. A group of researchers led by Justin Kruger, a professor at the NYU Stern School of Business,[20] conducted a series of studies that compared voice messages and email messages in terms of their ability to convey sarcasm, humor, and seriousness. Not surprisingly, they found that these emotions were communicated much more effectively via voice message than email. Participants detected sarcasm and humor more accurately when they listened to the message as opposed to reading it as a text. In one experiment, participants were given a list of twenty statements on topics such as the weather, food, and dating. Half the statements were sarcastic and half were serious. For example, a serious statement about dating was "I do not like first dates," and a sarcastic one was "I really enjoy dating because I like feeling as self-conscious and inadequate as possible." They were asked to choose ten statements they believed would be the easiest to classify as sarcastic or not, and to send them to another participant who would identify which ones were which. Half the participants were asked to type the statements, and the other half were asked to record them on a tape recorder. They were then asked to predict how many statements would be correctly identified as sarcastic or serious. The results clearly showed that those who heard the messages identified the sarcasm more accurately than those who read them. The results regarding humor were similar. While these findings are not surprising, there was one telling finding: the senders of the written messages were overconfident that their communications would be correctly interpreted. In other words, in email communication, emotions are not always detected the way they are intended, but those who send the messages are often overconfident and unaware of this fact. The researchers suggest that we are egocentric and assume that if we know the message was sarcastic or humorous, the other person will also understand that. However, people detect sarcasm, humor, and other emotions not only from the words that are said but from nonverbal communication: the tone of voice, the facial and bodily expressions, pauses, gestures, etc. Therefore, messages that are read without these cues may be easily misinterpreted, and the sender is unaware of that.

Take Another Look: Double-Check to Avoid Double Trouble

Always review your email before you send it. Double-check yourself if you meant your message to be sarcastic or humorous. If you did not get a response, consider calling to make sure your message was not misinterpreted.

Email and Productivity: A Double-Edged Sword

I remember what it was like to work before the days of email. I printed out each paper that I wrote and submitted it to a journal via airmail. A few weeks later, I would go to my physical mailbox in the department several times a day to check for a letter from the editor of the journal. Then, when the letter finally arrived, sometimes after a month or two, I continued the correspondence with the editor, each time sending it via airmail and waiting weeks for an answer. Today, I send an article via email, receive immediate confirmation, and then get an immediate response after it is reviewed.

There is no doubt that email has improved productivity at work in many ways. Immediate feedback is more efficient than feedback given two months later, when your mind is on other projects. However, email communication also has its shortcomings. The expectations for immediate response can be very stressful and interrupt your workflow. Responding to email as soon as it arrives requires task switching, which is time-consuming and lowers productivity. For many people, email overload has become a serious problem. Email messages distract people at work, and the need to answer email might disturb more important tasks that they have to perform. There is no question that when trying to concentrate on a particular task, whether it is reading a document or solving a problem, incoming messages and email are disrupting. It's better to refrain from checking your inbox while working on a project, and take an "email break" every hour or so.

Take a Break!

Take an email break for an hour if you are not expecting a very important message. Decide that you are not checking your mail during this time and only focus on your work. You will learn very quickly how this improves your performance.

These findings are very important. Decisions in negotiations are influenced by both cognition and emotions, and many negotiations are performed via email. On the one hand, emotion conveyed by email can be better controlled since the message can be reread and reviewed before it is sent. On the other hand, it can be misinterpreted. Therefore, review email before you send it; ask yourself if the emotion you are conveying is clear not only to you but to the recipient. Adding an emoji might help, but keep in mind your audience— emoji in work email can sometimes be seen as too casual and unprofessional. If there is no reply, or the reply suggests a misunderstanding, pick up the phone and make sure to clarify the message.

Yes, email and text messages often make our lives easier, but sometimes we still need to talk—and other times, we need a break. We've seen that although technology is important and useful for many aspects of our life and work, it can also disturb our attention and concentration, complicate communication, and disrupt our sleep. There are some relatively easy ways to decrease these disturbances. Try to leave the cell phone in another room for a while. If you are not expecting an important call, put it aside or turn it off. If you are at work on something that needs your attention, you'll get better results if you leave your cell phone somewhere else. Make sure your family knows the phone number at your workplace so they can reach you in case of emergency, and just forget about the phone. As studies show, the mere presence of it impairs attention and hurts performance.

Several apps can help you control smartphone use. For example, an app called Moment tracks how much you use your phone, and if you use it too much, it notifies you. This way, you can benefit from all the positive aspects of a smartphone but still have more time to spend on other things. Another app called AppDetox lets you tailor your smartphone usage. For example, you can restrict certain uses during work time and only leave email active, or you can restrict email when you want to relax.

Remember, our devices help us, but can also do us harm; learn to be selective with your phone use and be more intentional about checking your messages.

♫12

The Sound of Music
What Happens When We Listen at Work?

Music is the shorthand of emotion.
—LEO TOLSTOY

A few years ago I gave a talk in Puebla, Mexico, at an extremely interesting conference called la Ciudad de las Ideas—the City of Ideas. This conference presents innovative ideas in science, art, politics, business, entertainment, and more, and it brings inspiring speakers including Nobel Prize winners, eminent scientists, writers, and Oscar nominees. During the conference, we visited the youth orchestra founded by Ricardo Salinas Pliego, the owner of TV Azteca in Mexico. This orchestra is one of many in Mexico, and it offers a great opportunity for young people and an alternative to the violence many of them experience. The kids practice daily, and I had a chance to see them rehearse and also perform at the conference. It was a moving and exciting experience for me to see these kids and to see their heartfelt performance. Music empowered them, gave them something new, moving, and exciting. They were not the only ones who were emotional—I looked at the audience during the performance and saw from the expression on their faces how moved they were.

But the impact of music isn't limited to musicians and live audience members; music plays an important role for many people, providing an outlet, structure, and even meaning to their lives. Music is prevalent in everyday life, a central and important element for many people.

I'm sure most of you have experienced a feeling of relaxation listening to music. Indeed, music has therapeutic powers; it enhances emotional comfort and relaxation, and reduces anxiety, stress, blood pressure, and heart rate.[1] People who listened to music before a procedure, such as a colonoscopy or knee surgery, were less anxious.[2] Music also helps people with various disorders, such as PTSD, to reduce anxiety, to communicate, to socialize, and to express themselves.[3]

Music therapy can be helpful in restoring speech loss after an injury to the left hemisphere, which is responsible for verbal communication. On January 8, 2011, Congresswoman Gabby Giffords was shot during a constituent meeting held in a supermarket parking lot in Arizona. She suffered damage to the left hemisphere and had to learn to talk again. Music helped her regain her speech. In a very moving video that appeared on *20/20*, we can see how frustrated she was when she could not say the words she wanted, but then we watch her and her therapist sing together, "Let it shine, let it shine," and suddenly she can say the words. While the language center is in the left side of the brain, music exists in both hemispheres. Music therapy activates the brain, and gives the brain the ability to pave new pathways around damaged areas and create a new language area in the right hemisphere.

There are not strong enough words to emphasize the importance of music in our lives. But what is the influence of music at work? Many people listen to music not only in their leisure time or when they are driving or working out, but while they are working. A survey conducted in 2006 found that 80 percent of employees listen to music in the workplace about 35 percent of the time.[4] In some work settings, background music is played during business hours. In other cases, we choose when and what we want to listen to. And because it's so easy and tempting to listen while you work, it's important to know how it can affect you.

Since my book *Sensation* came out in 2014, showing the influence of physical sensations on our behavior, emotions, and cognition, I'm often asked about the effect of music on our job performance. Should we listen to music while we are at work or maybe only when we take a break? Does it matter what type of work we are doing, what type of music we are listening to? The answers to these questions are definitely not simple and depend on various factors. Let's take a deep dive into this complex issue.

The Mozart Effect: Does Listening to Classical Music Make You Smarter?

About twenty-five years ago, a group of researchers introduced a phenomenon they called "the Mozart effect."[5] They found that students who listened for ten minutes to Mozart's *Sonata for Two Pianos in D Major (K. 488)* performed better on cognitive tasks than those who listened to relaxation instructions or those who just sat in silence. This finding received a lot of attention. However, later studies suggested that music alone does not directly influence cognitive performance—there's more going on here, and it has to do with how music affects our emotions.

Emotional reactions include two dimensions: mood and intensity. We can be in a positive (e.g., happy, glad) or negative (e.g., sad) mood, and it can be characterized as more or less intense (high arousal and low arousal). Emotion is a psychological state, but it also involves physiological responses. When the emotion is intense, it generates profound changes in our cardiovascular, endocrine, and respiratory systems. Consequently, we have increased levels of heart rate, blood pressure, and adrenaline. For example, a friend of mine once told me about a professional meeting she attended with colleagues where her ideas and suggestions were rejected and everyone dismissed her. She was so upset and angry that when she told me about it, she actually started crying. This is an example of a negative mood (anger and frustration) with high intensity and arousal. In other cases, you can be angry or sad with low-level arousal and intensity. Someone I know once asked me for a ride home after a concert. I was really tired after a long day and wanted to go straight home, but she was standing and talking to friends, knowing that I was waiting for her. I was upset and angry, but it was with low intensity and arousal. Once she stopped talking and joined me, I almost forgot about my feelings. Both cases elicited anger, but in the first case, the anger was much more intense.

Let's take another example, this time of a positive emotion. You can be happy that you had a good day at work and you returned home to your family for a nice evening together. You experience a positive mood with low arousal. You can also be happy when you hear that you got a big promotion or that you were accepted to a prestigious university or were hired for the job you wanted so much. These are cases of a positive mood, but with a high degree of intensity and arousal, which is evidenced also in your physiological reactions. You feel that your heart is beating fast, it may be hard to breathe, and sometimes you want to run out in the street and shout how happy you are.

Several investigators have suggested that music does not directly influence cognitive performance, but rather influences the listener's mood and arousal, which can affect performance in several cognitive tasks.

Three psychologists from Toronto wanted to test how emotions might play into the Mozart effect.[6] They examined whether listening to various types of music that aroused different emotions would have a different influence on cognitive performance. Participants were divided into three groups. One group listened to Mozart's *Sonata for Two Pianos in D Major* for ten minutes, one group listened to Albinoni's *Adagio in G Minor for Strings and Organ* for ten minutes, and the third group sat in silence for ten minutes. If you are not familiar with these two pieces of music, please take a moment and listen to each of them on YouTube. You will notice immediately that the Mozart piece is fast and happy, while the Albinoni piece is slow and sad. Participants were then presented with a few items that were folded several times and asked to indicate how each item would look unfolded—a cognitive task to measure their spatial ability. In addition, they answered questions about their mood and rated their level of arousal. Participants did perform better on the cognitive task after listening to the Mozart sonata than after sitting in silence. There was no difference between the performance of those who listened to the music by Albinoni and those who sat in silence. In addition, those who listened to the Mozart sonata had a significantly higher positive mood and arousal and significantly lower negative mood, compared to those who listened to the music by Albinoni. It seems then that music that enhances arousal and positive mood influences our cognitive performance.

In a similar experiment,[7] participants listened for ten minutes to either Mozart or Albinoni and then completed a cognitive task. This time, they were given a subscale of the IQ test and filled out a questionnaire about their mood. Those who listened to Mozart performed better than those who listened to Albinoni. However, this was true only when there were differences in mood and arousal as a consequence of listening to the music. In other words, differences in cognitive performance were found only when listening to Mozart decreased the negative mood and increased the arousal level, while listening to Albinoni increased the negative mood and decreased the arousal.

While the previous studies examined performance on cognitive tasks, a study published in 2017 examined the influence of music on creativity in 584 schoolchildren.[8] The children were divided into three groups, two of which heard the same Mozart and Albinoni pieces used in the other study to induce positive or negative emotions; the control group did not listen to anything. The children were then tested again on creativity. The results clearly showed that *both* groups that listened to music (positive or negative) improved their performance on the creativity test compared to the control group. These results suggest that, at least for creativity, it might be the arousal rather than the mood that influences performance.

These studies show that when we listen to certain types of music *before* we start working, our performance increases. It seems that music affects cognitive performance through its indirect influence on our emotional reactions.

Background Music

One of the questions many people ask is whether it is good or bad to listen to music while they work. Should we have background music at the workplace, or when we sit next to our computer and work or study, or is it better to sit in a quiet room? Again, there is no one simple answer.

In 1940, the BBC launched a radio show entitled *Music While You Work*. In the decades since, many researchers have investigated the influence of background music on our cognitive functioning, memory, and learning. Their findings are not consistent.

Several early studies examined the effect of background music on performance and attitudes of employees in an industrial setting. For example, a study published in 1966 examined the influence of music on the performance and attitude of assembly-line personnel in a factory that manufactured skateboards.[9] For five weeks, four days a week, they played a different type of music each day. On the fifth day there was no music. They did not find any effect of the music on the quality and quantity of the work. However, the workers had very favorable attitudes toward listening to the music. Five years later, though, another research team found that music had a positive effect on the performance of workers who were engaged in a short-cycle, repetitive quality-control task.[10] A 1995 study found that employees who used headsets at work for four weeks showed an increase in their performance and satisfaction from the organization compared to those who did not.[11]

In a later and more in-depth study, Teresa Lesiuk, a professor of music education and music therapy at the University of Windsor, Canada, measured the effect of music listening on software developers from four different Canadian companies.[12] Their work requires creativity and is definitely not repetitive! Unlike in previous studies, the employees chose their own preferred music. Lesiuk's investigation lasted over several weeks. The first week of the study was the baseline week. Participants were asked to do what they normally do regarding their music-listening habits at work. In the second and third weeks, the researchers placed a music library in the workplace that included various types of music, and the workers were instructed to listen to music whenever they wanted to. They were allowed to listen (with headsets) within their office cubicles or on their personal music players. In the fourth week, the researchers removed the music library and told the workers not to listen to music at all during the workday. In the fifth week, the researchers returned the music library to the workplace. The results showed that listening to music undeniably increased positive moods among the workers. Their positive moods increased from the first week to the third and then dropped during the fourth week, when they couldn't listen to music. Moods improved once again during the fifth week, when they listened to music again. Going further, Lesiuk's team also examined the quality of work. They found that work quality dropped in the fourth week—the week without music—and increased once the workers started listening to music again. Furthermore, the workers needed to spend more time on tasks when they did not listen to music. It appears that when listening to music, these computer information system developers were in a better mood, exhibited a better quality of work, and were able to perform tasks more rapidly.

Studies show the advantage of listening to music in another domain of work: the operating room. Listening to preferred music in the operating room had a positive effect on the performance of plastic surgeons.[13]

However, not all studies show these findings. Many other studies have shown that music has negative influences on the execution of various cognitive tasks such as memory and reading comprehension, and have also found that performance was better in silence than with background music.[14]

A group of researchers conducted a meta-analysis study and compared the results of many studies that examined the influence of background music on various behaviors.[15] Based on their comparisons, they concluded that background music has a negative influence on reading tasks and a slight negative effect on memory tasks. In contrast, background music has a positive effect on emotional reactions and on performance in sports.

So does music enhance or decrease our performance? The fact that there are inconsistent and even contradictory findings is not surprising. You can't ask what the influence of music on our performance is without taking into consideration other factors, such as the genre, tempo, volume, and likability of the music, the type and complexity of the task, and the characteristics of the people who listen to the music. It depends on what type of music you are listening to—classical or jazz, hip-hop or heavy metal, fast or slow. Is the task that you are working on repetitive or boring, a complex task that needs attention, a memory task, a problem-solving task, or a task that needs creative thinking?

Type of Music

There are many music genres; pop, folk, classical, world music, show tunes, and so forth. Music can also be vocal or instrumental. Studies show that different types of music have different effects on our performance and mood. For example, music with more bass increases participants' feelings of power while certain types of music enhance abstract thinking skills.[16]

A team of researchers exposed participants to one of three conditions: *pop music, heavy metal,* or *classical music.*[17] Participants who listened to heavy metal had a significantly higher level of anxiety compared to those who heard either classical or pop music. Those who listened to classical and pop music reported they were more calm, relaxed, and less worried.

Uplifting music enhances our mood and even makes the world look brighter. A study conducted by British researchers found that participants perceived gray squares as brighter after listening to uplifting music and darker after listening to sad music.[18]

Several studies examined the influence of different types of music on reading comprehension. For example, one study from Wenzao Ursuline College of Languages in Taiwan gave 133 students three reading passages on various subjects, followed by several questions.[19] They divided the participants into three groups. The control group performed the reading comprehension task with no background music, one group listened to classical music, and the third group listened to a selection of some of the most popular hip-hop songs. Listening to hip-hop songs (but not to classical music) decreased cognitive performance. There was no difference between the control group, who worked with no background music, and the group who worked with classical background music. However, the participants who listened to the hip-hop songs performed poorly compared to the control group with no background music.

Another study also examined the effect of background music on reading comprehension, but instead of comparing two different genres, they varied the tempo and intensity of the same music.[20] Like so many other researchers, they chose Mozart's *Sonata for Two Pianos in D Major,* but they varied it. Together there were four conditions: *slow and loud, slow and soft, fast and loud,* and *fast and soft.* Each participant was given a passage to read for four minutes while listening to one version of the music, and was then asked several questions about that passage. Reading comprehension was not affected by slow or soft music, but when the music was fast and loud, it significantly disturbed reading comprehension.

Tune In for Better Performance

Try this: Before you work on something that demands analytic and/or creative thinking, take a break and listen for a few minutes to happy music that you like. Studies show it will improve your performance.

While you're working on something that demands your attention and concentration, such as solving problems or comprehending text, do not play upbeat and loud background music or music with vocals. It might have a negative impact on your performance. However, you can play slow and quiet instrumental music.

A study published in 2017, a collaboration between Dutch and Australian researchers, examined the influence of different types of music that arouse different moods on creativity.[21] Participants were divided into five groups and listened to various pieces of music that were found in previous studies to promote different moods. One group listened to calm music that enhances positive mood but is low on arousal; one group listened to happy music, which enhances positive mood and causes high arousal; one group listened to sad music that enhances sad mood but is low on arousal; and the fourth group listened to anxious music that enhances a negative mood but elicits high arousal. The fifth group was the silent group, the group that did not listen to any music. Those who listened to happy music had more creative and original ideas.

I Love These Songs—Should I Listen to Them at Work?

No less important than the type of music is the listener's personal preference. Some of us like jazz or hip-hop, others prefer classical music, and yet others prefer heavy metal. Some people like more relaxing music and others like lively, uplifting, or loud music. Many of us like several genres. I, for one, like all kinds of music, but if I can choose, my favorites are classical music and songs from the sixties. I love listening to the Platters, to Elvis, and to the Beatles, and I know most of the lyrics. We know what we like! It's logical to assume that the influence of music on our performance and mood depends also on its likability. Listening to music that we enjoy may improve our mood, and certain types of music increase our arousal. The question is: Does listening to music that we love also improve our performance at work?

First of all, we have to distinguish between listening to music prior to working or during work. In one study, participants listened to music that they either liked or disliked at either a fast or slow tempo.[22] Afterward, they were given a spatial rotation task, which measures the ability to mentally rotate an object. Participants were presented with two shapes; one was rotated, so that they didn't look alike. The participants were asked to decide whether these two shapes were identical. Performance was better after listening to music at a fast tempo, as compared to a slow tempo. However, at both tempos, participants performed better after listening to music that they liked rather than music they disliked.

What happens if we listen to liked or disliked music not prior to, but while we are working? Several studies conducted by British researchers examined this question.[23] The researchers compared participants' performance on memory tasks when they listened to either liked or disliked music or sat in a quiet room with no music. Performance was better in a quiet room with no music. Another study conducted in Taiwan divided eighty-nine workers from a university into four groups.[24] One group took an attention test without background music, and the participants of the other three groups listened to music while taking the test. One group listened to bestselling popular songs, one listened to five excerpts of classical music, and the third group listened to traditional Chinese music. Upon completing the attention task, participants rated how much they liked or disliked the background music on a five-point scale. Those who strongly liked or strongly disliked the background music performed more poorly on the attention task than those who sat in a quiet room. In other words, in all of these studies, both strongly liked and disliked music was a distraction and had a negative influence on work performance. Taken together, these findings suggest that listening to liked or uplifting music is beneficial before starting work, but if we listen to music we love while we are working, it is often detrimental and decreases our performance.

These results are not entirely surprising. It is well known that positive mood is related to performance and productivity. Liked or uplifting music enhances good mood and arousal. Therefore, if you listen to favored or cheerful music just before you start working, it enhances your mood and arousal, and consequently it may increase your performance. In contrast, if you listen to this music while you are working, it might be a distraction even though it enhances your mood. Music that you enjoy in the background may attract your attention more than quiet, unfamiliar, but pleasant music. It may disturb your performance on certain tasks that demand your full attention and focus. The best background music is music that workers don't feel strongly about one way or another.

However, when you take a break, do choose music that you like. Get up from your chair, get coffee, or just stand up and listen to the music. I like to take breaks, stand up or stretch, drink coffee, and listen to Elvis or the Beatles. I sometimes even dance when I'm alone in the room. That gives me the energy to get back to work. I turn the music off or put something else on, depending on the task I am doing.

Vocal or Instrumental

Another factor that might affect the influence of music is whether it is instrumental or vocal with lyrics. Several studies found that vocal music distracted performance on various cognitive tasks more than instrumental music.[25] One such study divided fourth-grade children into three groups and gave them a memory task.[26] One group listened to instrumental music while conducting the task, one to vocal music, and one had no music. Task performance was best with the instrumental music and worse with vocal music. That is, the instrumental music had a positive effect and the vocal music a negative effect on performance in the memory task. Another study conducted in Japan compared the performance of students who listened to vocal, instrumental, nature sound (the murmurings of a stream), and no music on several cognitive tasks.[27] Both the vocal music and the instrumental music had the most negative effect on performance, but the vocal music was perceived as the most annoying and distracting. It seems that, at least for some tasks, music with lyrics might be detrimental.

However, the lyrics of the song might not only distract our attention but also influence our mood and behavior in very special way.

The Impact of Lyrics on Our Behavior: Are You More Helpful When You Hear Songs with Prosocial Messages?

Do you think that when you listen to the words of "Help!" or "All You Need Is Love" by the Beatles, it affects your behavior? Do you think that you will be more helpful than if you listen to a neutral song? Several researchers investigated this question. They wanted to see if listening to songs with prosocial lyrics would enhance helping behavior. For example, two different studies exposed students to the songs "Help!" or "We Are the World" with prosocial lyrics such as "We are the ones who make a brighter day, so let's start giving," or to neutral songs such as "Englishman in New York" by Sting.[28] After listening to the songs, one of the research team came into the room and "accidentally" dropped a box with twenty pencils on the floor. The experimenter recorded how many pencils were picked up by the participants. Those who listened to the prosocial songs picked up significantly more pencils; they were more helpful. In another experiment, the participants heard either prosocial songs or neutral songs and were then told that there is a student who needs subjects for her thesis and asked if they would be willing to help her and participate in her study.[29] Of those who listened to prosocial songs, 68 percent were willing to help compared to only 28 percent of those who listened to neutral songs. In yet another study, participants listened to either prosocial or neutral songs.[30] They were then given two (UK) pounds for their participation and were told that they could donate that money to a nonprofit organization. Of those who listened to the prosocial songs, 53 percent donated compared to only 31 percent of those who listened to the neutral songs. Amazing! A French team conducted a field study in several restaurants.[31] In the restaurant, they played either songs with prosocial lyrics or neutral songs and recorded the tips of the guests in the restaurants. Those who were exposed to prosocial songs left more tips than those who were exposed to neutral songs. These studies clearly show that listening to songs with prosocial lyrics increases supportive behavior.

Even instrumental music with no lyrics may influence our helping behavior. In a field study conducted in two gyms, 646 students heard either up-tempo popular singles or avant-garde computer music while they were working out.[32] When they completed their workout, the researcher asked them to rate the music played in the gym on a scale ranging from "really annoying" to "really uplifting." Participants rated the computer avant-garde music as annoying and the up-tempo music as uplifting. The researcher then asked them to distribute leaflets to raise awareness for a fictitious sport charity to improve accessibility to sports for the disabled. Those who were exposed to the "uplifting" music were more willing to distribute leaflets supporting the charity. Since the researchers did not include a control group who listened to neutral music that was not especially uplifting but not avant-garde computer music, we can't be sure that it is not the computer avant-garde music that had negative influence rather than uplifting music having a positive influence on helping behavior. Nevertheless, the findings show that different types of music influence our willingness to help.

These results are important for organizations and workplaces. If indeed music with prosocial lyrics enhances helping behavior, it might be beneficial as background music just before people start working or at lunchtime. This might have an effect on the general atmosphere in the workplace.

Personality

Another factor we have to consider is personality. What is good and beneficial for one person might be distracting for another. Some individuals are less distracted by background music since they are better able to control their attention. Several studies found that introverts are more negatively affected by background music than extroverts.[33] Two researchers from Glasgow Caledonian University found that although high-arousal–inducing music reduced performance in most participants, introverts were more negatively affected and performed worse than extroverts in the presence of high-arousal music.[34]

Music and Physical Work

The sports center I go to offers a great selection of classes: fitness classes, different styles of yoga, Pilates, aerobics, water aerobics, and more. Obviously I can't go to all of them, and I choose the classes based on their level and the instructor. But there is a fitness class I try not to miss, and one of the main reasons is not the instructor but the music that the instructor plays during the class. It is uplifting, happy music, and I feel that it enhances my mood. I sometimes feel stressed or tired, and once I enter that class and start moving to the happy music, my mood changes.

Music during physical training classes varies according to the class, of course; what is appropriate for an aerobics class might not be appropriate for a yoga class. Often, gyms play well-known, popular songs as background music.

Studies are not entirely consistent, but some findings show that music has a positive effect on working out and exercising, and that people engaging in physical exercise work harder and longer when listening to fast-tempo music. For example, people who cycled while listening to music at various tempos worked faster with faster music and slower with slower music.[35] Other findings show that people exposed to music during muscle-endurance trials exhibited longer endurance times.[36] Self-selected music enhanced performance and enjoyment in sprint interval training, which is short bursts of high-intensity exercise combined with low-intensity aerobic recovery intervals.[37] Other findings suggest that background music acts as an external focus and distracts the participants' attention from their fatigue. It's interesting to note that in the case of physical performance, the distracting effect of music is beneficial whereas the same distraction is detrimental for cognitive performance.

These results can also be applied to the work environment. If your work is mainly physical (e.g., in construction, maintenance, gardening, farming, fitness training, carpentry, etc.), play background music. It will have a positive influence on your performance and may increase endurance and speed. You will probably work faster and be less tired.

What can we learn from all these studies?

It seems that there is no one simple answer about the influence of music on task execution. One thing is clear: If you listen to music before you start working, or on your breaks, it is likely to promote performance and reduce your anxiety and stress. Music has so many beneficial influences; it empowers us, reduces stress and anxiety, elevates our mood, has therapeutic powers, and improves performance on certain tasks. As for its influence on our work, we have to consider these findings against the type of work we do, and even the particular tasks we work on from day to day. Is your job more repetitive, or does it require lots of attention and creative thinking? Are you working alone, or will you collaborate with a team? Whether music will help or hinder you will probably change from day to day and depend on the task at hand. However, with this knowledge, you now know that taking a music break can have a positive result on your performance—and your overall mood on the job.

13

Tidy Desk, Tidy Mind?
Order and Disorder

It's pointless to have a nice clean desk, because it
means you're not doing anything.
—MICHIO KAKU

I used to meet with a friend every Tuesday. Her office was not far from mine, so I would stop by and we would go to lunch together. Every time I entered her office I felt guilty. It was so organized and clean: her desk only had the papers she was working on that day; all the rest were filed. I was really jealous. In contrast, I've been to many offices where I've wondered how the person finds anything among the clutter, with items piled on the desk and sometimes on the floor. I'm sure that the way an office looks says a lot about the person. However, the question I want to raise here is how a tidy and orderly (or disorderly) workplace affects a person's performance, decisions, and behavior.

The simplest and most obvious answer is that, indeed, it is easier to find what we are looking for in an organized work environment. A messy office, for example, can interfere with productivity, since it might take longer to find what we need at a specific moment. (I know this from experience—I can't begin to count the number of times I couldn't find an important document I had just printed!) My family and colleagues know that when I say I lost something that's supposed to be in the room, they are absolutely sure it is in the room and not lost. I usually find it eventually after checking and rechecking my drawers, moving things on my desk, and losing precious time. However, studies show that orderly and disorderly environments affect us and shape our behavior in less obvious and more complicated ways.

The Broken Windows Theory: Order and Morality

First, let's consider the effect of disorder. The "broken windows theory,"[1] introduced in the early 1980s by two social scientists, suggests that signs of disorder such as littering, graffiti, and broken windows encourage petty crimes and disorderly conduct. Indeed, the rate of petty crimes dropped significantly when the streets were cleaned, graffiti was removed, and broken windows were fixed.

Since then, the theory has become well known, and its derivative policy adopted by several cities. However, it was only in 2008 that a group of Dutch researchers conducted experimental studies in order to examine the theory.[2] These experiments were not conducted in the lab but in real-life situations. The researchers created two conditions: *orderly* or *disorderly*. In one experiment, people arriving at a garage to collect their cars saw a "no throughway" sign posted at the fence of the main entrance and were directed to another, more distant entrance. The fence was actually a temporary one set up by the researchers who also posted a sign prohibiting locking bicycles to the fence. In the orderly condition, the fence was totally clear of bicycles, while for the disorderly condition, the researchers arranged for bicycles to be leaning or hanging on the fence. The results were amazing. In the disorderly condition, significantly more people (82 percent) disobeyed the no-entrance sign and walked through the entrance they were not supposed to, whereas in the orderly condition, only 27 percent trespassed. Just the fact that there were bikes leaning on the fence, where they were not supposed to be, significantly increased the number of people who disobeyed the no-entrance sign, even though it was not about bikes. This directly supports the broken windows theory.

The researchers conducted another experiment, this time in an alley used to park bicycles. In the disorderly condition the walls were covered with graffiti, while in the orderly condition the walls were clean. The researchers attached a flyer with "Happy Holiday" greetings to each bicycle and waited to see whether the bicycle owners, upon collecting their bikes, would carelessly throw away the flyer and litter the alley. Again, the results were striking. In the orderly condition (walls without graffiti), only 33 percent littered whereas in the disorderly condition, 69 percent littered.

In a third experiment, the researchers placed an envelope containing a five-euro bill at the lip of a public mailbox in such a way that the envelope and its content protruded conspicuously. Here there were three conditions: the *orderly condition*, in which the mailbox was free of graffiti and the ground around it clean with no litter; *disorderly condition number one,* in which the mailbox was covered with graffiti but the ground was clean; and *disorderly condition number two,* in which the mailbox was clean but the ground was littered. The researchers then observed the behavior of people passing by the mailbox or posting a letter. The results were again quite clear. More people stole the envelope when the mailbox was covered with graffiti or the ground was littered than when the setting was clean, free of graffiti, and without litter. This is further corroboration of the fact that allowing petty crimes, such as littering, can lead to other unethical and immoral behaviors.

Other studies found that physical cleanliness influences morality. One study, for example, found that participants who sat in a room with a clean scent shared a sum of money they received in a fairer way compared to those who sat in a room with no particular scent.[3] In a second experiment, subjects who were seated in a clean-scented room (sprayed with Windex) agreed more often to volunteer for Habitat for Humanity, a charitable nonprofit organization.

These results have direct implications for the workplace. The scent of Windex or other cleaning materials can enhance reciprocity and prosocial behavior and in general encourage more moral behavior—all important factors in the workplace. So here is another reason for thoroughly cleaning your office and not just getting rid of the dust.

A study by researchers from the University of Chicago examined the association between organized and disorganized rooms and another aspect of unethical behavior—cheating.[4] The researchers presented 105 participants with a series of digital images of urban and natural environments and asked them to rate each scene on a seven-point scale ranging from very disorderly to very orderly. They found that environments with asymmetrical lines and curvy broken edges were more often rated as disorderly. In a separate experiment, they gave participants two minutes to solve a math task with several problems. Upon finishing the task, participants were divided into two groups and presented with either disorderly or orderly scenes based on the rating of the participants in the first experiment. After being exposed to the scenes, the participants were asked to grade their own performance on the task, giving them the opportunity to cheat. For each problem, all they had to do was answer yes or no to the question: Did you get it right? They were given money for each correct answer. They could have easily cheated and were sure that there was no way they would be caught. What they did not know was that the researchers had a way of determining their actual performance so they could find out whether or not the participants cheated. Participants who were exposed to disorderly scenes were 35 percent more likely to cheat than those who were exposed to the orderly scenes.

Order and Self-Control

So people cheat more in a disorganized room. Is it possible that a disorganized and messy room influences our self-control? Rui (Juliet) Zhu, a professor of marketing in Beijing, has conducted many studies on the influence of environmental factors on our behavior. Dr. Zhu and her graduate student led several experiments to examine whether disorganized environments decrease self-regulation and the ability to control our emotions and impulses.[5] In the first study, they assigned 150 students to three groups: *disorganized*, *organized*, and *control*. In the *disorganized group*, the students sat in an office where various office supplies such as paper and paper cups were scattered on the shelves. In the *organized group*, the same objects were arranged on the shelves in an orderly manner. In the *control group* the shelves were empty. Each participant was presented with a list of ten different items (some of them quite expensive, such as a ski vacation or a high-end speaker) and was asked to indicate the highest price that he or she was willing to pay in order to buy it. Those who sat in the disorganized room gave higher prices compared to the other two groups. That is, they were more impulsive and willing to pay more money for the various items. In a second experiment, the participants were again assigned to three groups: *organized, disorganized,* and *control.* This time, they were given the Stroop Task (the test I describe in chapter 9, where participants see different color words and have to name the color of the ink, not the printed word). Upon completion of the task, the participants answered how burned-out and overworked they felt. Those who sat in the disorganized room performed poorly compared to those who sat in the organized room or the control group. It was more difficult for them to name the ink color and hence took them longer. They also felt more depleted, more burned-out, and more overworked compared to participants in the other two groups. These studies show that there is a relationship between environmental orderliness and self-regulation. Disorganized environments can be depleting and affect both behavior and cognition, leading to poorer performance on tasks that demand attention.

Make Room for Thoughts

Organize your workspace and keep it neat. Not only is it much more pleasant to work in a tidy environment and easier to find things, but it helps you organize your thoughts. Moreover, not keeping things tidy and sitting in a messy environment depletes your psychological resources and causes poor performance.

Order and Social Conventions

A group of researchers from the University of Minnesota conducted several studies to investigate the influence of an organized environment on adherence to social conventions such as charitable donations and healthy eating.[6] Participants were assigned to either a neat or disorganized room. Both rooms were right next to each other, the same size, and with the same lighting conditions. The only difference was how orderly they were. The disorganized room had an array of scattered office items and papers, while the neat room had no scattered items and appeared very neat. All the students filled out a questionnaire, which took about ten minutes. The questionnaire was in fact a ploy to get them to sit either in an orderly or disorderly room. At the end of the questionnaire, to assess their giving behavior, the students were asked to donate a certain amount to charity for children. In addition, the researchers also wanted to examine the influence of a neat room on healthy eating—a desirable behavior. Hence, on the way out, each student was allowed to take either a chocolate bar or an apple. The results were amazing! Those who sat in the neat room donated considerably more than those in the untidy room and chose the healthy apple significantly more often than the chocolate. The researchers concluded that "an orderly (vs. disorderly) environment leads to more desirable, normatively good behaviors. Sitting in a tidy room led to healthier food choices and greater financial support of a charitable institution relative to sitting in a cluttered room."[7]

These studies suggest that an untidy office or desk might decrease self-control and self-regulation, which may lead to more impulsive and even unethical behavior, whereas a neat and organized office encourages desirable and conventional behaviors.

It must be said that this does not mean that if an office is clean then no one will behave impulsively or unethically, or that if the office is dirty then people will behave impulsively and unethically. These results do suggest, however, that an orderly environment can encourage desirable and even moral behavior while a disorderly environment tends to encourage more impulsive and sometimes unethical behavior.

Take a Clean Break

If you are easily distracted or prone to indulging impulses while you're supposed to be working (online shopping breaks?), then spending a few minutes cleaning your office and organizing your work surface may help you to curb those impulses.

Disorder: Not Always a Disadvantage?

But before singing the praises of orderliness and vowing to overhaul each and every environment under our control, let us consider another influence of disorderly environment. In some specific work situations, an untidy desk can be beneficial and even crucial. These are situations that require creativity. There's a saying often attributed to Albert Einstein that goes, "If a cluttered desk is a sign of a cluttered mind, of what, then, is an empty desk a sign?" A photo taken from Einstein's office on the day that he died shows a messy desk with cluttered papers and books. Various sites show photos of messy desks of creative people like Mark Twain or J. K. Rowling. Is it possible that messy desks or offices are related to creativity?

In 2013, the same researchers who found the association between orderly behavior and adherence to convention investigated the influence of orderly and disorderly rooms on creativity.[8] They wanted to test the hypothesis that an orderly room would boost conventional behavior while a disorderly and untidy room would stimulate creativity and unconventional thinking. In one study they asked participants to come up with new ideas for using ping-pong balls. Half the participants sat in a messy room and the other half in a tidy room. Participants in both rooms came up with a similar number of ideas. However, the ideas were coded for creativity by independent raters, and those who sat in the messy room received higher creativity scores.

In the next experiment, participants were again seated in either a tidy or disorderly room. This time they were asked to imagine they were in a snack bar and had to choose a smoothie with a boost of various ingredients. Next to the ingredients the researchers added either a "New" sign or a "Classic" sign. The word *new* cued *novelty* and the word *classic* cued *convention*. When the flavor boost had the "New" sign next to it, those who sat in the disorderly room were more likely to choose it than those sitting in the orderly room. In contrast, when the sign said "Classic," those who sat in the orderly room chose it more often than those who sat in the disorderly room.

Studies suggest that a room that is in disorder inspires unconventional and creative behavior and leads its occupants to gravitate toward the novel and unconventional, while an orderly room encourages a person to toe the line in terms of social conventions. So a messy desk can sometimes be beneficial and promote creativity. These findings have implications for workplaces in which a premium is placed on creativity and out-of-the-box thinking—advertising, marketing, research, software development, ad hoc task forces, etc. Make no mistake: This does not imply that if you mess up a room everyone will suddenly become more creative. Certainly not. It does suggest, however, that a little clutter may, in certain circumstances, enhance an unconventional out-of-the-box view of things. It does not mean that creative people often have messy desks. However, the studies cited above show that sometimes a messy desk is related to creativity.

Indeed, creativity is becoming ever more important for many jobs and industries—so we'll explore the surprising factors that may help us cultivate it (far beyond an untidy workspace) in the next chapter.

Bless This Mess

The only time a disorganized office can be an advantage is when you are working on a problem that demands creativity. An office that is too organized, where everything is exactly in its place, might inhibit creativity. So allow a little disorder when you are working on creative tasks—but not too much, especially if you work on different types of tasks.

14

Creativity

An Essential Skill for the Twenty-First Century

I've always been an optimist and I suppose that is rooted in my belief that the power of creativity and intelligence can make the world a better place.
—Bill Gates

We stand on the brink of a technological revolution that will fundamentally alter the way we live, work, and relate to one another. In its scale, scope, and complexity, the transformation will be unlike anything humankind has experienced before . . ."[1]

This is according to Klaus Schwab, founder and executive chairman of the World Economic Forum, signaling the historic shifts fast occurring in our modern world.

Schwab asserts that the head-spinning pace of advancement in technology and artificial intelligence represents the dawning of a Fourth Industrial Revolution. Did I say "dawning"? It was already past dawn by the time we gave it a name. This revolution is expanding and making important strides that affect millions on an almost daily basis.

Our world and its technologies and industries are constantly changing. Once upon a time we threw out our black-and-white TVs. Years later it was the VCR. Then it was floppy disks, soon after diskettes. (Future students of ancient history and archaeology might smile charitably on the extinct companies Borders, Woolworth, Amoco, or Blockbuster.) Today, new technologies are sprouting up so fast and in so many directions and disciplines that it dizzies the mind.

Businesses are continually taken by surprise by the frequent disruptions and are constantly forced to examine and rethink the way they operate. In order to survive, they must align themselves with the fast-changing environment and continuously innovate. This has far-reaching implications for industry, the labor market, and people in general. It is particularly important for anybody who works and wants to develop a career.

So what does all this have to do with creativity? And what does this have to do with the average person? Actually, a whole lot, as we shall see.

In a 2016 report entitled "The Future of Jobs," the World Economic Forum issued a projection of the top ten skills most needed in the labor market for the year 2020 as compared with 2015.[2] The changes within five years, a brief sliver of time in terms of historical human progress, were unexpectedly sudden: from its humble beginnings at the tenth spot in 2015, creativity skyrocketed to number three in the list, eclipsing "negotiation" and even "service orientation" in today's required skills. In addition, a total newcomer to the list is "cognitive flexibility," which is related to creativity.

Top Ten Skills in 2015

1. Complex problem-solving
2. Coordinating with others
3. People management
4. Critical thinking
5. Negotiation
6. Quality control
7. Service orientation
8. Judgment and decision-making
9. Active listening
10. Creativity

Top Ten Skills in 2020

1. Complex problem-solving
2. Critical thinking
3. Creativity
4. People management
5. Coordinating with others
6. Emotional intelligence
7. Judgment and decision-making
8. Service orientation
9. Negotiation
10. Cognitive flexibility

In a 2018 report from the World Economic Forum, creativity was still predicted to be number 3 in demanded skills for 2022, same as in 2018. Analytic thinking and innovation, which are related to creativity, were in first place.[3]

According to the Forum, "These developments will transform the way we live, and the way we work. Some jobs will disappear, some jobs will grow, and jobs that don't even exist today will become commonplace. What is certain is that the future workforce will need to align its skill set to keep pace."[4] In today's world of fast-changing (and even disappearing) platforms, technologies, and terminology, it seems axiomatic and rather obvious that one needs to have cognitive flexibility, imagination, and creativity in order to perform at a consistently high level in a dynamic and fluid environment.

Indeed, three years after the World Economic Forum report was issued in 2016, a new LinkedIn analysis of hundreds of thousands of job postings in 2019 found that creativity was the most demanded skill.[5] According to a study from the McKinsey Global Institute, at least 60 percent of all occupations can be automated to a significant extent with existing technology.[6] Creativity, however, will be sought and hard to replace.

Businesses will need to cultivate creativity in their corporate cultures and environments, not by only hiring creative people, but by purposefully encouraging their employees' creative powers. And individual workers should also concentrate on developing these skills.

This might sound scary to some, who may ask, "What if I am just not a creative person? Is creativity something that I have or don't have? And if I'm 'not creative,' what will happen to me?"

The good news is that there are strategies and practices for increasing creativity, as we shall see. But before we talk about how to develop it, let us first get a handle on it.

What Is Creativity?

So, what is creativity exactly? Is it an inborn trait? A state of mind? Something either you have or you don't? Or something you can learn and develop and improve? Creativity is a rather evasive concept that's hard to articulate. But for us to be on the same page, we need a working definition. So, for our purposes, we define creativity thusly: *Creativity is the formation of novel and original ideas that are workable and useful.* In other words, creativity—the kind that matters pretty much to everyone in their personal and business lives—is aimed at finding effective and implementable ways of upgrading the present situation.

When tackling a creative project, people employ two separate and distinct cognitive styles, or ways of thinking, each of them crucial to creativity: *divergent* thinking and *convergent* thinking.

Divergent thinking explores a variety of ideas, not systematically, but rather through free-floating associations that spark an assortment of concepts. Some ideas might hold promise while others might seem to be "silly" imaginings. Divergent thinking in its purest (best!) form is free to go wherever it pleases, unrestricted by limits, unbound from reality, unbowed to "logic." It is a wild youngster romping through an endless park, stopping here, scampering about, exploring there. Divergent thinking generates a flow of ideas, remote associations, and unexpected combinations that, when taken together, may form the raw material of any creative undertaking. It is a style of thinking characterized by fluency, flexibility, and originality.

Convergent thinking, in contrast, is a process that follows logical steps in order to arrive at a single correct solution. Unlike divergent thinking, which spews out a stream of ideas, convergent thinking typically seeks a unified solution to a problem or task. Once the novel ideas have been generated, they must be carefully examined and evaluated to see which are workable, effective, and implementable. Divergent thinking generates ideas that must be winnowed down to the best serviceable solution. This is where convergent thinking comes in—to review and analyze and test on the way to finding the solution.

To illustrate divergent and convergent thinking, there's the apocryphal story of a sculptor who, when asked about the difficulties of sculpting an elephant, replied: "All I do is chip away at whatever doesn't look like an elephant." Divergent thinking delivers and dumps a huge slab of varicolored marble into the workshop. Convergent thinking, waiting patiently, is the sculptor. Both styles of thinking are essential to the creative process.

In order to measure creativity, researchers commonly employ two tests: the Alternative Uses Task (AUT) and the Remote Associates Test (RAT).

AUT measures divergent thinking by asking subjects to find as many uses as possible for an object, say, a brick.[7] The answers are then assessed based on flexibility, fluidity, and originality. Flexibility is measured by the number of categories used for the object. For example, using a brick as a doorstop is one category; using it to flatten a chicken breast is another. The first idea is not high on originality, as many people think of it; the second idea is statistically rated as being original and scores points for the category of use and originality. To suggest using the brick as a window stop would not be considered original nor would it constitute a different category than a doorstop. Here it is divergent thinking that is being measured since there is no one correct answer, and the possibilities are endless.

The next is RAT. Several decades ago, Sarnoff Mednick, a well-known psychology professor who contributed to the study of creativity, created this test.[8] The RAT measures convergent thinking by presenting test subjects with three words and asking them to find a fourth word related to all three of them. For example, what is the fourth word in the sequence following the words *falling, movie,* and *dust*? The answer is *star* (*falling star, movie star,* and *stardust*). Another example would be *manners, tennis,* and *round*; the solution is *table* (*table tennis, table manners,* and *round table*). Here it is convergent thinking that is being measured since each question has only one correct answer. Certainly, one needs to be creative and think outside the box to arrive at a solution, but this is a systematic scan of our knowledge that tests the hypothesis, whether arrived at in a logical manner or through a sudden insight.

One's aptitude for divergent and convergent thinking might seem like an innate, unchanging aspect of one's personality, but that's not all there is to the story.

What Are the Factors That Promote Creativity?

Studies show that three major forces affect creative performance, particularly in the workplace. They are:

1. Creative personality
2. The social-organizational environment
3. The physical work environment[9]

To be sure, some people can draw on creativity more easily, and some are more naturally creative than others; this is what researchers mean by "creative personality." However, organizational and situational factors also influence creativity beyond the individual differences among workers. Clearly, of these three factors, we can exert a degree of control on two of them: our social and physical environments. And herein lies the hope—for companies seeking to improve their bottom line and for individuals who want to be more creative. The supposedly "given" variable of "creative personality," well, that can be tweaked to our advantage and actually boosted if we do it in an informed manner.

Creative Personality

What factors define a naturally creative personality?

A group of researchers in Germany found that *openness to experience* is one of the foremost characteristics of creative thinking.[10] People who are open to experience are more curious, untraditional, and imaginative; as a result they expose themselves to a much larger set of ideas and directions including the unusual and unexpected.

Another personality characteristic found to correlate with creativity is *proactive personality*. People who score high on proactive personality are those who identify opportunities, take the initiative, anticipate problems, and seek to influence the environment. They initiate solutions and are not intimidated by obstacles. They search for new ideas all the time. They are more creative in the workplace.[11]

Cognitive styles—the way people perceive and solve problems, and make decisions—are also related to creativity. For example, some people are more intuitive and make fast decisions while others are more conventional, formal, and methodical. Some are better when the problem requires the free flow of novel ideas (divergent thinking), whereas others are better when the problem requires more analytic and systematic thinking (convergent thinking).

The Social-Organizational Environment

In the workplace, creativity is affected by organizational and social factors as well as the physical environment. We know that a positive innovation climate, support from supervisors and coworkers, the feeling of not being controlled and evaluated, and organizational resources (such as time and personnel) all contribute to creativity in the workplace.

Given that companies can, within limitations, manipulate their social and physical environments, it only makes sense for them to do so in a way geared toward enhancing creativity. So how can businesses do this?

Is there an association between rewards and creativity? One meta-analysis looked at the results of sixty studies that examined this question.[12] These studies found that creativity was positively related to rewards that were *contingent upon being creative* rather than the completion of a task. Employees have to know that creativity is valued and rewarded. Employees perform better when they feel encouraged to think of new ideas and are given the time to do so, without being pressured. This is very important! Deadlines and pressures to perform are perceived as threats that we react to naturally by pushing ourselves to avoid them, lest we pay a penalty. Negative pressure may lead to forced thinking—precisely what sabotages creativity.

When people are motivated by fear of a negative outcome, such as losing their job or being demoted for poor performance, they usually take fewer risks, are less flexible, and thus less creative. Such pressure leads to forced and unimaginative thinking. In contrast, when workers are motivated by a creativity-contingent reward, they take more risks, are more flexible in their thinking, and readily bounce ideas back and forth. In short, they perform with greater creativity. This sort of supportive environment should include positive reinforcement for creativity as well as allowing workers to feel less controlled and more autonomous in their work.

The Physical Environment

Aside from personality and organizational factors, there are certain factors in the physical environment that influence and enhance creativity.

Color and Creativity: Red Alert

As we saw in chapter 9, colors carry intrinsic meaning and can influence our emotions, behavior, and impressions of other people. But can colors affect our cognitive performance and creativity? Well, studies show that colors can, in fact, influence us on all those levels.

The primary colors red and blue carry many meanings for us. The color red is associated with danger, stop signs, and the red ink teachers use to correct papers. The color blue is associated with the ocean and sky, which are related to openness and tranquility. Do the colors red and blue influence our cognitive performance? Different cognitive tasks in the workplace demand different types of thinking. Some demand more creative thinking, some demand more analytic systematic skills, and some, such as proofreading or memorizing documents, require more focused attention. Two well-known researchers on creativity, Ravi Mehta from the University of Illinois and Rui (Juliet) Zhu from the Cheung Kong Graduate School of Business, conducted a series of studies that was published in the prestigious journal *Science*.[13] They examined the influence of the colors red and blue on problems that require creativity and problems that require mainly focused attention. In one study, participants were given the AUT; they had to indicate as many uses for a brick as they could think of in one minute. One group saw the question written on a red background, one group on a blue background, and a third group on a neutral white background. Several independent judges rated the creativity of each answer on a nine-point scale, where 1 was lacking creativity and 9 was very creative. For example, one creative answer suggested "using the brick as a scratching post for animals (for their nails)." The findings were quite surprising. While there was no difference between the groups in the *number of uses* they suggested, those who saw the question on the blue background thought of more *creative* uses than participants in the two other conditions. The color blue enhanced creativity and influenced the quality of the answers.

In another study, participants were given a different creative task, this time five items from the RAT. Again, there were three groups: one group who saw the task written on a blue background, one on red, and one on a neutral color. The blue condition group gave more correct answers than the other two groups. They were more creative.

In yet other study, participants were given a sheet of paper with drawings of twenty different parts. They were asked to use any five parts they wanted to draw a toy for a child. One group received drawings with red parts and the other group received blue parts. The toys they created were evaluated by several judges for their creativity and practicality. The toys drawn with blue parts were evaluated as more creative than those drawn with the red parts. In contrast, the toys composed of the red parts were judged as more practical.

It seems that the color blue, which is associated with openness and tranquility, signals a calm and safe environment where people may try more innovative approaches and think more creatively. The researchers suggest that the color blue activates what researchers call "approach motivation" (a desire or motivation to move toward something rather than avoiding it), therefore enhancing thinking and innovative ideas.

Several studies have shown that the color red impairs performance not only in creative tasks, but also in problem-solving in achievement settings.[14] For example, in one study, three groups of students were each assigned an identification number and given an anagram test in which they were required to unscramble sequences of letters into words (like rearranging "BELTA" into "TABLE"). All the students received the same anagrams; the difference was in the color of participants' numbers written at the upper right-hand corner of each page. For one group of students, the participant's number was written in red; for another group the number was written in green; for a third group it was written in black. Again, these were the only differences between the three groups. The subtle red test number had an almost unbelievable effect: students with a red number performed significantly worse, correctly solving fewer anagrams than those who had a green or a black number. Other achievement tasks showed similar results in both verbal and mathematic tests. The researchers suggested that the color red, which is associated with danger and failure (the red ink of a teacher), activated avoidance behavior, which in achievement settings under time constraints impairs performance.

Other studies showed, however, that in tasks that demand mainly attention and memory, such as proofreading, rather than problem-solving, the sense of danger aroused by the color red induces an avoidance reaction and vigilance, which means paying attention.[15] Consequently, it enhances performance.

The findings above show that red and blue can influence our cognitive performance, depending on the type of problem. These results have direct implications for the workplace and for students.

The Best Ideas Come Out of the Blue

Try this: If you are working on something that requires creativity, are brainstorming, working on a new project, or designing something new, try to have something blue in the room; it could be a picture, a blue wall, or even office accessories such as the color of your computer screen.

Avoid the color red when you have to be creative or solve problems that demand analytic thinking; it might impair your performance. If, however, you are working on a task that demands systematic and focused attention, such as memorization or carefully reading instructions, the color red might enhance your performance.

People who try to look for a better place to work or a better and more exciting job are often said to be moving on to "greener pastures." It's not surprising that the idiom to express something more promising uses the color green. Green is related to growth and improvement. We observe the growth of green grass and plants and use expressions like *green thumb* and *going green*. As noted earlier, many studies have found that positive motivation enhances creativity. Green is associated with physical and psychological growth, and with positive things such as awareness of the environment.

Andrew Elliot, Markus Maier, and Stephanie Lichtenfeld from the University of Munich in Germany, who have greatly contributed to the study of the influence of colors on our behavior, examined whether the color green might cue positive motivation and enhance creativity.[16]

In one experiment, participants sat in front of a computer and were shown a black number inside a rectangle. Half of them were shown a green rectangle and the other half a white one. They were then given a version of the AUT where they had to write down as many different and creative ways to use a tin can as they could think of. Participants who viewed the green rectangle prior to taking the creativity test performed better than those who viewed the white rectangle. In a second experiment, the participants received the test material in a binder. In the middle of the first page there was a wide rectangle with the word *Ideas* in black ink. One group had a green rectangle and the other group had a gray rectangle. Two seconds later, the participants turned the page and completed the creativity task. This time they were given another creativity test—they were asked to draw as many different objects from a geometric figure as they could. Again, those who saw the green rectangle exhibited more creativity than those who saw the gray rectangle.

In two additional experiments, the researchers compared green not only to gray or to white, but also to the colors red and blue. Those who were exposed to a green rectangle evidenced more creativity than those who were exposed to a blue, red, or gray one.

Have a Green Moment

Try this: When you are working on a task that demands creativity, take a minute or two several times during the day to stare at a green surface; it can be a picture, a photo, or an image on the computer that has mainly green elements. Compare your performance to days without these "green moments."

These four different experiments clearly indicate that people who were exposed to the color green, even for a short time, exhibited greater creativity in different creativity tasks. These results have direct implications for the workplace. Exposing employees to the color green either by hanging paintings with a lot of green, or painting some of the objects in the office green, even just an object like the doorknob or handrail, might be enough to enhance creativity. Green plants might do the job as well. Plants also have another specific influence on employees, as we saw in chapter 4.

Think Different: Logos and Photos

In one study, conducted during the height of Apple's prestige, 341 students were exposed to either the Apple logo (associated with cutting-edge innovation, nonconformity, creativity, and the "Think Different" campaign) or the IBM logo (perceived as smart, responsible, and traditional). Exposure to the logos was subliminal; it was so fleeting (only thirty milliseconds) that the students weren't even aware of it. Then the students were given the AUT. Those who were exposed to the Apple logo thought of significantly more creative and novel uses for a brick than those exposed to the IBM logo. And remember, they were not even aware they had seen the logos! These results suggest that any brand or photo associated with creativity and innovation can enhance the creativity of those who are exposed to it. This is an example of an easily implementable change in the workplace (in this case, the exposure of employees to meaningful symbols) that can yield real and lasting benefits. (One might wonder, naturally, if this means people will be more creative on Macs than on PCs. Many "creative types" seem to have Macs, and business types seem to use PCs—generally. It would make for an intriguing study!)

Light and Creativity

In chapter 2, we saw that bright light has a positive influence on mood, well-being, and performance. However, sometimes when people are in a dim room or even think of darkness, they are more creative. Sounds strange, but a series of studies conducted in Germany seem to show it's true.[17]

In the first study, the participants were asked to describe a situation in which they had been in a dark or in a bright location. Then they were given a creative task: to draw the aliens they might meet if they were visiting another planet. Aliens drawn by participants who thought of a dark location were rated by independent coders as more creative than those of participants who thought of a bright location. In the second study, participants were asked to find and circle twelve words in a word search puzzle. The words for one group were all related to darkness (e.g., black, night, cave), and for the other group the words were related to brightness (e.g., sun, ray, day). There was also a control group that had neutral words (e.g., shoes, house). Participants were then given the AUT. Those in the group with words related to darkness were more creative in their responses than those in the other two groups.

In the third experiment, participants actually sat in a dim office, in a bright office, or in a control room that was brighter than the dim room but not as bright as the bright room. They were given another creativity task, this time four creative insight problems. Those who sat in the dark room exhibited more creativity. The participants were also asked how free from constraints they felt. Those in the dim, dark room felt freer from constraints than those in the bright room or the control room—suggesting that when we feel freer from limitations we can be more creative.

This seems somewhat confusing because other studies demonstrate that bright light enhances performance. However, I believe these results suggest that brightness spurs industriousness and dimness spurs creativity. A songwriter and editor told me that he hangs around with artists, musicians, and writers, and very few of them create in bright light; "I have noticed I *create* in dimmer light, but fine-tune (edit and revise) in brighter light," he wrote. "I think this is not uncommon." Although light usually has a positive influence, sometimes, when we are stuck and are looking for creative solutions, it might be useful to sit in a dim room for a while, alone, free from constraints.

Thinking Outside the Box and Other Metaphors

We all know the metaphor "thinking outside the box." It means thinking creatively, differently, less conventionally, and in a less structured way. An interesting experiment headed by Professor Angela Leung from Singapore Management University found that *actually sitting outside a box* will enhance our creativity.[18] The researchers divided the participants into three groups and asked them to take the RAT. Participants in one group took the test sitting inside a five-foot-square box. Participants in the second group were taking the test sitting outside the box. Participants in the third group had no box. The researchers found that those who sat outside a box solved more problems correctly than those who literally sat inside a box or those who sat in a room with no box at all.

If this is not surprising enough, another study found that you don't need a real box—sometimes photos are enough.[19] In the first experiment, one group was shown an image of a box and a brain outside the box. The second group was shown an image of a fish, and the third group was not shown any image. All the groups were then given the RAT. Those who were shown the image of the brain and the box got higher scores.

In another experiment, one group of participants was shown an image of a burned-out light bulb, representing the negative metaphor of being *burned out*. The second group was shown an image of an illuminated light bulb, and the third group was shown an image of a fish. A fourth group was not shown any image. Participants who viewed the burned-out light bulb were less creative than participants from the other three groups. As unbelievable as these findings seem, they suggest how we can easily increase our creativity by just looking at the right photos.

In yet another study,[20] the researchers used a different metaphor, *shedding light on the problem*, or the symbol of the light bulb as a sign of insight. They gave participants a problem you might be familiar with: connecting four dots arranged in a square by drawing three connected lines. The participants were told they could not lift the pencil from the paper. This is an insight problem. You have to realize that although the dots are arranged in a square, you can go outside the square. Once people have this insight they can easily solve the problem. About a minute after the participants were given the problem, the experimenter said that it was a little dark in the room and then turned on either a light bulb or a fluorescent light. More of those who sat in a room with the light bulb were able to solve the problem. The presence of the light bulb activated insight. Let me emphasize: just the fact that participants saw a light bulb enhanced their creativity!

Need a Flash of Inspiration?

Easy and effective: Light an area of your office with a simple light bulb, even when you dim the room. Alternatively, use an image of a light bulb. A dim room with a light bulb is a great combination to enhance creativity when you are looking for an idea or an innovative solution.

Fluidity and Creativity

Creativity is described as the opposite of rigid thought, the ability to flexibly move in various directions and from one thought to another—also sometimes called "fluid thinking." Indeed, studies found that subjects who were encouraged to walk around a room were significantly more creative than subjects who were seated or asked to walk along a straight line. However, is it possible that just tracing fluid lines could enhance creativity? Researchers conducted several experiments to test this hypothesis.[21] In each experiment of the study, participants were asked to trace either three fluid or three nonfluid drawings. The fluid drawings had curved lines, whereas the nonfluid drawings were angular. In all other aspects, the two sets of drawings were the same. The participants were then given various tasks that examine different domains of creativity. In one experiment, they were asked to write creative uses for a newspaper, and in another they were given the RAT. In all three experiments, those who traced fluid lines got higher scores on creative thinking.

I Want to Be Creative . . . but I Keep Going Around in Circles!

Good! When you are thinking about an innovative solution, a new idea for a project, or anytime you need to draw on your creativity, take a piece of paper and doodle—but remember, don't draw straight lines, only wavy or curved lines. Or, try to get up and walk around—but again not in straight lines, but rather around the room or the building. Both of these circular and seemingly trivial actions ease the mind and free it from stereotypical thinking—crucial ingredients to inducing a creative mindset.

Imagine You Are a Creative Person

A study conducted by researchers from the University of Maryland examined whether just imagining you are a creative person can enhance your creativity.[22]

In this study, ninety-six undergraduate students were administered the AUT to write as many uses as they could for ten different objects. The students were divided into three groups. The only difference between the groups was that the members of one group were told to imagine they were eccentric poets. The members of the second group were told to imagine that they were strict librarians. The third group was a control group that was not told anything. An eccentric poet and a librarian were chosen based on the stereotypes that a poet is a creative person while a librarian is not. (The researchers emphasize that they do not think real librarians are uncreative, but that this is a stereotype held by many people.) The answers were scored on fluency (which means the number of ideas generated) and originality. As for originality, those who were in the *poet condition* scored significantly higher than those who were in the control group and those who were in the *librarian condition*. Participants in the rigid librarian condition scored lower on fluency than those in the poet condition. The scores of the control group were in the middle. The researchers conducted a second study, similar to the first one. This time participants received the same task, but before the first five objects some of the participants were told to imagine that they were eccentric poets and some that they were rigid librarians. Then, for the next five objects, they switched. When the participants were told to imagine they were poets, they were significantly more fluent and more original than when they were told to imagine they were librarians.

These results show that creativity can be enhanced if we imagine that we are creative people. Try to do that the next time you are working on an insight problem or when you try to generate new and innovative ideas. Think of your-self not necessarily as an eccentric poet but as a creative person, an inventor, an artist, or any profession that you believe is creative. You can also imagine that you are a certain person you know that you believe to be a creative person.

Want to Be Creative? Don't Think of Yourself

Try to solve this insight problem, which demands a novel, creative solution:

> A prisoner was attempting to escape from a tower. He found a rope in
> his cell that was half as long enough to permit him to reach the ground

safely. He divided the rope in half, tied the two parts together, and escaped. How could he have done this?

The solution is that he divided the rope lengthwise. Participants in a study were given this problem to solve, but half of them were asked to imagine themselves in the tower trying to escape, whereas the other half imagined they were solving the problem for someone else who was in the tower. Only 48 percent of those who imagined themselves in the tower solved the problem, while 66 percent of those who imagined that they were doing it for someone else managed to solve the problem.

This implies that when we are trying to be creative and come up with innovative ideas or solutions, we should think about solving it for someone else rather than for ourselves. This is simple guidance that might make the difference for people who are working on a complex project.

Larks or Owls: The Best Time of Day

People often define themselves as either morning or evening individuals. I know that I do my best work early in the morning, so I leave the less complicated tasks, such as answering email or checking my bank accounts, for the evening, when I know I can't focus and can't think creatively. However, Benjamin Franklin's famous saying, "early to bed and early to rise makes a man healthy, wealthy, and wise," does not hold true for people who work better at night. It seems logical to assume, then, that people will be more creative at their optimal time. Morning people will be more creative in the morning, and evening people will be more creative in the evening. However, research shows that this is not the case.

In one study,[23] participants were divided into groups of morning or evening types based on their answers to a "morningness/eveningness" questionnaire that asked about their sleep habits and performance at different times of the day. Since not everyone can fit into one of these two categories, only those who were clearly morning or evening people (223 out of the 428) were analyzed further. Participants were asked to solve three insight problems and three analytic problems. To understand what these are, let's look at two examples.

For instance, one of the analytic problems given to the participants was the flower problem:

> Four women, Anna, Emily, Isabel, and Yvonne, receive a bunch of flowers from their partners Tom, Ron, Ken, and Charlie. The following information is known: Anna's partner, Charlie, gave her a huge bouquet of her favorite blooms, which aren't roses. Tom gave daffodils to his partner (not Emily). Yvonne received a dozen lilies, but not from Ron. What types of flowers (carnations, daffodils, lilies, or roses) were given to each woman and who is her partner?

An example of an insight problem that was given to the participants was the coin dealer problem:

> A dealer in antique coins got an offer to buy a beautiful bronze coin. The coin had an emperor's head on one side and the date 544 BC stamped on the other. The dealer examined the coin, but instead of buying it, he called the police. Why?

The difference between the two types of problems is quite clear. To solve the flower problem, you have to work systematically. You have to check each possibility until you solve the whole problem. For example, Charlie is with Anna, and Tom gave daffodils, while Yvonne got lilies, but not from Ron. That means that Ken is Yvonne's partner. And so you continue to work incrementally toward the solution until you work out all the partners and flower combinations.

Insight problems are very different. It's not enough to examine them systematically. You have to think of different ways and alternatives, and often feel stuck until the solution suddenly "hits" you. Before you move to the next paragraph, please take a few moments and try to solve the insight problem. Ask yourself if you are a morning or an evening person and whether now is the best time for you to answer this problem.

The answer is that coins could not have had "BC" stamped on them, since the concept of BC (Before Christ) did not exist at the time.

The researchers wanted to examine whether people are more creative at their peak time. The results were surprising. For the analytic problems, the time of day did not make a difference, even for participants not at their optimal time of day. However, and contrary to what we might think, participants in a nonoptimal condition solved the insight problems better than participants at their optimal time. No wonder the study was titled: "When the non-optimal is optimal."

In order to understand these findings, you have to remember that solving analytical problems requires avoiding distractions. This is not the case with insight problems. Insight problems demand creative thinking, which means looking for novel solutions rather than working systematically. Studies have shown that at the nonoptimal time of day, people have less ability to avoid distractions and are more influenced by previous information. Random thoughts and distractions that we avoid during our peak time might actually help to solve creative problems.

So we might not always be at our best when we're at our peak time. Some problem-solving efforts might benefit from the nonoptimal time of the day. Reading and comprehension, for example, is best done at your peak time, whether it's morning or evening. However, when it comes to creativity, we often have more original ideas at our nonoptimal time of the day. So for certain types of problems, working when we are not at our best might, in fact, be beneficial.

These results have important implications. If you have to work on analytical problems that demand focused attention and concentration, try to work on them at your optimal time of day. However, if you work on problems that demand more creative solutions and novel ideas, try to work on them at your nonoptimal time. The fact that it is harder for you to concentrate and focus, and that you are more influenced by distractions, might help you see the problem in a different way, and it might bring new ideas.

Time for a Break or for a No-Brainer?

Mind wandering often disturbs performance. Think of a situation in which you were trying to concentrate and work on a task that demanded your full attention, but your mind kept wandering to other things. In this case, the mind wandering probably had a negative influence on your performance. However,

The Rewards of Being a "Slacker"

Most people have an optimal time of day when they feel they are at their best, whether in the morning, evening, or afternoon. Some of us are night owls, some early birds, and others in between may feel most potent during the afternoon hours. If you are able to organize your day and divide your work, make it a point to tend to tasks that demand attention and analytical thinking at your optimal time of the day. However, if the task you face demands creativity and novel ideas, it's best to tackle it at your "worst" time of day! So if you are an early bird, make sure to attack your creative task in the evening, and vice versa for night owls. When your mind and physiology are less perked up, less vigilant than at your "peak" hours, the muse of creativity awakens and is allowed to roam more freely. In other words, when your mental machinery is slack rather than standing upright at attention and being hyperalert, the creativity flows. A creative tip that is as productive as it is counterintuitive!

recent studies have shown that mind wandering may be beneficial to finding creative solutions. Indeed, people who come up with brilliant ideas or solve particularly thorny problems frequently report how the spark of inspiration "just came to them"—for example, while walking in nature, driving, taking a shower, or just resting or even dreaming. Conversely, consciously trying to *force* a creative outcome leads to agitation and frustration.

Several studies examined whether engaging in unrelated, random thoughts would enhance creativity. In one study, each participant was given the AUT for two objects.[24] Their answers were coded for creativity and represented the baseline. The participants were then assigned to four different groups. Two of the groups were given an "incubation period" of twelve minutes: one group was given a demanding task that required attention and concentration and the other was given an easy, undemanding task. The third group was simply given a break—the participants were asked to sit quietly and wait for twelve minutes. A fourth group did not receive an incubation period or a break.

Immediately after, each of the participants was given four different rounds of the AUT. Two of the problems were the same as before and two were new. Those who had an undemanding "incubation period" task showed greater improvement than those who had a tough incubation task, got a break, and did not have a break at all. It seems that certain unrelated thoughts that enable our minds to wander enhance creative solutions.

Another study found similar results.[25] One group of participants was given several boring tasks, such as reading the telephone numbers from a phone book, followed by a creative task. The control group was just given the creative task. The participants who engaged in the boring preliminary task showed more creativity in the second task than those in the control group.

The results of these studies do not suggest that workers should be bored or work on repetitive, undemanding tasks all day long. They do suggest, however, that sometimes it might be beneficial to allow or even encourage first working on a repetitive and easy task for a while, before tackling a problem that requires a creative solution. This opens the way for multiple thoughts and snippets of ideas to come forth and jumble around like lottery balls—the ideal medium for breeding creative ideas.

Meditation and Mindfulness

Some perceive the practice of meditation as just sitting still, relaxing, and doing nothing. This is far from true. Meditation is a deliberate practice of mental discipline. Meditation and mindfulness techniques have been touted for years as highly beneficial for reducing stress, elevating mood, increasing powers of concentration, improving memory, enhancing immune function, increasing happiness, and more. Numerous scientific studies back these claims. And, notably, meditation can also enable greater creative output.

In a simple study, researchers divided subjects into two groups.[26] One group received meditation training and meditated thirty minutes every day for a week. The second group, the control group, was trained to simply relax. After the training, participants were given tasks that tested creativity. Findings showed impressively higher scores for people who meditated compared to those who simply relaxed. This suggests that even brief training in meditation can be effective.

In another study, participants were assigned to either a mindfulness or a control group.[27] The mindfulness group listened for ten minutes to instructions on non-judgmental awareness and learning to accept sensations in the body. The control group listened to a recording about natural history. They were then given problems that required insight (the prisoner problem or the coin problem, mentioned earlier in this chapter) and problems that didn't (such as the flower problem, also explained earlier in this chapter). Participants who had the brief mindfulness training solved the insight problems better, but not the noninsight problems.

In a study published in the *Harvard Business Review* entitled "Can 10 Minutes of Meditation Make You More Creative?" the researchers sought to confirm that creativity is among the earliest benefits of mindfulness meditation.[28] Specifically, they wanted to see whether a few minutes of mindfulness meditation would be enough to boost creativity. They divided 129 participants into three groups and assigned a creative task: generate as many business ideas as possible for using drones.

Before the participants began brainstorming ideas, one group was guided through a ten-minute recorded mindfulness session, a second group through a ten-minute fake meditation (being asked to allow their minds to relax and wander freely), and the third group was told to immediately begin brainstorming ideas.

Each group of participants generated approximately the same number of ideas. The main difference was that the meditators generated a wider range of ideas. Some of the creative ideas of the meditators included using drones for gardening (cutting plants, watering, pruning), security (extinguishing fires, monitoring, alerts), maintenance (washing windows), and zoo maintenance (feeding giraffes). In other words, practicing meditation revealed dimensions unseen by the non-meditators. In a further study, the researchers asked twenty-four senior managers at a large organization to meditate for twelve minutes and then to generate ideas about a certain subject. Most participants said that meditation helped them to clear their heads and come up with more original solutions.

Digging deeper, a group of researchers from Leiden University in the Netherlands asked practitioners of meditation to engage in two different forms of mindfulness meditation:

1. Open Monitoring, where subjects are asked to observe present-moment phenomena and simply notice any thought, emotion, or sensation without judgment; and

2. Focused Attention, where subjects fix their focus on a single object, say a candle, to the exclusion of all other stimuli.

After each meditation session, the participants took the AUT and RAT. The researchers discovered that Open Monitoring meditation was far more effective in enhancing divergent thinking, a key engine of creativity. Focused Attention meditation, not surprisingly, was more strongly related to convergent thinking, which is vital for narrowing down options and formulating a practicable solution.[29]

It appears that well-developed observation skills, which are enhanced by Open Monitoring meditation, increase cognitive flexibility and reduce cognitive rigidity, essential to the creative process. In building upon the above study, Dutch psychologist Matthijs Baas asserts that the ability to observe is closely related to one's openness to experience, a personality trait shown by studies to be one of the strongest indicators of creative success.[30] If you can learn how to meditate, you will see it will help you in several aspects of your life.

This advice also applies widely to organizations. Convinced of the benefits of mediation, Google has adopted a corporate mindfulness program for its employees called "Search Inside Yourself." Other major companies that embrace and support meditation in their corporate culture include Apple, Nike, WarnerMedia and AstraZeneca,[31] Goldman Sachs and Medtronic,[32] and the US Army.[33] Indeed, in cases where creativity is the lifeblood of an organization, decision-makers are sure to have a wider range of ideas arriving at their desks if they cultivate the practice of meditation among their employees.

Clearly, the corporate world and labor market are undergoing rapid changes. Studies and surveys show that one of the most important skills for pursuing a career, and for the business world, is creativity. I hope that this chapter has illustrated that there's more to creativity than your given personality—it is a skill that can be developed, just like any other.

With creativity as a top skill, businesses will need to shrewdly cultivate it in their organizations. As we've seen, creativity in the workplace is affected not only by the characteristics of the people and by the social environment, but also by environmental factors and through the use of various techniques. Individuals and organizations that seek creativity should welcome all possible tools and tricks they can employ. The findings of the studies included in this chapter suggest relatively easy ways to enhance creativity, for example, by tracing curved fluid lines, hanging photos that represent metaphors such as a bright light bulb, sitting outside a box, enhancing the colors blue and green in the office space, and taking short meditation breaks.

The trajectory of the modern economy clearly points to the ever-increasing importance of creativity as a desired skill. Businesses and job seekers should take heed, inform themselves, and act accordingly, lest they fall behind.

EPILOGUE

In this book, I hoped to deliver science-based findings that can make us happier, more satisfied, and more successful at work.

After penning the final word of the final chapter, after months of demanding literature research and more months of intensive writing, revising, and polishing, I sent the finished manuscript to the "cloud"—and of course to my publisher. There was one more thing I had to do: come up with a nice title. I had a temporary one, but I felt it was not good enough. I was looking for a nice, catchy name that would describe what the book is about.

Always disciplined, I booted up my computer and sat down to work. I adjusted my body into a comfortable position, gazed at the screen, and took a deep breath. I glanced at the clock. Here we go!

There I stayed.

Ten minutes, twenty, the good part of an hour. During that time all I was able to produce were several titles I was not satisfied with. I was stuck—it was total writer's block.

Pressured and flustered, with no inspiration or angle to pursue, I followed my own advice in the book I had just finished writing. The one with no title.

I knew from the studies presented in the book that when stuck, it's a good idea to take a break and do something else—to remove yourself from the situation. I also knew that it's preferable to take a walk in nature, to recover from mental fatigue and enhance performance creativity. I knew that a walk outdoors might be the boost I needed to find the perfect title.

Okay, Thalma, I thought to myself. *It's time to do something.*

Since finding a title is primarily a creative task, unlike reading and sum-marizing an article, I knew I had to let my mind wander and free-associate. I turned to the chapter I wrote on creativity. (I needed an insurance policy in case my usually reliable seashore wouldn't help this time!) The science offered several ways to enhance my creativity, including walking in circles and looking at something green and something blue. I thought I'd start with these tips and then, if they didn't work, try the others in that chapter—whatever works!

I turned off the computer, got up from my desk, and treated myself to a beau-tiful stroll on the beach, one of my favorite natural settings. At that time of the day there weren't many people around, and I walked along the shore, listening to the sound of the waves, watching the water and the seagulls. I remembered that sci-ence showed how being exposed to blue space, looking at water, positively influ-ences us and has a restorative value as well as increases our cognitive performance. I also walked part of the way in circles, turning back and forth. I was looking at the sea (something blue) and also looking at green squares that I found on my phone via the internet. All this time, my mind was wandering and free-associating. I was thinking about the tips I decided to try and about the others that I had not tried yet, and hoped one of them would work for me. And then it hit me; the book contains many takeaways backed by science for improving one's working life. Tips and cues from all sorts of directions, many unexpected, some newly discovered. Some when you really need it—in a job interview, a negotiation, talking with your boss, improving performance, needing to be creative, and more. These takeaways are offered to you, like a large menu of stuff that works. You can choose whatever works for you and makes you happier, more successful, more productive, and more creative at work. In short, to enlarge your palette of strategies, tactics, and "hacks" that surpass popular knowledge and present you with multiple opportu-nities to gain an edge. It is all about finding *Whatever Works!*

This book doesn't touch on typical job concerns like salary and benefits, although they are important, of course. This book is about the smaller things, sometimes unnoticed or unappreciated, such as the physical features of the office. Furthermore, we have gone beyond common knowledge and rather fuzzy intuition to offer concrete steps that put you at an advantage.

For instance, everyone *knows* that smartphones distract our attention, so if there is an important task at hand that demands concentration or creativity, we should silence our cell phones. Pretty much a no-brainer. But as we saw in the chapter on smartphones, turning off your cell phone but leaving it within your visual field, or even accessible to you physically, has been proven to be measurably distracting. It is only when the cell phone is completely out of sight and hidden away somewhere, in a drawer or in another room, for instance, that its seductive pull is neutralized and we can achieve peak concentration.

Or consider the value of diversity in a working team or task force. Certainly, we all pay lip service to the ideal of social diversity and praise its merits. And it only makes sense that a heterogeneous team will have more opinions expressed and offer different perspectives. However, it may not be common knowledge that the mere presence on a team of someone from a different culture, ethnicity, or mother tongue, *even if that person sits motionless and never once utters a word*, will instantly widen and enrich the entire group's thinking patterns and make the team more original and effective.

We've seen that there are specific moments in a negotiation when you can strategically express anger or disappointment in order to sway your negotiating partner toward the outcome you desire. We have also included studies that show how you can enhance your creativity at work, and how to restore your mental fatigue and enhance your well-being at your job.

The advice given in this book, all based on research, can make all the difference and can help to make our working lives better. They can be used when you need to perform, land a job, win a negotiation, keep your team happy and productive, ask for a raise, or simply be happier and more fulfilled in the workplace. Science shows us that the keys to more productive, creative, and happier working lives are well within our reach; however, it is up to us to put into practice *whatever works*—for ourselves, for our teams, and, if we have the power, for the entire organization.

It is my sincere wish that you profit from the insights in this book and see your life upgraded. In that case, our time together will have been truly valuable and enriching for both of us.

ACKNOWLEDGMENTS

Writing this book has been a journey, and I am grateful to the numerous people who accompanied me and provided support, encouragement, and advice. Without them I could not have completed the book. A huge thank-you to the teams at BenBella and at Levine Greenberg Rostan. BenBella's fine staff was a delight to work with. I am grateful to Glenn Yeffeth, the publisher, who believed in me when he first saw the proposal. I particularly want to thank my brilliant editor, Claire Schulz, for her beautiful and careful editing and suggestions. Claire is the kind of editor that every writer hopes to work with. She read the text multiple times and provided her comments, questions, ideas, and suggestions (always insisting they were only suggestions), improved my writing and thinking, and made the book better. Thank you, Claire. Special thanks to the BenBella production team: Sarah Avinger, the art director, deputy production manager Jessika Rieck, copy editor Scott Calamar, and my marketer, Lindsay Marshall.

I owe many thanks to my agent, Lindsay Edgecombe, of the Levine Greenberg Rostan Literary Agency. This is the second book on which I have worked with Lindsay, and she is the best literary agent a writer could ever hope to work with. This book would not have been possible without her guidance and assistance. Lindsay believed in the book and kept on believing all through the three years it took me to write it. She helped me from the first stage of the proposal, recognized the importance of this book even before I did, and encouraged me to write it. Thank you, Lindsay!

Special thanks to Harvey Frenkel and to Dalit Shmueli for reading several parts of this book and providing valuable insights, suggestions, and comments. They both improved my writing and I owe them many thanks.

I want to thank my research assistant, Yonathan Brand, for the help I received from him, and for responding to many requests regarding bibliography information. He worked under time pressure and was always efficient and attentive. I also thank Dani Yagil for suggesting some of the titles that I loved.

I am deeply grateful to the late Woolf Marmot for supporting my book. He and his late wife, Helene, were always true friends of me and my husband. Woolf was an amazing person, extremely smart, generous, and fun to be with, and I feel fortunate I had him as a friend.

I am also grateful to the School of Psychological Sciences at Tel Aviv University, my second home.

As always, I want to thank my family. My amazing children, Orly Lobel and Dory Lobel, are definitely role models for me and inspire me to grow. Orly is a law professor who wrote several successful and important books, and she is giving talks all over the world. Dory is a successful musician who plays and performs in many countries. They are both extremely creative and productive while managing to raise beautiful families. They are always supportive and true inspiration for me.

There is not a day I don't think of my son Dani, and he is a source of strength for me. I feel the loss of him and his presence every day. I know that he could have contributed many ideas with his sharp and deep mind, and I often find myself thinking of what he would have said.

My grandchildren Danielle, Elinor, Natalie, Dean, Libby, and Adam are an endless source of wonder, pride, joy, and laughter. They are the sunshine of my life. Their sense of wonder and curiosity, their innocence, and their eagerness to learn motivates me to write and explore.

My son-in-law, On Amir, my daughter-in-law, Keren Kohen-Lobel, my brother, Raffi Jacobson, and his partner, Rick Sylvester, are always wonderfully supportive and encouraging.

My late parents, Dora and Hillel Jacobson, were always there for me, believed in me, and taught me to do and pursue whatever I want. I wish they could read this book.

Finally I want to thank my husband, David Lobel, for always encouraging me, believing in me, supporting me, and being there for me and for tolerating the long hours I spent in front of the computer. Thank you, David.

NOTES

Chapter 1: The Office Layout

1. Siu-Kei Wong et al., "Sick building syndrome and perceived indoor environmental quality: A survey of apartment buildings in Hong Kong," *Habitat International* 33, no. 4 (October 2009): 463–71, https://doi.org/10.1016/j.habitatint.2009.03.001; Yousef Al Horr et al., "Occupant productivity and office indoor environment quality: A review of the literature," *Building and Environment* 105 (August 2016): 369–89, https://doi.org/10.1016/j.buildenv.2016.06.001.
2. US Environmental Protection Agency, Indoor Environments Division, Office of Radiation and Indoor Air: Indoor Air Quality and Student Performance (Washington, DC, 2000), 1–4, https://my.airrestoreusa.com/wp-content/uploads/2015/04/STUDY-Indoor-Air-Quality-Student-Performance-8-1-00.pdf.
3. Ron Friedman, "Why Our Cubicles Make Us Miserable," *Psychology Today*, April 13, 2015, https://www.psychologytoday.com/us/blog/glue/201504/why-our-cubicles-make-us-miserable.
4. Emily Van Zandt, "Studies show open offices are distraction magnets. But there are ways to make it work," *Washington Business Journal*, May 17, 2018, https://www.bizjournals.com/washington/news/2018/05/17/studies-show-open-offices-are-distraction-magnets.html.
5. Ethan S. Bernstein and Stephen Turban, "The impact of the 'open' workspace on human collaboration," *Philosophical Transactions of the Royal Society B* 373, no. 1753 (July 2018), https://doi.org/10.1098/rstb.2017.0239; Jena McGregor, "Open office plans are as bad as you thought," *Washington Post*, July 18, 2018, https://www.washingtonpost.com/business/2018/07/18/open-office-plans-are-bad-you-thought/?noredirect=on.

6. Maria Konnikova, "The Open-Office Trap," *New Yorker*, January 7, 2014, https://
    www.newyorker.com/business/currency/the-open-office-trap.
7. Jan H. Pejtersen et al., "Sickness absence associated with shared and open-plan
    offices—a national cross sectional questionnaire survey," *Scandinavian Journal of
    Work Environment & Health* 37, no. 5 (September 2011): 376–82, https://doi
    .org/10.5271/sjweh.3167.
8. Manna Navai and Jennifer A. Veitch, "Acoustic Satisfaction in Open-Plan Offices:
    Review and Recommendations" (Ottawa: Institute for Research in Construction,
    2003), 1–22, http://citeseerx.ist.psu.edu/viewdoc/download?doi=10.1.1.5.1910
    &rep=rep1&type=pdf; Vinesh G. Oomen, Mike Knowles, and Isabella Zhao,
    "Should Health Service Managers Embrace Open Plan Work Environments?: A
    Review," *Asia Pacific Journal of Health Management* 3, no. 2 (2008): 37–43, https://
    search.informit.com.au/documentSummary;dn=424236471220718;res=IELAPA;
    Mahbob Rashid and Craig Zimring, "A Review of the Empirical Literature on the
    Relationships Between Indoor Environment and Stress in Health Care and Office
    Settings: Problems and Prospects of Sharing Evidence," *Environment and Behavior*
    40, no. 2 (March 2008): 151–90, https://doi.org/10.1177/0013916507311550;
    Aram Seddigh et al., "Concentration requirements modify the effect of office type
    on indicators of health and performance," *Journal of Environmental Psychology* 38
    (June 2014): 167–74, https://doi.org/10.1016/j.jenvp.2014.01.009; Jungsoo Kim
    and Richard de Dear, "Workspace satisfaction: The privacy-communication trade-
    off in open-plan offices," *Journal of Environmental Psychology* 36 (December 2013):
    18–26, https://doi.org/10.1016/j.jenvp.2013.06.007; Tobias Otterbring et al.,
    "The relationship between office type and job satisfaction: Testing a multiple medi-
    ation model through ease of interaction and well-being," *Scandinavian Journal of
    Work Environment & Health* 44, no. 3 (2018): 330–34, https://doi.org/10.5271/
    sjweh.3707.
9. Christine Castor et al., "Changes in work conditions and impact on workers'
    health: The case of collective syndrome in workers of a French administration
    office in March 2017," *Revue d'Épidémiologie et de Santé Publique* 66, no. 5 (July
    2018): S263, https://doi.org/10.1016/j.respe.2018.05.075.
10. Bernstein and Turban, "The impact of the 'open' workspace on human
    collaboration."
11. Nick Perham et al., "Mental arithmetic and non-speech office noise: an explo-
    ration of interference-by-content," *Noise & Health* 15 (2013): 73–8, https://doi
    .org/10.4103/1463-1741.107160.
12. Helena Jahncke et al., "Open-plan office noise: Cognitive performance and res-
    toration," *Journal of Environmental Psychology* 3, no. 4 (2011): 373–82, http://dx
    .doi.org/10.1016/j.jenvp.2011.07.002.
13. Aram Seddigh et al., "The association between office design and performance on
    demanding cognitive tasks," *Journal of Environmental Psychology* 42 (June 2015):
    172–81, https://doi.org/10.1016/j.jenvp.2015.05.001.

14. Gary Evans and Dana Johnson, "Stress and Open-Office Noise," *Journal of Applied Psychology* 85, no. 5 (October 2000): 779–83, http://dx.doi.org/10.1037/0021-9010.85.5.779.

15. Valtteri Hongisto, Annu Haapakangas, and Miia Haka, "Task performance and speech intelligibility—a model to promote noise control actions in open offices" (Foxwoods: 9th International Congress on Noise as a Public Health Problem, ICBEN, 2008), 1–8, https://pdfs.semanticscholar.org/dd87/aaf8cbb02dcfe9e3e b5b319d019cf1c9243b.pdf.

16. Niklas Halin et al., "Effects of Speech on Proofreading: Can Task-Engagement Manipulations Shield Against Distraction?," *Journal of Experimental Psychology: Applied* 20, no. 1 (March 2014): 69–80, https://doi.org/10.1037/xap0000002; Niklas Halin et al., "A shield against distraction," *Journal of Applied Research in Memory and Cognition* 3, no. 1 (March 2014): 31–6, https://doi.org/10.1016/j .jarmac.2014.01.003; Marijke Keus van de Poll, "Unmasking the effects of masking on performance: The potential of multiple-voice masking in the office environment," *Journal of the Acoustical Society of America* 138, no. 2 (2015): 807, https://doi.org/10.1121/1.4926904.

17. Brendan Norman and Daniel Bennett, "Are mobile phone conversations always so annoying? The 'need-to-listen' effect re-visited," *Behaviour & Information Technology* 33, no. 12 (January 2014): 1294–305, https://doi.org/10.1080/01 44929X.2013.876098; John E. Marsh et al., "Why are background telephone conversations distracting?," *Journal of Experimental Psychology: Applied* 24, no. 2 (2018): 222–35, http://dx.doi.org/10.1037/xap0000170.

18. Marsh et al., "Why are background telephone conversations distracting?"

19. Haapakangas et al., "Effects of Five Speech Masking Sounds on Performance and Acoustic Satisfaction. Implications for Open-Plan Offices," *Acta Acustica united with Acustica* 97, no. 4 (2011): 641–55, https://doi.org/10.3813/AAA.918444; Marijke Keus van de Poll, "Unmasking the effects of masking on performance: The potential of multiple-voice masking in the office environment," *The Journal of the Acoustical Society of America* 138, no. 2 (2015): 807, https://doi.org/10.1121/1.4926904.

20. Ravi Mehta, Rui (Juliet) Zhu, and Amar Cheema, "Is Noise Always Bad? Exploring the Effects of Ambient Noise on Creative Cognition," *Journal of Consumer Research* 39, no. 4 (December 2012): 784–99, https://doi.org/10.1086/665048.

21. David Burkus, "Why You Can Focus in a Coffee Shop but Not in Your Open Office," *Harvard Business Review*, October 18, 2017, https://hbr.org/2017/10 /why-you-can-focus-in-a-coffee-shop-but-not-in-your-open-office.

22. Alison Hirst and Christina Schwabenland, "Doing gender in the 'new office,'" *Gender, Work & Organization* 25, no. 2 (March 2018): 159–76, https://doi.org /10.1111/gwao.12200.

23. Christina Bodin Danielsson et al., "The relation between office type and workplace conflict: A gender and noise perspective," *Journal of Environmental Psychology* 42 (June 2015): 161–71, https://doi.org/10.1016/j.jenvp.2015.04.004.

24. Nathan Bos et al., "Workplace Satisfaction Before and After Move to an Open Plan Office—Including Interactions with Gender and Introversion," *Proceedings of the Human Factors and Ergonomics Society Annual Meeting* 61, no. 1 (2018): 455–9, https://doi.org/10.1177/1541931213601594.

25. Steve Lohr, "Don't Get Too Comfortable at That Desk," *New York Times*, October 6, 2017, https://www.nytimes.com/2017/10/06/business/the-office-gets-remade-again.html.

26. Rianne Appel-Meulenbroek, Peter Groenen, and Ingrid Janssen, "An end-user's perspective on activity-based office concepts," *Journal of Corporate Real Estate* 13, no. 2 (2011): 122–35, https://doi.org/10.1108/14630011111136830.

27. Eline Meijer, Monique H. W. Frings-Dresen, and Judith Sluiter, "Effects of office innovation on office workers' health and performance," *Ergonomics* 52, no. 9 (2009): 1027–38, https://doi.org/10.1080/00140130902842752.

28. Lina Engelen et al., "Is activity-based working impacting health, work performance and perceptions? A systematic review," *Building Research & Information* 47, no. 4 (2019): 468–79, https://doi.org/10.1080/09613218.2018.1440958.

29. Tobias Otterbring et al., "The relationship between office type and job satisfaction: Testing a multiple mediation model through ease of interaction and well-being," *Scandinavian Journal of Work Environment & Health* 44, no. 3 (2018): 330–34, https://doi.org/10.5271/sjweh.3707.

Chapter 2: Let There Be Light

1. Femke Beute and Yvonne de Kort, "Let the sun shine! Measuring explicit and implicit preference for environments differing in naturalness, weather type and brightness," *Journal of Environmental Psychology* 36 (December 2013): 162–78, https://doi.org/10.1016/j.jenvp.2013.07.016.

2. Mohamed Boubekri et al., "Impact of Windows and Daylight Exposure on Overall Health and Sleep Quality of Office Workers: A Case-Control Pilot Study," *Journal of Clinical Sleep Medicine* 10, no. 6 (2014): 603–11, http://dx.doi.org/10.5664/jcsm.3780.

3. Yousef Al Horr et al., "Occupant productivity and office indoor environment quality: A review of the literature," *Building and Environment* 105 (August 2016): 369–89, https://doi.org/10.1016/j.buildenv.2016.06.001; Ihab Elzeyadi, *Daylighting-Bias and Biophilia: Quantifying the Impact of Daylighting on Occupants Health* (Oregon: US Green Building Council, 2011), 1–9, https://www.usgbc.org/sites/default/files/OR10_Daylighting%20Bias%20and%20Biophilia.pdf.

4. Antoine U. Viola et al., "Blue-enriched white light in the workplace improves self-reported alertness, performance and sleep quality," *Scandinavian Journal of Work, Environment & Health* 34, no. 4 (August 2008): 297–306, https://doi.org/10.5271/sjweh.1268.

5. Pietro Badia et al., "Psychophysiological and behavioral effects of bright and dim light," *Journal of Sleep Research* 19 (1990): 387; Melanie Ruger et al., "Weak relationships between suppression of melatonin and suppression of sleepiness/ fatigue in response to light exposure," *Journal of Sleep Research* 14, no. 3 (September 2005): 221–7, https://doi.org/10.1111/j.1365-2869.2005.00452.x; Christian Cajochen et al., "Dose-response relationship for light intensity and ocular and electroencephalographic correlates of human alertness," *Behavioural Brain Research* 115, no. 1 (October 2000): 75–83, https://doi.org/10.1016/S0166 -4328(00)00236-9; Christian Cajochen et al., "High Sensitivity of Human Melatonin, Alertness, Thermoregulation, and Heart Rate to Short Wavelength Light," *Journal of Clinical Endocrinology & Metabolism* 90, no. 3 (March 2005): 1311–16, https://doi.org/10.1210/jc.2004-0957; Karin Smolders, Yvonne de Kort, and Stéphanie M. van den Berg, "Daytime light exposure and feelings of vitality: Results of a field study during regular weekdays," *Journal of Environmental Psychology* 36 (December 2013): 270–9, https://doi.org/10.1016/j .jenvp.2013.09.004; Jan L. Souman et al., "Acute alerting effects of light: A systematic literature review," *Behavioural Brain Research* 337 (January 2018): 228– 39, https://doi.org/10.1016/j.bbr.2017.09.016.

6. Karin C. H. J. Smolders and Yvonne de Kort, "Bright light and mental fatigue: Effects on alertness, vitality, performance and physiological arousal," *Journal of Environmental Psychology* 39 (September 2014): 77–91, https://doi.org/10 .1016/j.jenvp.2011.12.003.

7. Anna Steidle and Lioba Werth, "In the spotlight: Brightness increases self-awareness and reflective self-regulation," *Journal of Environmental Psychology* 39 (2014): 40–50, https://doi.org/10.1016/j.jenvp.2013.12.007.

8. Jingyi Lu, Zhengyan Liu, and Zhe Fang, "Hedonic products for you, utilitarian products for me," *Judgment and Decision Making* 11, no. 4 (July 2016): 332–41, http://journal.sjdm.org/16/16428a/jdm16428a.pdf.

9. Xun (Irene) Huanga, Ping Dong, and Aparna A. Labroo, "Feeling disconnected from others: The effects of ambient darkness on hedonic choice," *International Journal of Research in Marketing* 35, no. 1 (March 2018): 144–53, https://doi .org/10.1016/j.ijresmar.2017.12.005.

10. Chen-Bo Zhong, Vanessa K. Bohns, and Francesca Gino, "Good Lamps Are the Best Police: Darkness Increases Dishonesty and Self-Interested Behavior," *Psychological Science* 21, no. 3 (March 2010): 311–4, https://doi.org/10.1177 /0956797609360754.

11. Wen-Bin Chiou and Ying-Yao Cheng, "In broad daylight, we trust in God! Brightness, the salience of morality, and ethical behavior," *Journal of Environmental Psychology* 36 (December 2013): 37–42, https://doi.org/10.1016/j.jenvp .2013.07.005.

12. Pronobesh Banerjee, Promothesh Chatterjee, and Jayati Sinha, "Is It Light or Dark? Recalling Moral Behavior Changes Perception of Brightness," *Psychological Science* 23, no. 4 (March 2012): 407–9, https://doi.org/10.1177/0956797611432497.

Chapter 3: I Am Too Cold, I Am Too Hot

1. Li Lan, Zhiwei Lian, and Li Pan, "The effects of air temperature on office workers' well-being, workload and productivity-evaluated with subjective ratings," *Applied Ergonomics* 42, no. 1 (March 2010): 29–36, https://doi.org/10.1016/j .apergo.2010.04.003.

2. Peter A. Hancock and Ioannis Vasmatzidis, "Effects of heat stress on cognitive performance: the current state of knowledge," *International Journal of Hyperthermia* 19, no. 3 (2003): 355–72, https://doi.org/10.1080/0265673021000054630.

3. Amar Cheema and Vanessa M. Patrick, "Is It Light or Dark? Recalling Moral Behavior Changes Perception of Brightness," *International Conference on Information Management, Innovation Management and Industrial Engineering* (2009): 533–6, https://doi.org/10.1109/ICIII.2009.286.

4. Johne Marjo, "Too hot? Too cold? Temperature wars flare at work," *Globe and Mail*, December 15, 2017, https://www.theglobeandmail.com/report-on -business/too-hot-too-cold-temperature-wars-flare-at-work/article4303843/.

5. Forrest Burnson, "How to Improve Employee Morale and Productivity Through Smart Climate Control," Software Advice, July 16, 2015, https://www.software advice.com/resources/improve-employee-productivity-with-climate-control/.

6. R. D. Pepler and R. E. Warner, "Temperature and Learning: An experimental study. Paper No 2089" (Lake Placid: Transactions of ASHRAE annual meeting, 1967), 211–9.

7. Olli Seppänen, William J. Fisk, and Q. H. Lei, "Effect of temperature on task performance in office environment," in *Proceeding of the 5th International Conference on Cold Climate Heating* (Berkeley, CA: Ernest Orlando Lawrence Berkeley National Laboratory, 2006), 219–20.

8. Alan Hedge, "Linking environmental conditions to productivity" (class lecture, Cornell University, Ithaca, NY, 2004).

9. Derek Clements-Croome, *Creating the productive workplace, Second Edition*, (Abingdon: Routledge, 2006); Charlie Huizenga et al., *Window performance for human thermal comfort: Final Report to the National Fenestration Rating Council* (Berkeley: University of California, February 2006), https://escholarship.org/uc /item/6rp85170; Olli A. Seppänen and William Fisk, "Some Quantitative Relations between Indoor Environmental Quality and Work Performance or Health," *HVAC&R Research* 12 (2006): 957–73, https://doi.org/10.1080/10789669.2006 .10391446.

10. Amar Cheema and Vanessa M. Patrick, "Influence of Warm versus Cool Temperatures on Consumer Choice: A Resource Depletion Account," *Journal of Marketing Research* 49, no. 6 (2012): 984–95, https://doi.org/10.1509/jmr.08.0205.

11. Henna Häggblom et al., "The effect of temperature on work performance and thermal comfort-laboratory experiment," in *Proceedings of indoor air 2011, the 12th International Conference on Indoor Air Quality and Climate* (Santa Cruz, CA: International Society of Indoor Air Quality and Climate, 2011), 519–25; Henna

Maula et al., "The effect of slightly warm temperature on work performance and comfort in open-plan offices—a laboratory study," *Indoor Air* 26, no. 2 (April 2016): 286–97, https://doi.org/10.1111/ina.12209.

12. Roberta Sellaro et al., "Preferred, but not objective temperature predicts working memory depletion," *Psychological Research* 79, no. 2 (March 2005): 282–8, https://doi.org/10.1007/s00426-014-0558-4.

13. Monica Hesse, "Cynthia Nixon asked to turn down the AC. It isn't silly. It's symbolic," *Washington Post*, August 29, 2018, https://www.washingtonpost .com/lifestyle/style/cynthia-nixon-asked-to-turn-down-the-ac-it-isnt-silly-its -symbolic/2018/08/29/a0b83eee-ab0c-11e8-8a0c-70b618c98d3c_story.html.

14. American Society of Heating, Refrigerating and Air-Conditioning Engineers, *ASHRAE Standard Thermal Environmental Conditions for Human Occupancy* (Atlanta, Ga, 2017), https://www.ashrae.org/technical-resources/bookstore/standard -55-thermal-environmental-conditions-for-human-occupancy.

15. Sami Karjalainen, "Gender differences in thermal comfort and use of thermostats in everyday thermal environments," *Building and Environment* 42, no. 4 (2007): 1594–603, https://doi.org/10.1016/J.BUILDENV.2006.01.009.

16. Joon Ho Choi, Azizan Aziz, and Vivian Loftness, "Investigation on the impacts of different genders and ages on satisfaction with thermal environments in office buildings," *Building and Environment* 45, no. 6 (2010): 1529–35, https://doi .org/10.1016/j.buildenv.2010.01.004.

17. Jéssica Kuntz Maykot, Ricardo Forgiarini Rupp, and Enedir Ghisi, "Assessment of gender on requirements for thermal comfort in office buildings located in the Brazilian humid subtropical climate," *Energy and Buildings* 158 (2018): 1170–83, https://doi.org/10.1016/j.enbuild.2017.11.036.

18. Kei Nagashima et al., "Thermal regulation and comfort during a mild-cold exposure in young Japanese women complaining of unusual coldness," *Journal of Applied Physiology* 92, no. 3 (March 2002): 1029–35, https://doi.org/10.1152 /japplphysiol.00399.2001.

19. Boris Kingma and Wouter van Marken Lichtenbelt, "Energy consumption in buildings and female thermal demand," *Nature Climate Change* 5, (2015): 1054–6, https://doi.org/10.1038/nclimate2741.

20. Sybil Derrible and Matthew Reeder, "The cost of over-cooling commercial buildings in the United States," *Energy and Buildings* 108 (December 2015): 304–6, https://doi.org/10.1016/j.enbuild.2015.09.022.

21. Tom Y. Chang and Agne Kajackaite, "Battle for the thermostat: Gender and the effect of temperature on cognitive performance," *PLoS One* 14, no. 5 (May 2019): e0216362, https://doi.org/10.1371/journal.pone.0216362.

22. Cheema and Patrick, "Influence of Warm versus Cool Temperatures on Consumer Choice: A Resource Depletion Account."

23. Lawrence E. Williams and John A. Bargh, "Experiencing Physical Warmth Promotes Interpersonal Warmth," *Science* 322 (October 2008): 606–7, https://doi .org/10.1126/science.1162548.

24. Yoona Kang, "Physical temperature effects on trust behavior: the role of insula," *Social Cognitive and Affective Neuroscience* 6, no. 4 (September 2011): 507–15, https://doi.org/10.1093/scan/nsq077.

25. Janina Steinmetz and Thomas Mussweiler, "Breaking the ice: How physical warmth shapes social comparison consequences," *Journal of Experimental Social Psychology* 47, no. 5 (2011): 1025–8, https://doi.org/10.1016/j.jesp.2011.03.022.

26. Adam J. Fay and Jon K. Maner, "Embodied effects are moderated by situational cues: Warmth, threat, and the desire for affiliation," *British Journal of Social Psychology* 54, no. 2 (June 2015): 291–305, https://doi.org/10.1111/bjso.12088.

27. John Bargh and Idit Shalev, "The Substitutability of Physical and Social Warmth in Daily Life," *Emotion* 12, no. 1 (February 2012): 154–62, https://doi.org/10.1037/a0023527; Zhansheng Chen, Kai-Tak Poon, and C. Nathan DeWall, "Cold Thermal Temperature Threatens Belonging: The Moderating Role of Perceived Social Support," *Social Psychological and Personality Science* 6, no. 4 (2015): 439–46, https://doi.org/10.1177/1948550614562843.

28. Thalma Lobel, *Sensation: The New Science of Physical Intelligence* (New York: Atria Books/Simon & Schuster, 2014).

29. Xun (Irene) Huang et al., "Warmth and conformity: The effects of ambient temperature on product preferences and financial decisions," *Journal of Consumer Psychology* 24, no. 2 (April 2014): 241–50, https://doi.org/10.1016/j.jcps.2013.09.009.

30. Janina Steinmetz and Ann-Christin Posten, "Physical temperature affects response behavior," *Journal of Experimental Social Psychology* 70 (May 2017): 294–300, https://doi.org/10.1016/j.jesp.2016.12.001.

31. Yonat Zwebner, Leonard Lee, and Jacob Goldenberg, "The temperature premium: Warm temperatures increase product valuation," *Journal of Consumer Psychology* 24, no. 2 (April 2014): 251–9, https://doi.org/10.1016/j.jcps.2013.11.003.

Chapter 4: Take a Walk in Nature

1. World Health Organization, "Mental health in the workplace" (Geneva Switzerland, 2019), http://www10.who.int/mental_health/in_the_workplace/en/.

2. Bum Jin Park et al., "Physiological effects of Shinrin-yoku (taking in the atmosphere of the forest) in a mixed forest in Shinano Town, Japan," *Scandinavian Journal of Forest Research* 23, no. 3 (2008): 278–83, https://doi.org/10.1080/02827580802055978; Bum Jin Park et al., "Physiological Effects of Forest Recreation in a Young Conifer Forest in Hinokage Town, Japan," *Silva Fennica* 43, no. 2 (2009): 291–301, http://www.metla.fi/silvafennica/full/sf43/sf432291.pdf; Bum Jin Park et al., "The physiological effects of Shinrin-yoku (taking in the forest atmosphere or forest bathing): evidence from field experiments in 24 forests across Japan," *Environmental Health and Preventive Medicine* 15 (January 2010): 18–26, https://doi.org/10.1007/s12199-009-0086-9.

3. Park et al., "The physiological effects of Shinrin-yoku (taking in the forest atmosphere or forest bathing): evidence from field experiments in 24 forests across Japan."

4. Ahmad Hassan et al., "Effects of Walking in Bamboo Forest and City Environments on Brainwave Activity in Young Adults," *Evidence-Based Complementary and Alternative Medicine* 2018 (2018): 1–9, https://doi.org/10.1155/2018/9653857.

5. Gregory N. Bratman et al., "The benefits of nature experience: Improved affect and cognition," *Landscape and Urban Planning* 138 (June 2015): 41–50, https://doi.org/10.1016/j.landurbplan.2015.02.005.

6. Kurt Beil and Douglas Hanes, "The Influence of Urban Natural and Built Environments on Physiological and Psychological Measures of Stress—A Pilot Study," *International Journal of Environmental Research and Public Health* 10, no. 4 (2013): 1250–67, https://doi.org/10.3390/ijerph10041250.

7. Joke Luttik, "The value of trees, water and open space as reflected by house prices in the Netherlands," *Landscape and Urban Planning* 48, no. 3–4 (May 2000): 161–7, https://doi.org/10.1016/S0169-2046(00)00039-6.

8. Mathew White et al., "Blue space: The importance of water for preference, affect, and restorativeness ratings of natural and built scenes," *Journal of Environmental Psychology* 30, no. 4 (December 2010): 482–93, https://doi.org/10.1016/j.jenvp.2010.04.004.

9. Sebastian Völker et al., "Do perceived walking distance to and use of urban blue spaces affect self-reported physical and mental health?," *Urban Forestry & Urban Greening* 29 (January 2018): 1–9, https://doi.org/10.1016/j.ufug.2017.10.014.

10. Joanne K. Garrett, "Urban blue space and health and wellbeing in Hong Kong: Results from a survey of older adults," *Health & Place* 55 (January 2019): 100–10, https://doi.org/10.1016/j.healthplace.2018.11.003; Daniel Nutsford et al., "Residential exposure to visible blue space (but not green space) associated with lower psychological distress in a capital city," *Health & Place* 39 (May 2016): 70–8, https://doi.org/10.1016/j.healthplace.2016.03.002.

11. Mireia Gascon et al., "Outdoor blue spaces, human health and well-being: A systematic review of quantitative studies," *International Journal of Hygiene and Environmental Health* 220, no. 8 (November 2017): 1207–21, https://doi.org/10.1016/j.ijhch.2017.08.004.

12. George MacKerron and Susana Mourato, "Happiness is greater in natural environments," *Global Environmental Change* 23, no. 5 (October 2013): 992–1000, https://doi.org/10.1016/j.gloenvcha.2013.03.010.

13. Won Sop Shin, "The influence of forest view through a window on job satisfaction and job stress," *Scandinavian Journal of Forest Research* 22, no. 3 (2007): 248–53, https://doi.org/10.1080/02827580701262733.

14. Agnes E. Van den Berg, Anna Jorgensen, and Edward R. Wilson, "Evaluating restoration in urban green spaces: Does setting type make a difference?," *Landscape and Urban Planning* 127 (July 2014): 173–81, https://doi.org/10.1016/j.landurbplan.2014.04.012.

15. Jesper J. Alvarsson, Stefan Wiens, and Mats E. Nilsson, "Stress Recovery during Exposure to Nature Sound and Environmental Noise," *International Journal of Environmental Research and Public Health* 7, no. 3 (2010): 1036–46, https://doi .org/10.3390/ijerph7031036.

16. Jacob A. Benfield, B. Derrick Taff, Peter Newman, and Joshua Smyth, "Natural Sound Facilitates Mood Recovery," *Ecopsychology* 6, no. 3 (2014): 183–8, http:// doi.org/10.1089/eco.2014.0028.

17. John D. Mayer and Yvonne N. Gaschke, "The Brief Mood Introspection Scale (BMIS)," *Journal of Personality and Social Psychology* 55 (1988): 102–11.

18. Rachel Kaplan and Stephen Kaplan, *The Experience of Nature: A Psychological Perspective* (Cambridge: Cambridge University Press, 1989); Stephen Kaplan, "The restorative benefits of nature: Toward an integrative framework," *Journal of Environmental Psychology* 15, no. 3 (September 1995): 169–82, https://doi .org/10.1016/0272-4944(95)90001-2.

19. Marc G. Berman, John Jonides, and Stephen Kaplan, "The cognitive benefits of interacting with nature," *Psychological Science* 19, no. 12 (2008): 1207–12, http:// dx.doi.org/10.1111/j.1467-9280.2008.02225.x.

20. Rita Berto, "Exposure to restorative environments helps restore attentional capacity," *Journal of Environmental Psychology* 25, no. 3 (September 2005): 249–59, https://doi.org/10.1016/j.jenvp.2005.07.001.

21. Kate E. Lee et al., "40-second green roof views sustain attention: The role of micro-breaks in attention restoration," *Journal of Environmental Psychology* 42 (2015): 182–9, https://doi.org/10.1016/j.jenvp.2015.04.003.

22. Ruth K. Raanaas et al., "Benefits of indoor plants on attention capacity in an office setting," *Journal of Environmental Psychology* 33, no. 1 (March 2011): 99–105, https://doi.org/10.1016/j.jenvp.2010.11.005.

23. Tina Bringslimark, Terry Hartig, and Grete Grindal Patil, "Psychological Benefits of Indoor Plants in Workplaces: Putting Experimental Results into Context," *Hortscience* 42, no. 3 (2007): 581–7, https://doi.org/10.21273/HORTSCI.42.3.581.

24. Tina Bringslimark, Grete Grindal Patil, and Terry Hartig, "Adaptation to Windowlessness: Do Office Workers Compensate for a Lack of Visual Access to the Outdoors?," *Environment and Behavior* 43, no. 4 (2011): 469–87, https://doi .org/10.1177/0013916510368351.

25. Chen-Yen Chang and Ping-Kun Chen, "Human Response to Window Views and Indoor Plants in the Workplace," *Hortscience* 40, no. 5 (August 2005): 1354–9, https://doi.org/10.21273/HORTSCI.40.5.1354.

Chapter 5: Wordless Interactions

1. Janine Willis and Alexander Todorov, "First Impressions: Making Up Your Mind After a 100-Ms Exposure to a Face," *Psychological Science* 17, no. 7 (2006): 592–8, https://doi.org/10.1111/j.1467-9280.2006.01750.x.

2. Murray R. Barrick et al., "Candidate characteristics driving initial impressions during rapport building: Implications for employment interview validity," *Journal of Occupational and Organizational Psychology* 85, no. 2 (June 2012): 330–52, https://doi.org/10.1111/j.2044-8325.2011.02036.x; Allen I. Huffcutt, "From Science to Practice: Seven Principles for Conducting Employment Interviews," *Applied H.R.M. Research; Radford* 12, no. 1 (2010): 121–36.

3. Debby Mayne, "7 Tips on Proper Handshake Etiquette," Updated February 10, 2019, https://www.thespruce.com/handshake-etiquette-p2-1216847.

4. Greg L. Stewart et al., "Exploring the Handshake in Employment Interviews," *Journal of Applied Psychology* 93, no. 5 (2008): 1139–46, https://doi.org/10.1037/0021-9010.93.5.1139.

5. William F. Chaplin, "Handshaking, gender, personality, and first impressions," *Journal of Personality and Social Psychology* 79, no. 1 (2000): 110–7, http://dx.doi.org/10.1037/0022-3514.79.1.110; Greg L. Stewart et al., "Exploring the Handshake in Employment Interviews," *Journal of Applied Psychology* 93, no. 5 (2008): 1139–46, https://doi.org/10.1037/0021-9010.93.5.1139.

6. Juliana Schroeder et al., "Handshaking promotes deal-making by signaling cooperative intent," *Journal of Personality and Social Psychology* 116, no. 5 (2019): 743–68, https://doi.org/10.1037/pspi0000157.

7. Joao Avelino et al., "The Power of a Hand-Shake in Human-Robot Interations," in *Proceeding of 2018 IEEE/RSJ International Conference on Intelligent Robots and Systems (IROS)* (Madrid, Spain, 2018), https://doi.org/ doi.org/10.1109/IROS.2018.8593980.

8. Sanda Dolcos et al., "The Power of a Handshake: Neural Correlates of Evaluative Judgments in Observed Social Interactions," *Journal of Cognitive Neuroscience* 24, no. 12 (December 2012): 2295–305, https://doi.org/10.1162/jocn_a_00295.

9. Yuta Katsumi et al., "When Nonverbal Greetings 'Make It or Break It': The Role of Ethnicity and Gender in the Effect of Handshake on Social Appraisals," *Journal of Nonverbal Behavior* 41, no. 4 (December 2017): 345–65, https://doi.org/10.1007/s10919-017-0257-0.

10. Paul Watson, "Martial Arts Academy Shows How To Defend Against Trump's Handshake," AskMen, https://in.askmen.com/entertainment-news/1115774/article/martial-arts-academy-shows-how-to-defend-against-trumps-handshake.

11. Tanya L. Chartrand and John A. Bargh, "The Chameleon Effect: The Perception-Behavior Link and Social Interaction," *Journal of Personality and Social Psychology* 76, no. 6 (1999): 893–910, https://doi.org/10.1037/0022-3514.76.6.893.

12. Tanya L. Chartrand and John A. Bargh, "The unbearable automaticity of being," *American Psychologist* 54, no. 7 (1999): 462–79, http://dx.doi.org/10.1037/0003-066X.54.7.462; Jessica L. Lakin and Tanya L. Chartrand, "Using Nonconscious Behavioral Mimicry to Create Affiliation and Rapport," *Psychological Science* 14, no. 4 (2003): 334–9, https://doi.org/10.1111/1467-9280.14481.

13. William W. Maddux, Elizabeth Mullen, and Adam D. Galinsky, "Chameleons bake bigger pies and take bigger pieces: Strategic behavioral mimicry facilitates negotiation outcomes," *Journal of Experimental Social Psychology* 44, no. 2 (March 2008): 461–8, https://doi.org/10.1016/j.jesp.2007.02.003.

14. Chartrand and Bargh, "The Chameleon Effect: The Perception-Behavior Link and Social Interaction."

15. Jeremy N. Bailenson and Nick Yee, "Digital Chameleons: Automatic Assimilation of Nonverbal Gestures in Immersive Virtual Environments," *Psychological Science* 16, no. 10 (October 2005): 814–9, https://doi.org/10.1111/j.1467-9280.2005.01619.x.

16. Rick B. van Baaren et al., "Mimicry for money: Behavioral consequences of imitation," *Journal of Experimental Social Psychology* 39, no. 4 (July 2003): 393–8, https://doi.org/10.1016/S0022-1031(03)00014-3; Céline Jacob and Nicolas Guéguen, "The effect of employees' verbal mimicry on tipping," *International Journal of Hospitality Management* 35 (December 2013): 109–11, https://doi.org/10.1016/j.ijhm.2013.05.006.

17. Lakin and Chartrand, "Using Nonconscious Behavioral Mimicry to Create Affiliation and Rapport."

18. Johan C. Karremans and Thijs Verwijmeren, "Mimicking Attractive Opposite-Sex Others: The Role of Romantic Relationship Status," *Personality and Social Psychology Bulletin* 34, no. 7 (May 2008): 939–50, https://doi.org/10.1177/0146167208316693.

19. Kipling D. Williams, Christopher K. T. Cheung, and Wilma Choi, "Cyberostracism: Effects of being ignored over the Internet," *Journal of Personality and Social Psychology* 79, no. 5 (2000): 748–62, https://doi.org/10.1037/0022-3514.79.5.748.

20. Kipling D. Williams, "The Pain of Exclusion," *Scientific American Mind* 21, no. 6 (2011): 30–7, https://www.jstor.org/stable/24943221.

21. Jessica L. Lakin, Tanya L. Chartrand, and Robert M. Arkin, "I Am Too Just Like You: Nonconscious Mimicry as an Automatic Behavioral Response to Social Exclusion," *Psychological Science* 19, no. 8 (August 2008): 816–22, https://doi.org/10.1111/j.1467-9280.2008.02162.x.

22. Marina Kouzakova, Rick van Baaren, and Advan Knippenberg, "Lack of behavioral imitation in human interactions enhances salivary cortisol levels," *Hormones and Behavior* 57 (April 2010): 421–6, https://doi.org/10.1016/j.yhbeh.2010.01.011.

23. Robin J. Tanner et al., "Of Chameleons and Consumption: The Impact of Mimicry on Choice and Preferences," *Journal of Consumer Research* 34, no. 6 (April 2008): 754–66, https://doi.org/10.1086/522322.

24. Céline Jacob et al., "Retail salespeople's mimicry of customers: Effects on consumer behavior," *Journal of Retailing and Consumer Services* 18, no. 5 (September 2011): 381–8, https://doi.org/10.1016/j.jretconser.2010.11.006.

25. Rick B. van Baaren et al., "Mimicry and Prosocial Behavior," *Psychological Science* 15, no. 1 (January 2004): 71–4, https://doi.org/10.1111/j.0963-7214.2004.01501012.x.

26. N. Pontus Leander, Tanya L. Chartrand, and John A. Bargh, "You Give Me the Chills: Embodied Reactions to Inappropriate Amounts of Behavioral Mimicry," *Psychological Science* 23, no. 7 (2012): 772–9, https://doi.org/10.1177/0956797611434535.

27. Liam C. Kavanagh, "When It's an Error to Mirror: The Surprising Reputational Costs of Mimicry," *Psychological Science* 22, no. 10 (2011): 1274–6, https://doi.org/10.1177/0956797611418678.

28. Mariëlle Stel et al., "Mimicking disliked others: Effects of a priori liking on the mimicry-liking link," *European Journal of Social Psychology* 14, no. 5 (August 2010): 867–80, https://doi.org/10.1002/ejsp.655; Leander, Chartrand, and Bargh, "You Give Me the Chills: Embodied Reactions to Inappropriate Amounts of Behavioral Mimicry."

29. Amy Dalton, Tanya Chartrand, and Eli Finkel, "The Schema-Driven Chameleon: How Mimicry Affects Executive and Self-Regulatory Resources," *Journal of Personality and Social Psychology* 98, no. 4 (April 2010): 605–17, http://dx.doi.org/10.1037/a0017629.

Chapter 6: We Need to Talk

1. Shirli Kopelman, Ashleigh Shelby Rosette, and Leigh Thompson, "The three faces of Eve: Strategic displays of positive, negative, and neutral emotions in negotiations," *Organizational Behavior and Human Decision Processes* 99, no. 1 (January 2006): 81–101, https://doi.org/10.1016/j.obhdp.2005.08.003.

2. Marwan Sinaceur and Larissa Z. Tiedens, "Get mad and get more than even: When and why anger expression is effective in negotiations," *Journal of Experimental Social Psychology* 3, no. 3 (May 2006): 314–22, https://doi.org/10.1016/j.jesp.2005.05.002.

3. Gert-Jan Lelieveld et al., "Disappointed in you, angry about your offer: Distinct negative emotions induce concessions via different mechanisms," *Journal of Experimental Social Psychology* 58 (February 2017): 31–43, https://doi.org/10.1016/j.joep.2016.09.003.

4. Andreas Jäger, David D. Loschelder, and Malte Friese, "Using self-regulation to overcome the detrimental effects of anger in negotiations," *Psychological Science* 23, no. 4 (March 2012): 407–9, https://doi.org/10.1177/0956797611432497.

5. Andreas Jäger, David D. Loschelder, and Malte Friese, "Using Self-regulation to Successfully Overcome the Negotiation Disadvantage of Low Power," *Frontiers in Psychology* 8 (2017): 271, https://doi.org/10.3389/fpsyg.2017.00271.

6. Amy J. C. Cuddy, Caroline A. Wilmuth, and Dana R. Carney, "The Benefit of Power Posing Before a High-Stakes Social Evaluation," *Harvard Business*

School Working Paper 13-027 (September 2012), https://dash.harvard.edu/handle/1/9547823.

7. Stéphane Côté, Ivona Hideg, and Gerben A. van Kleef, "The consequences of faking anger in negotiations," *Journal of Experimental Social Psychology* 23, no. 4 (March 2012): 407–9, https://doi.org/10.1177/0956797611432497.

8. Hajo Adam and Jeanne M. Brett, "Everything in moderation: The social effects of anger depend on its perceived intensity," *Journal of Experimental Social Psychology* 76 (May 2018): 12–18, https://doi.org/10.1016/j.jesp.2017.11.014.

9. Marwan Sinaceur et al., "Hot or cold: Is communicating anger or threats more effective in negotiation?," *Journal of Applied Psychology* 96, no. 5 (2011): 1018–32, http://dx.doi.org/10.1037/a0023896.

10. Alice H. Eagly, *Sex Differences in Social Behavior: A Social-role Interpretation* (Mahwah, NJ: Lawrence Erlbaum Associates, 1987); Alice H. Eagly and Wendy Wood, "Social Role Theory," in *The Handbook of Theories of Social Psychology: Volume 2*, ed. Paul A. M. Van Lange, Arie W. Kruglanski, and E. Tory Higgins (Newbury Park, CA: SAGE Publications Ltd, 2012), chapter 49, http://dx.doi.org/10.4135/9781446249222.n49.

11. Victoria L. Brescoll and Eric Luis Uhlmann, "Can an Angry Woman Get Ahead?: Status Conferral, Gender, and Expression of Emotion in the Workplace," *Psychological Science* 19, no. 3 (March 2008): 268–75, https://doi.org/10.1111/j.1467-9280.2008.02079.x.

12. Jessica M. Salerno and Liana C. Peter-Hagene, "One Angry Woman: Anger Expression Increases Influence for Men, but Decreases Influence for Women, During Group Deliberation," *Law and Human Behavior* 39, no. 6 (2015): 581–92, http://dx.doi.org/10.1037/lhb0000147.

13. Jessica M. Salerno et al., "Closing With Emotion: The Differential Impact of Male Versus Female Attorneys Expressing Anger in Court," *Law and Human Behavior* 42, no. 4 (2018): 385–401, http://dx.doi.org/10.1037/lhb0000292.

14. Alice F. Stuhlmacher and Amy E. Walters, "Gender differences in negotiation outcome: A meta-analysis," *Personnel Psychology* 52, no. 3 (1999): 653–77, https://doi.org/10.1111/j.1744-6570.1999.tb00175.x; Jens Mazei et al., "A meta-analysis on gender differences in negotiation outcomes and their moderators," *Psychological Bulletin* 141, no. 1 (2015): 85–104, https://doi.org/10.1037/a0038184.

15. Mazei et al., "A meta-analysis on gender differences in negotiation outcomes and their moderators."

16. Hannah Riley Bowles, Linda Babcock, and Lei Lai, "Social incentives for gender differences in the propensity to initiate negotiations: Sometimes it does hurt to ask," *Organizational Behavior and Human Decision Processes* 103, no. 1 (May 2007): 84–103, https://doi.org/10.1016/j.obhdp.2006.09.001.

17. Katharina G. Kugler et al., "Gender Differences in the Initiation of Negotiations: A Meta-Analysis," *Psychological Bulletin* 144, no. 2 (2018): 198–222, http://dx.doi.org/10.1037/bul0000135.

18. Gert-Jan Lelieveld et al., "Does Communicating Disappointment in Negotiations Help or Hurt? Solving an Apparent Inconsistency in the Social-Functional Approach to Emotions," *Journal of Personality and Social Psychology* 105, no. 4 (2013): 605–20, https://doi.org/10.1037/a0033345.

19. Russell Cropanzano and Marie S. Mitchell, "Social Exchange Theory: An Interdisciplinary Review," *Journal of Management* 31, no. 6 (March 2012): 874–900, https://doi.org/10.1177/0149206305279602.

20. Sebastian Kube, Michel André Maréchal, and Clemens Puppe, "The Currency of Reciprocity: Gift Exchange in the Workplace," *American Economic Research* 102, no. 4 (June 2012): 1644–62, 10.1257/aer.102.4.1644.

21. Micro Tonin and Michael Vlassopoulos, "Corporate Philanthropy and Productivity: Evidence from an Online Real Effort Experiment," *Journal of Consumer Management Science* 61, no. 8 (August 2015): 1795–811, https://doi.org/10.1287/mnsc.2014.1985.

22. Thomas Gilovich, Amit Kumar, and Lily Jampol, "A wonderful life: experiential consumption and the pursuit of happiness," *Journal of Consumer Psychology* 25, no. 1 (January 2015): 152–65, https://doi.org/10.1016/j.jcps.2014.08.004; Lily Jampol and Thomas Gilovich, "Surprise! Purchase type determines whether expectation disconfirmation is fun or upsetting," *Association for Consumer Research* 42 (2014): 788, http://acrwebsite.org/volumes/1017611/volumes/v42/NA-42; Cindy Chan and Cassie Mogilner, "Experiential gifts foster stronger social relationships than material gifts," *Journal of Consumer Research* 43, no. 6 (April 2017): 913–31, https://doi.org/10.1093/jcr/ucw067.

23. Peter A. Caprariello and Harry T. Reis, "To do, to have, or to share? Valuing experiences over material possessions depends on the involvement of others," *Journal of Personality and Social Psychology* 104, no. 2 (2013): 199–215, http://dx.doi.org/10.1037/a0030953.

24. Leaf Van Boven and Thomas Gilovich, "To Do or to Have? That Is the Question," *Journal of Personality and Social Psychology* 85, no. 6 (2003): 1193–202, https://doi.org/10.1037/0022-3514.85.6.1193.

25. Travis J. Carter and Thomas Gilovich, "The Relative Relativity of Material and Experiential Purchases," *Journal of Personality and Social Psychology* 98, no. 1 (2010): 146–59, https://doi.org/0.1037/a0017145.

26. Amit Kumar and Thomas Gilovich, "Some 'Thing' to Talk About? Differential Story Utility from Experiential and Material Purchases," *Personality and Social Psychology Bulletin* 41, no. 10 (2015): 1320–31, https://doi.org/10.1177/0146167215594591; Amit Kumar, Matthew A. Killingsworth, and Thomas Gilovich, "Waiting for Merlot: Anticipatory Consumption of Experiential and Material Purchases," *Psychological Science* 25, no. 10 (August 2014): 1924–31, https://doi.org/10.1177/0956797614546556.

Chapter 7: Sticky Fingers

1. Maryam Kouchaki and Sreedhari D. Desai, "Anxious, threatened, and also unethical: How anxiety makes individuals feel threatened and commit unethical acts," *Journal of Applied Psychology* 100, no. 2 (2015): 360–75, http://dx.doi .org/10.1037/a0037796.

2. Maryam Kouchaki and Isaac H. Smith, "The Morning Morality Effect: The Influence of Time of Day on Unethical Behavior," *Psychological Science* 25, no. 1 (2014): 95–102, https://doi.org/10.1177/0956797613498099.

3. Brian C. Gunia, Christopher M. Barnes, and Sunita Sah, "The Morality of Larks and Owls: Unethical Behavior Depends on Chronotype as Well as Time of Day," *Psychological Science* 25, no. 12 (October 2014): 2272–4, https://doi.org/10 .1177/0956797614541989.

4. Francesca Gino et al., "Unable to resist temptation: How self-control depletion promotes unethical behavior," *Organizational Behavior and Human Decision Processes* 115, no. 2 (July 2011): 191–203, https://doi.org/10.1016/j.obhdp .2011.03.001.

5. Hengchen Dai et al., "The Impact of Time at Work and Time Off from Work on Rule Compliance: The Case of Hand Hygiene in Health Care," *Journal of Applied Psychology* 100, no. 3 (2015): 846–62, http://dx.doi.org/10.1037/a0038067.

6. Christopher M. Barnes et al., "Lack of sleep and unethical conduct," *Journal of Personality and Social Psychology* 115, no. 2 (July 2011): 169–80, https://doi .org/10.1016/j.obhdp.2011.01.009.

7. Vic Schlitzer, "Millennials: Does big paycheck Trump ethical responsibility?," Bentley University, https://www.bentley.edu/news/millennials-does-big-paycheck -trump-ethical-responsibility.

8. Matthew Jenkin, "Millennials want to work for employers committed to values and ethics," *The Guardian*, May 5, 2015, https://www.theguardian.com /sustainable-business/2015/may/05/millennials-employment-employers-values -ethics-jobs.

Chapter 8: Diversity in the Workplace

1. Catalyst, "2008 Catalyst Census of Women Board Directors of the Fortune 500," updated January 12, 2009, https://www.catalyst.org/research/2008-catalyst -census-of-women-board-directors-of-the-fortune-500/.

2. Renée B. Adams and Daniel Ferreira, "Women in the boardroom and their impact on governance and performance," *Journal of Financial Economics* 94, no. 2 (November 2009): 291–309, https://doi.org/10.1016/j.jfineco.2008.10.007; M. K. Julizaerma Zulkarnain and Mohamad Sori, "Gender Diversity in the Boardroom and Firm Performance of Malaysian Public Listed Companies,"

Procedia—Social and Behavioral Sciences 65, no. 3 (December 2012): 1077–85, https://doi.org/10.1016/j.sbspro.2012.11.374.

3. "Press Release: Large-cap companies with at least one woman on the board have outperformed their peer group with no women on the board by 26% over the last six years, according to a report by Credit Suisse Research Institute," July 31, 2012, https://www.credit-suisse.com/about-us-news/en/articles/media-releases/42035 -201207.html.

4. Anh D. Pham and Anh T. P. Hoang, "Does Female Representation on Board Improve Firm Performance? A Case Study of Non-financial Corporations in Vietnam," *Beyond traditional probabilistic methods in economics. ECONVN 2019. Studies in computational intelligence* 809 (2019): 497–509, https://link.springer .com/chapter/10.1007/978-3-030-04200-4_36.

5. Cristian L. Dezsö and David Gaddis Ross, "Does female representation in top management improve firm performance? A panel data investigation," *Strategic Management Journal* 33, no. 9 (September 2012): 1072–89, https://doi .org/10.1002/smj.1955.

6. Richard Orlando et al., "Employing an innovation strategy in racially diverse workforces: Effects on firm performance," *Group & Organization Management* 28, no. 1 (March 2003): 107–26, https://search.proquest.com/docview/203375015.

7. Samuel R. Sommers, "On racial diversity and group decision making: Identifying multiple effects of racial composition on jury deliberations," *Journal of Personality and Social Psychology* 90, no. 4 (2006): 597–612, http://dx.doi .org/10.1037/0022-3514.90.4.597.

8. Richard B. Freeman and Wei Huang, "Collaboration: Strength in diversity," *Nature* 513, no. 7518 (2013): 305, https://www.nature.com/news/collaboration -strength-in-diversity-1.15912.

9. Thomas Barta, Markus Kleiner, and Tilo Neumann, "Is there a payoff from top-team diversity?," *McKinsey Quarterly* (April 2012): 1–3, https://www.mckinsey .com/business-functions/organization/our-insights/is-there-a-payoff-from-top -team-diversity.

10. Katherine W. Phillips, "How Diversity Makes Us Smarter," *Scientific American*, October 1, 2014, https://www.scientificamerican.com/article/how-diversity-makes -us-smarter/.

11. Sheen S. Levine et al., "Ethnic diversity deflates price bubbles," *PNAS* 111, no. 52 (2014): 18524–9, https://doi.org/10.1073/pnas.1407301111.

12. Sheen S. Levine et al., "Ethnic diversity deflates price bubbles."

13. Daniel Kahneman, *Thinking, Fast and Slow* (New York: Farrar, Straus and Giroux, 2011).

14. Boaz Keysar, Sayuri L. Hayakawa, and Sun Gyu An, "The Foreign-Language Effect: Thinking in a Foreign Tongue Reduces Decision Biases," *Psychological Science* 23, no. 6 (2012): 661–8, https://doi.org/10.1177/0956797611432178.

15. Albert Costa et al., "'Piensa' twice: On the foreign language effect in decision making," *Cognition* 130, no. 2 (February 2014): 236–54, https://doi.org/10.1016/j.cognition.2013.11.010.

16. Albert Costa et al., "Your Morals Depend on Language," *PLoS One* 9, no. 4 (2014): e94842, https://doi.org/10.1371/journal.pone.0094842; Heather Cipolletti, Steven McFarlane, and Christine Weissglass, "The Moral Foreign-Language Effect," *Philosophical Psychology* 29, no. 1 (2016): 23–40, https://doi.org/10.1080/09515089.2014.993063; Janet Geipela, Constantinos Hadjichristidis, and Luca Surian, "How foreign language shapes moral judgment," *Journal of Experimental Social Psychology* 59 (July 2015): 8–17, https://doi.org/10.1016/j.jesp.2015.02.001.

Chapter 9: Will This Tie Get Me Hired or Fired?

1. Miriam Berger, "Women in Japan were told not to wear glasses to work. Their response has been fiery," *Washington Post,* November 8, 2019, https://www.washingtonpost.com/world/2019/11/08/women-japan-were-told-not-wear-glasses-work-their-response-has-been-fiery/.

2. "Social Psychology Lecture, UCLA, Matthew Lieberman, Ph.D.," YouTube video, 1:22:43, "UCLACourses," September 29, 2009, https://www.youtube.com/watch?v=Vl7Ead_YAxc.

3. John T. Malloy, *Dress for Success* (New York: Peter H. Wyden, 1975).

4. Guy Gherardi et al., "Are we dressed to impress? A descriptive survey assessing patients' preference of doctors' attire in the hospital setting," *Clinical Medicine* 9, no. 6 (December 2009): 519–24, https://doi.org/10.7861/clinmedicine.9-6-519.

5. Miles Landry et al., "Patient Preferences for Doctor Attire: The White Coat's Place in the Medical Profession," *Ochsner Journal* 13, no. 3 (September 2013): 334–42, https://www.ncbi.nlm.nih.gov/pmc/articles/PMC3776508/.

6. Bettina Hannover and Ulrich Kühnen, "'The clothing makes the self' via knowledge activation," *Journal of Applied Social Psychology* 32, no. 12 (2013): 2513–25, http://dx.doi.org/10.1111/j.1559-1816.2002.tb02754.x.

7. Adrian Furnham, Pui Shuen Chan, and Emma Wilson, "What to wear? The influence of attire on the perceived professionalism of dentists and lawyers," *Journal of Applied Social Psychology* 43, no. 9 (September 2013): 1838–50, https://doi.org/10.1111/jasp.12136.

8. Noola K. Griffiths, "'Posh music should equal posh dress': an investigation into the concert dress and physical appearance of female soloists," *Psychology of Music* 38, no. 2 (2009): 159–77, https://doi.org/10.1177/0305735608100372.

9. Peter Glick et al., "Evaluations of Sexy Women In Low- and High-Status Jobs," *Psychology of Women Quarterly* 29, no. 4 (December 2005): 389–95, https://doi.org/10.1111/j.1471-6402.2005.00238.x.

10. Peter Glick et al., "Beyond Prejudice as Simple Antipathy: Hostile and Benevolent Sexism Across Cultures," *Journal of Personality and Social Psychology* 79, no. 5 (November 2000): 763–775, https://doi.org/10.1037//0022-3514.79.5.763.

11. Melissa L. Wookey, Nell A. Graves, and J. Corey Butler, "Effects of a Sexy Appearance on Perceived Competence of Women," *Journal of Social Psychology* 149, no. 1 (February 2009): 116–8, https://doi.org/10.3200/SOCP.149.1.116-118.

12. Neil Howlett et al., "Unbuttoned: The Interaction Between Provocativeness of Female Work Attire and Occupational Status," *Sex Roles* 72 (February 2015): 105–16, https://doi.org/10.1007/s11199-015-0450-8.

13. Regan A. R. Gurung et al., "Dressing 'in code': Clothing rules, propriety, and perceptions," *Journal of Social Psychology* 158, no. 5 (2018): 553–7, https://doi.org/10.1080/00224545.2017.1393383.

14. Silvia Bellezza, Francesca Gino, and Anat Keinan, "The Red Sneakers Effect: Inferring Status and Competence from Signals of Nonconformity," *Journal of Consumer Research* 41, no. 1 (June 2014): 35–54, https://doi.org/10.1086/674870.

15. Vanessa Friedman, "Does This Dress Make Me Look Guilty?," *New York Times*, April 25, 2019, https://www.nytimes.com/2019/04/25/fashion/anna-sorokin-elizabeth-holmes-card-b-court-fashion.html.

16. Brian P. Meier, Michael D. Robinson, and Gerald L. Clore, "Why Good Guys Wear White: Automatic Inferences About Stimulus Valence Based on Brightness," *Psychological Science* 15, no. 2 (February 2004): 82–7, https://doi.org/10.1111/j.0963-7214.2004.01502002.x.

17. Mark G. Frank and Thomas Gilovich, "The dark side of self- and social perception: Black uniforms and aggression in professional sports," *Journal of Personality and Social Psychology* 54, no. 1 (1988): 74–85, https://doi.org/10.1037/0022-3514.54.1.74.

18. Andrew J. Elliot and Daniela Niesta, "Romantic Red: Red Enhances Men's Attraction to Women," *Journal of Personality and Social Psychology* 95, no. 5 (2008): 1150–64, https://doi.org/10.1037/0022-3514.95.5.1150.

19. Katherine A. Karl, Leda McIntyre Hall, and Joy V. Peluchette, "City Employee Perceptions of the Impact of Dress and Appearance: You Are What You Wear," *Public Personnel Management* 42, no. 3 (2013): 452–70, https://doi.org/10.1177/0091026013495772.

20. Hajo Adam and Adam D. Galinsky, "Enclothed cognition," *Journal of Experimental Social Psychology* 48, no. 4 (July 2012): 918–25, https://doi.org/10.1016/j.jesp.2012.02.008.

21. Michael L. Slepian et al., "The Cognitive Consequences of Formal Clothing," *Social Psychological and Personality Science* 16, no. 6 (2015): 661–8, https://doi.org/10.1177/1948550615579462.

22. Dennis Dreiskaemper et al., "Influence of red jersey color on physical parameters in combat sports," *Journal of Sport & Exercise Psychology* 35, no. 1 (2013): 44–9, https://doi.org/10.1123/jsep.35.1.44.

23. Michael W. Kraus and Wendy Berry Mendes, "Sartorial Symbols of Social Class Elicit Class-Consistent Behavioral and Physiological Responses: A Dyadic Approach," *Journal of Experimental Psychology: General* 143, no. 6 (December 2014): 2330–40, http://dx.doi.org/10.1037/xge0000023.

Chapter 10: Judging a Book by Its Cover

1. Lauren A. Rivera, "Hiring as Cultural Matching: The Case of Elite Professional Service Firms," *American Sociological Review* 77, no. 6 (November 2012): 999–1022, https://doi.org/10.1177/0003122412463213.
2. Charles C. Ballew and Alexander Todorov, "Predicting political elections from rapid and unreflective face judgments," *PNAS* 104, no. 46 (November 2006): 17948–53, https://doi.org/10.1073/pnas.0705435104; Alexander Todorov et al., "Inferences of Competence from Faces Predict Election Outcomes," *Science* 308, no. 5728 (June 2005): 1623–6, https://doi.org/10.1126/science.1110589; Alexander Todorov, Manish Pakrashi, and Nikolaas N. Oosterhof, "Evaluating Faces on Trustworthiness After Minimal Time Exposure," *Social Cognition* 27, no. 6 (2009): 813–33, https://doi.org/10.1521/soco.2009.27.6.813; Janine Willis and Alexander Todorov, "First Impressions: Making Up Your Mind After a 100-Ms Exposure to a Face," *Psychological Science* 17, no. 7 (2006): 592–8, https://doi.org/10.1111/j.1467-9280.2006.01750.x; John A. Bargh et al., "Automaticity in social-cognitive processes," *Trends in Cognitive Science* 16, no. 12 (December 2012): 593–605, https://doi.org/10.1016/j.tics.2012.10.002.
3. Soo Kim, "Unusual flight attendant requirements: the good, the bad and the beautiful," *Telegraph*, March 31, 2016, https://www.telegraph.co.uk/travel/news/unusual-flight-attendant-requirements-the-good-the-bad-the-beautiful.
4. Alice H. Eagly et al., "What Is Beautiful Is Good, But . . . : A Meta-Analytic Review of Research on the Physical Attractiveness Stereotype," *Psychological Bulletin* 110, no. 1 (July 1991): 109–28, https://doi.org/10.1037/0033-2909.110.1.109; Judith H. Langlois et al., "Maxims or Myths of Beauty? A Meta-Analytic and Theoretical Review," *Psychological Bulletin* 126, no. 3 (May 2000): 390–423, https://doi.org/10.1037/0033-2909.126.3.390; Edward P. Lemay Jr., Margaret S. Clark, and Aaron Greenberg, "What Is Beautiful Is Good Because What Is Beautiful Is Desired: Physical Attractiveness Stereotyping as Projection of Interpersonal Goals," *Personality and Social Psychology Bulletin* 36, no. 3 (2010): 339–53, https://doi.org/10.1177/0146167209359700.
5. Karen Dion, Ellen Berscheid, and Elaine Walster, "What is beautiful is good," *Journal of Personality and Social Psychology* 24, no. 3 (1972): 285–90, http://dx.doi.org/10.1037/h0033731.
6. Megumi Hosoda, Eugene F. Stone-Romero, and Gwen Coats, "The effects of physical attractiveness on job-related outcomes: A meta-analysis of experimental studies," *Personnel Psychology* 56, no. 2 (2003): 431–62, https://doi

.org/10.1111/j.1744-6570.2003.tb00157.x; Enbar Toledano, "May the best (looking) man win: The unconscious role of attractiveness in employment decisions," *Cornell HR Review* (May 2013), http://digitalcommons.ilr.cornell.edu /chrr/48/.

7. Tracy Vaillancourt and Aanchal Sharma, "Intolerance of sexy peers: intrasexual competition among women," *Aggressive Behavior* 37, no. 6 (December 2011): 569–77, https://doi.org/10.1002/ab.20413; Tracy Vaillancourt, "Do human females use indirect aggression as an intrasexual competition strategy?," *Philosophical Transactions of the Royal Society B* 368, no. 1631 (December 2013), https:// doi.org/10.1098/rstb.2013.0080.

8. Sara E. Gutierres, Douglas T. Kenrick, and Jenifer J. Partch, "Beauty, dominance, and the mating game: Contrast effects in self-assessment reflect gender differences in mate selection," *Personality and Social Psychology Bulletin* 25, no. 9 (1999): 1126–34, http://dx.doi.org/10.1177/01461672992512006.

9. Maria Agthe, Matthias Spörrle, and Jon K. Maner, "Does Being Attractive Always Help? Positive and Negative Effects of Attractiveness on Social Decision Making," *Personality and Social Psychology Bulletin* 37, no. 8 (2011): 1042–54, https:// doi.org/10.1177/0146167211410355.

10. Marc F. Luxen and Fons J. R. Van De Vijver, "Facial attractiveness, sexual selection, and personnel selection: when evolved preferences matter," *Journal of Organization Behavior* 27, no. 2 (March 2006): 241–55, https://doi.org/10.1002/ job.357.

11. Ibid.

12. Bradley J. Ruffle and Ze'ev Shtudiner, "Are Good-Looking People More Employable?," *Management Science* 61, no. 8 (August 2015): 1760–76, https://doi .org/10.1287/mnsc.2014.1927.

13. Juan M. Madera and Michelle R. Hebl, "Discrimination against facially stigmatized applicants in interviews: An eye-tracking and face-to-face investigation," *Journal of Applied Psychology* 97, no. 2 (2012): 317–30, http://dx.doi.org/10 .1037/a0025799.

14. Juan M. Madera, "Facial Stigmas in Dyadic Selection Interviews: Affective and Behavioral Reactions Toward a Stigmatized Applicant," *Journal of Hospitality & Tourism Research* 40, no. 4 (2016): 456–75, https://doi.org/10.1177 /1096348013503996.

15. Stefanie K. Johnson et al., "Physical Attractiveness Biases in Ratings of Employment Suitability: Tracking Down the 'Beauty is Beastly' Effect," *The Journal of Social Psychology* 150, no. 3 (2010): 301–18, https://doi.org/10.1080/00224 540903365414.

16. Margaret Lee et al., "Perceived Entitlement Causes Discrimination Against Attractive Job Candidates in the Domain of Relatively Less Desirable Jobs," *Journal of Personality and Social Psychology* 114, no. 3 (2018): 422–42, http://dx.doi .org/10.1037/pspi0000114.

17. Sunyoung Lee et al., "When beauty helps and when it hurts: An organizational context model of attractiveness discrimination in selection decisions," *Organizational Behavior and Human Decision Processes* 128 (May 2015): 15–28, https://doi .org/10.1016/j.obhdp.2015.02.003.

18. Jaume Masip, Eugenio Garrido, and Carmen Herrero, "Facial appearance and judgments of credibility: The effects of facial babyishness and age on statement credibility," *Genetic, Social, and General Psychology Monographs* 129, no. 3 (August 2003): 269–311; Diane S. Berry and Leslie Zebrowitz McArthur, "Some Components and Consequences of a Babyface," *Journal of Personality and Social Psychology* 48, no. 2 (1985): 312–23, http://dx.doi.org/10.1037/0022-3514.48.2.312; Diane S. Berry and Sheila Brownlow, "Were the Physiognomists Right?: Personality Correlates of Facial Babyishness," *Personality and Social Psychology Bulletin* 15, no. 2 (1989): 266–79, https://doi.org/10.1177/0146167289152013; Leslie Zebrowitz, *Reading Faces: Window To The Soul?* (New York: Routledge, 1997); Diane S. Berry and Leslie Zebrowitz-McArthur, "What's in a Face?: Facial Maturity and the Attribution of Legal Responsibility," *Personality and Social Psychology Bulletin* 14, no. 1 (1988): 23–33, https://doi.org/10.1177/0146167288141003.

19. Leslie A. Zebrowitz and Joann M. Montepare, "Appearance DOES Matter," *Science* 308, no. 5728 (June 2005): 1565–6, https://doi.org/10.1126/science .1114170; Nicholas O. Rule and Nalini Ambady, "The Face of Success: Inferences From Chief Executive Officers' Appearance Predict Company Profits," *Psychological Science* 19, no. 2 (2008): 109–11, https://doi.org/10.1111/j.1467 -9280.2008.02054.x; Leslie A. Zebrowitz and Joann M. Montepare, "Social Psychological Face Perception: Why Appearance Matters," *Social and Personality Psychology Compass* 2, no. 3 (May 2008): 1497–517, https://doi.org/10.1111/j .1751-9004.2008.00109.x.

20. Zebrowitz, *Reading Faces: Window To The Soul?*; Joann M. Montepare and Leslie A. Zebrowitz, "Person Perception Comes of Age: The Salience and Significance of Age in Social Judgments," *Advances in Experimental Social Psychology* 30 (1998): 93–161, https://doi.org/10.1016/S0065-2601(08)60383-4.

21. Caroline F. Keating et al., "Do Babyfaced Adults Receive More Help? The (Cross-Cultural) Case of the Lost Resume," *Journal of Nonverbal Behavior* 27, no. 2 (June 2003): 89–109, https://doi.org/10.1023/A:1023962425692.

22. Gerald J. Gorn, Yuwei Jiang, and Gita Venkataramani Johar, "Babyfaces, Trait Inferences, and Company Evaluations in a Public Relations Crisis," *Journal of Consumer Research* 35, no. 1 (June 2008): 36–49, https://doi.org/10.1086/529533.

23. Juliana Schroeder and Nicholas Epley, "The Sound of Intellect: Speech Reveals a Thoughtful Mind, Increasing a Job Candidate's Appeal," *Journal of Personality and Social Psychology* 26, no. 6 (2015): 877–91, https://doi.org/10 .1177/0956797615572906.

24. Jack W. Bradbury and Sandra L. Vehrencamp, *Principles of Animal Communication 2nd Edition* (Sunderland: Sinauer Associates, 2011); William A. Searcy

and Stephen Nowicki, *The Evolution of Animal Communication: Reliability and Deception in Signaling Systems* (Princeton, NJ: Princeton University Press, 2005).

25. Jody Kreiman and Diana Sidtis, *Foundations of voice studies: An interdisciplinary approach to voice production and perception* (Hoboken, NJ: Wiley-Blackwell, 2011); Katarzyna Pisanski and Gregory A. Bryant, "The Evolution of Voice Perception," in *The Oxford Handbook of Voice Studies,* ed. Nina Eidsheim and Katherine Meizel (Oxford: Oxford University Press, 2016); David A. Puts, Benedict C. Jones, and Lisa M. DeBruine, "Sexual Selection on Human Faces and Voices," *The Journal of Sex Research* 49 (2012): 227–43, https://doi.org/10.1080/00224499.2012.658924.

26. David R. Feinberg et al., "Manipulations of fundamental and formant frequencies influence the attractiveness of human male voices," *Animal Behaviour* 69, no. 3 (March 2005): 561–8, https://doi.org/10.1016/j.anbehav.2004.06.012; David A. Puts, Benedict C. Jones, and Lisa M. DeBruine, "Sexual Selection on Human Faces and Voices," *The Journal of Sex Research* 49 (2012): 227–43, https://doi.org/10.1080/00224499.2012.658924.

27. Feinberg et al., "Manipulations of fundamental and formant frequencies influence the attractiveness of human male voices."

28. David A. Puts et al., "Men's voices as dominance signals: vocal fundamental and formant frequencies influence dominance attributions among men," *Evolution and Human Behavior* 28, no. 5 (September 2007): 340–4, https://doi.org/10.1016/j.evolhumbehav.2007.05.002.

29. Cara C. Tigue et al., "Voice pitch influences voting behavior," *Evolution and Human Behavior* 33, no. 3 (May 2012): 210–6, https://doi.org/10.1016/j.evolhumbehav.2011.09.004.

30. Casey A. Klofstad, Rindy C. Anderson, and Susan Peters, "Sounds like a winner: voice pitch influences perception of leadership capacity in both men and women," *Proceeding of the Royal Society B* 279, no. 1738 (2012): 2698–704, https://doi.org/10.1098/rspb.2012.0311; Casey A. Klofstad, "Candidate Voice Pitch Influences Election Outcomes," *Political Psychology* 37, no. 5 (October 2016): 725–38, https://doi.org/10.1111/pops.12280.

31. Rindy C. Anderson and Casey A. Klofstad, "Preference for Leaders with Masculine Voices Holds in the Case of Feminine Leadership Roles," *PLoS One* 7, no. 12 (December 2012): 1–4, https://doi.org/10.1371/journal.pone.0051216.

32. Kelyn J. Montano et al., "Men's voice pitch influences women's trusting behavior," *Evolution and Human Behavior* 38, no. 3 (May 2017): 293–7, https://doi.org/10.1016/j.evolhumbehav.2016.10.010.

33. Jovana Vukovic et al., "Variation in perceptions of physical dominance and trustworthiness predicts individual differences in the effect of relationship context on women's preferences for masculine pitch in men's voices," *Journal of Personality and Social Psychology* 102, no. 1 (February 2011): 37–48, https://doi.org/10.1348/000712610X498750.

34. Montano et al., "Men's voice pitch influences women's trusting behavior."

35. William J. Mayew, Christopher A. Parsons, and Mohan Venkatachalam, "Voice pitch and the labor market success of male chief executive officers," *Evolution and Human Behavior* 34, no. 4 (July 2013): 243–8, https://doi.org/10.1016/j .evolhumbehav.2013.03.001.

Chapter 11: Switching On and Off

1. "Number of smartphones sold to end users worldwide from 2007 to 2020," Telecommunications, Statista, August 2019, https://www.statista.com/statistics /263437/global-smartphone-sales-to-end-users-since-2007/; "Mobile Fact Sheet," Internet & Technology, Pew Research Center, June 12, 2019, https://www.pew research.org/internet/fact-sheet/mobile/.
2. Jason Gilbert, "Smartphone Addiction: Staggering Percentage Of Humans Couldn't Go One Day Without Their Phone," HuffPost, last modified August 16, 2012, https://www.huffpost.com/entry/smartphone-addiction-time-survey _n_1791790?guccounter=1.
3. Sara Thomée, Annika Härenstam, and Mats Hagberg, "Mobile phone use and stress, sleep disturbances, and symptoms of depression among young adults—a prospective cohort study," *BMC Public Health* 11, no. 1 (2011): 66–76, https:// bmcpublichealth.biomedcentral.com/articles/10.1186/1471-2458-11-66.
4. Éilish Duke and Christian Montag, "Smartphone addiction, daily interruptions and self-reported productivity," *Addictive Behaviors Reports* 6 (December 2017): 90–5, https://doi.org/10.1016/j.abrep.2017.07.002.
5. Sabine Sonnentag and Undine Kruel, "Psychological detachment from work during off-job time: The role of job stressors, job involvement, and recovery-related self-efficacy," *European Journal of Work and Organizational Psychology* 15, no. 2 (2006): 197–217, https://doi.org/10.1080/13594320500513939; Sabine Sonnentag, "Psychological Detachment From Work During Leisure Time: The Benefits of Mentally Disengaging From Work," *Current Directions in Psychological Science* 21, no. 2 (2012): 114–8, https://doi.org/10.1177/0963721411434979.
6. Leslie A. Perlow, *Sleeping with Your Smartphone: How to Break the 24/7 Habit and Change the Way You Work* (Boston: Harvard Business Review Press, 2012).
7. Janne Grønli et al., "Reading from an iPad or from a book in bed: the impact on human sleep. A randomized controlled crossover trial," *Sleep Medicine* 21 (May 2016): 86–92, https://doi.org/10.1016/j.sleep.2016.02.006.
8. Matthew A. Christensen et al., "Direct Measurements of Smartphone Screen-Time: Relationships with Demographics and Sleep," *PLoS One* 11 (2016): e0165331, https://doi.org/10.1371/journal.pone.0165331.
9. Klodiana Lanaj, Russell E. Johnson, and Christopher M. Barnes, "Beginning the workday yet already depleted? Consequences of late-night smartphone use and sleep," *Organizational Behavior and Human Decision Processes* 124, no. 1 (May 2014): 11–23, https://doi.org/10.1016/j.obhdp.2014.01.001.

10. Christopher M. Barnes, "I'll sleep when I'm dead: Managing those too busy to sleep," *Organizational Dynamics* 40, no. 1 (2011): 18–26, http://dx.doi.org/10.1016/j.orgdyn.2010.10.001.

11. Nathaniel Barr et al., "The brain in your pocket: Evidence that Smartphones are used to supplant thinking," *Computers in Human Behavior* 48 (July 2015): 473–80, https://doi.org/10.1016/j.chb.2015.02.029.

12. Wade C. Jacobsen and Renata Forste, "The Wired Generation: Academic and Social Outcomes of Electronic Media Use Among University Students," *Cyberpsychology, Behavior and Social Networking* 14, no. 5 (2011): 275–80, https://doi.org/10.1089/cyber.2010.0135.

13. Andrew Lepp, Jacob E. Barkley, and Aryn C. Karpinski, "The relationship between cell phone use, academic performance, anxiety, and Satisfaction with Life in college students," *Computers in Human Behavior* 31 (February 2014): 343–50, https://doi.org/10.1016/j.chb.2013.10.049.

14. Brittany A. Harman and Toru Sato, "Cell phone use and grade point average among undergraduate university students," *College Student Journal* 45, no. 3 (2011): 544–9, https://psycnet.apa.org/record/2011-24677-009; Wade C. Jacobsen and Renata Forste, "The Wired Generation: Academic and Social Outcomes of Electronic Media Use Among University Students," *Cyberpsychology, Behavior and Social Networking* 14, no. 5 (2011): 275–80, https://doi.org/10.1089/cyber.2010.0135; Eileen Wood et al., "Examining the impact of off-task multi-tasking with technology on real-time classroom learning," *Computers & Education* 58, no. 1 (January 2012): 365–74, https://doi.org/10.1016/j.compedu.2011.08.029; Arnold D. Froese et al., "Effects of classroom cell phone use on expected and actual learning," *College Student Journal* 46, no. 2 (2012): 323–32, https://psycnet.apa.org/record/2012-19556-009; Chris A. Bjornsen and Kellie J. Archer, "Relations Between College Students' Cell Phone Use During Class and Grades," *Scholarship of Teaching and Learning in Psychology* 1, no. 4 (2015): 326–36, http://dx.doi.org/10.1037/stl0000045.

15. Min-Hee Lee et al., "Structural Brain Network Abnormalities in Subjects with Internet Addiction," *Journal of Mechanics in Medicine and Biology* 17, no. 7 (2017): 1740031, https://doi.org/10.1142/S0219519417400310.

16. Seungyeon Lee et al., "The Effects of Cell Phone Use and Emotion-regulation Style on College Students' Learning," *Applied Cognitive Psychology* 31, no. 3 (May/June 2017): 360–6, https://doi.org/10.1002/acp.3323.

17. Bill Thornton et al., "The Mere Presence of a Cell Phone May be Distracting: Implications for Attention and Task Performance," *Social Psychology* 45 (2014): 479–88, https://doi.org/10.1027/1864-9335/a000216.

18. Adrian F. Ward et al., "Brain Drain: The Mere Presence of One's Own Smartphone Reduces Available Cognitive Capacity," *Journal of the Association for Consumer Research* 2, no. 2 (April 2017): 140–54, http://dx.doi.org/10.1086/691462.

19. Sara Radicati and Justin Levenstein, *Email Statistics Report, 2013–2017*, http://www.radicati.com/wp/wp-content/uploads/2013/04/Email-Statistics-Report-2013-2017-Executive-Summary.pdf.

20. Justin Kruger et al., "Egocentrism over e-mail: Can we communicate as well as we think?," *Journal of Personality and Social Psychology* 89, no. 6 (2005): 925–36, http://dx.doi.org/10.1037/0022-3514.89.6.925.

Chapter 12: The Sound of Music

1. Joke Bradt and Cheryl Dileo, "Music for stress and anxiety reduction in coronary heart disease patients," *Cochrane Database Systematic Review* 28, no. 12 (2013): CD006577, https://doi.org/10.1002/14651858.CD006577.pub3.

2. "How music can help you heal," Harvard Health Publishing, Harvard Medical School, February 2016, https://www.health.harvard.edu/mind-and-mood/how-music-can-help-you-heal.

3. Holly Covington, "Therapeutic Music for Patients with Psychiatric Disorders," *Holistic Nursing Practice* 15, no. 2 (January 2001): 59–69, https://doi.org/10.1097/00004650-200101000-00009.

4. Anneli B. Haake, "Individual music listening in workplace settings: An exploratory survey of offices in the UK," *Musicae Scientiae* 15, no. 1 (March 2011): 107–29, https://doi.org/10.1177/1029864911398065.

5. Frances H. Rauscher, Gordon L. Shawa, and Katherine N. Ky, "Listening to Mozart enhances spatial-temporal reasoning: towards a neurophysiological basis," *Neuroscience Letters* 185, no. 1 (February 1995): 44–7, https://doi.org/10.1016/0304-3940(94)11221-4.

6. William Forde Thompson, E. Glenn Schellenberg, and Gabriela Husain, "Arousal, Mood, and The Mozart Effect," *Psychological Science* 12, no. 3 (May 2001): 248–51, https://doi.org/10.1111/1467-9280.00345.

7. E. Glenn Schellenberg et al., "Exposure to music and cognitive performance: tests of children and adults," *Psychology of Music* 35, no. 1 (January 2007): 5–19, https://doi.org/10.1177/0305735607068885.

8. Wu-Jing He, Wan-Chi Wong, and Anna N. N. Hui, "Emotional Reactions Mediate the Effect of Music Listening on Creative Thinking: Perspective of the Arousal-and-Mood Hypothesis," *Frontiers in Psychology* 8 (2017): 1680, https://doi.org/10.3389/fpsyg.2017.01680.

9. Richard I. Newman Jr., Donald L. Hunt, and Fen Rhodes, "Effects of music on employee attitude and productivity in a skateboard factory," *Journal of Applied Psychology* 50, no. 6 (1966): 493–6, https://doi.org/10.1037/h0024046.

10. J. G. Fox and E. D. Embrey, "Music—an aid to productivity," *Applied Ergonomics* 3, no. 4 (December 1972): 202–5, https://doi.org/10.1016/0003-6870(72)90101-9.

11. Greg R. Oldham et al., "Listen While You Work? Quasi-Experimental Relations Between Personal-Stereo Headset Use and Employee Work Responses," *Journal of Applied Psychology* 80, no. 5 (1995): 547–64, 10.1037/0021-9010.80.5.547.

12. Teresa Lesiuk, "The effect of music listening on work performance," *Psychological of Music* 33, no. 2 (2005): 173–191, https://doi.org/10.1177/0305735605050650.

13. Shelby R. Lies, MD, Andrew Y. Zhang, MD, "Prospective Randomized Study of the Effect of Music on the Efficiency of Surgical Closure," *Aesthetic Surgery Journal* 35, no. 7 (2015): 858–63, https://doi.org/10.1093/asj/sju161; Afaaf BS Shakir et al., "The Effects of Music on Microsurgical Technique and Performance: A Motion Analysis Study," *Annals of Plastic Surgery* 78, no. 5 (May 2017): S243–S247, https://doi.org/10.1097/SAP.0000000000001047.

14. Gianna Cassidy and Raymond A. R. MacDonald, "The effect of background music and background noise on the task performance of introverts and extraverts," *Psychology of Music* 38, no. 3 (May 2017): 293–7, https://doi.org/10.1016/j.evolhumbehav.2016.10.010; Adrian Furnham and Lisa Strbac, "Music is as distracting as noise: the differential distraction of background music and noise on the cognitive test performance of introverts and extraverts," *Ergonomics* 45, no. 3 (2002): 203–17, https://doi.org/10.1080/00140130210121932; Stacey Dobbs, Adrian Furnham, and Alastair McClelland, "The effect of background music and noise on the cognitive test performance of introverts and extraverts," *Applied Cognitive Psychology* 25, no. 2 (March/April 2011): 307–13, https://doi.org/10.1002/acp.1692; Sarah Ellen Ransdell and Lee A. Gilroy, "The effects of background music on word processed writing," *Computers in Human Behavior* 17, no. 2 (March 2001): 141–8, https://doi.org/10.1016/S0747-5632(00)00043-1; Stacey A. Anderson and Gerald B. Fuller, "Effect of music on reading comprehension of junior high school students," *School Psychology Quarterly* 25, no. 3 (September 2010): 178–87, https://doi.org/10.1037/a0021213; Eddie A. Christopher and Jill Talley Shelton, "Fertile Green: Green Facilitates Creative Performance." *Journal of Applied Research in Memory and Cognition* 6, no. 2 (June 2017): 167–73, https://doi.org/10.1016/j.jarmac.2017.01.012.

15. Juliane Kämpfe, Peter Sedlmeier, and Frank Renkewitz, "The impact of background music on adult listeners: A meta-analysis," *Psychology of Music* 39, no. 4 (2011): 424–48, https://doi.org/10.1177/0305735610376261.

16. Dennis Y. Hsu et al., "The Music of Power: Perceptual and Behavioral Consequences of Powerful Music," *Social Psychological and Personality Science* 6, no. 1 (2015): 75–83, https://doi.org/10.1177/1948550614542345.

17. Christopher Rea, Pamelyn MacDonald, and Gwen Carnes, "Listening to classical, pop, and metal music: An investigation of mood," *Emporia State Research Studies* 42, no. 1 (2010): 1–3, https://esirc.emporia.edu/bitstream/handle/123456789/381/205.1.1.pdf?sequence=1.

18. Joydeep Bhattacharya and Job P. Lindsen, "Music for a Brighter World: Brightness Judgment Bias by Musical Emotion," *PloS One* 11, no. 2 (2016): e0148959, https://doi.org/10.1371/journal.pone.0148959.

19. Peter Tze-Ming Chou, "Attention Drainage Effect: How Background Music Effects Concentration in Taiwanese College Students," *Journal of the Scholarship of Teaching and Learning* 10, no. 1 (January 2010): 36–46, https://eric.ed.gov/?id=EJ882124.

20. William Forde Thompson, E. Glenn Schellenberg, and Adriana Katharine Letnic, "Fast and loud background music disrupts reading comprehension," *Psychology of Music* 40, no. 6 (2012): 700–8, https://doi.org/10.1177/0305735611400173.

21. Simone M. Ritter and Sam Ferguson, "Happy creativity: Listening to happy music facilitates divergent thinking," *PloS One* 12, no. 9 (2017): e0182210, https://doi.org/10.1371/journal.pone.0182210.

22. Nick Perham and Tom Withey, "Liked Music Increases Spatial Rotation Performance Regardless of Tempo," *Current Psychology* 31, no. 2 (May 2012): 168–81, http://dx.doi.org/10.1007/s12144-012-9141-6.

23. Nick Perham and Joanne Vizard, "Can preference for background music mediate the irrelevant sound effect?," *Applied Cognitive Psychology* 25, no. 4 (July/August 2011): 625–31, https://doi.org/10.1002/acp.1731.

24. Rong-Hwa Huang and Yi-Nuo Shih, "Effects of background music on concentration of workers," *Work* 38, no. 4 (2011): 383–7, https://doi.org/10.3233/WOR-2011-1141.

25. Adrian Furnham and Anna Bradley, "Music while you work: the differential distraction of background music on the cognitive test performance of introverts and extraverts," *Applied Cognitive Psychology* 11, no. 5 (October 1997): 445–55, https://doi.org/10.1002/(SICI)1099-0720(199710)11:5<445::AID-ACP472>3.0.CO;2-R; Adrian Furnham, "Person-organization-outcome fit," in *Personality and Individual Differences in the Workplace*, ed. B. Roberts and R. Hogan (Washington, DC: APA, 2001), 223–51.

26. Anna O'Hare, "The Effect of Vocal and Instrumental Background Music on Primary School Pupils' Verbal Memory Using a Sentence Recall Task," *Student Psychology Journal* 2 (2011): 1–11, https://psychology.tcd.ie/spj/past_issues/issue02/Empirical%20Studies/(3)%20Anna%20O'Hare.pdf.

27. Makoto Iwanaga and Takako Ito, "Disturbance Effect of Music on Processing of Verbal and Spatial Memories," *Perceptual and Motor Skills* 94, no. 3 (2002): 1251–8, https://doi.org/10.2466/pms.2002.94.3c.1251.

28. Tobias Greitemeyer, "Effects of Songs With Prosocial Lyrics on Prosocial Behavior: Further Evidence and a Mediating Mechanism," *Personality and Social Psychology Bulletin* 35, no. 11 (2009): 1500–11, https://doi.org/10.1177/0146167209341648; Patrick Edward Kennedy, "The Relationship Between Prosocial Music and Helping Behaviour and its Mediators: An Irish College Sample," *Journal of European Psychology Students* 4, no. 1 (2013): 1–15, http://doi.org/10.5334/jeps.av.

29. Tobias Greitemeyer, "Effects of Songs With Prosocial Lyrics on Prosocial Behavior: Further Evidence and a Mediating Mechanism," *Personality and Social*

Psychology Bulletin 35, no. 11 (2009): 1500–11, https://doi.org/10.1177/01461 67209341648.

30. Tobias Greitemeyer, "Effects of songs with prosocial lyrics on prosocial thoughts, affect, and behavior," *Journal of Experimental Social Psychology* 45, no. 1 (January 2009): 186–90, https://doi.org/10.1016/j.jesp.2008.08.003.

31. Céline Jacob, Nicolas Guéguen, and Gaëlle Boulbry, "Effects of songs with prosocial lyrics on tipping behavior in a restaurant," *International Journal of Hospitality Management* 29, no. 4 (December 2010): 761–3, https://doi.org/10.1016/j.ijhm.2010.02.004.

32. Adrian C. North, Mark Tarrant, and David J. Hargreaves, "The Effects of Music on Helping Behavior: A Field Study," *Environment and Behavior* 36, no. 2 (March 2004): 266–75, https://doi.org/10.1177/0013916503256263.

33. Adrian Furnham and Lisa Strbac, "Music is as distracting as noise: the differential distraction of background music and noise on the cognitive test performance of introverts and extraverts," *Ergonomics* 45, no. 3 (2002): 203–17, https://doi.org/10.1080/00140130210121932; Goran Belojevic, Vesna Ž. Slepčević, and Branko Jakovljevic, "Mental performance in noise: the role of introversion," *Journal of Environmental Psychology* 21, no. 2 (June 2001): 209–13, https://doi.org/10.1006/jevp.2000.0188; Stacey Dobbs, Adrian Furnham, and Alastair McClelland, "The effect of background music and noise on the cognitive test performance of introverts and extraverts," *Applied Cognitive Psychology* 25, no. 2 (March/April 2011): 307–13, https://doi.org/10.1002/acp.1692.

34. Gianna Cassidy and Raymond A. R. MacDonald, "The effect of background music and background noise on the task performance of introverts and extraverts," *Psychology of Music* 35, no. 3 (July 2007): 517–37, https://doi.org/10.1177/0305735607076444.

35. Attila Szabo, A. Small, and M. Leigh, "The effects of slow- and fast-rhythm classical music on progressive cycling to voluntary physical exhaustion," *Journal of Sports Medicine and Physical Fitness* 39, no. 3 (September 1999): 220–5, https://europepmc.org/abstract/med/10573664.

36. Lee Crust, "Carry-Over Effects of Music in an Isometric Muscular Endurance Task," *Perceptual and Motor Skills* 98, no. 3 (2004): 985–91, https://doi.org/10.2466/pms.98.3.985-991.

37. Matthew J. Stork et al., "Music enhances performance and perceived enjoyment of sprint interval exercise," *Medicine & Science in Sports & Exercise* 47, no. 5 (May 2015): 1052–60, https://doi.org/10.1249/MSS.0000000000000494.

Chapter 13: Tidy Desk, Tidy Mind?

1. James Q. Wilson and George L. Kelling, "Broken Windows: The police and neighborhood safety," *The Atlantic Online*, March 1982, http://www.lakeclaire.org/docs/BrokenWindows-AtlantaicMonthly-March82.pdf.

2. Kees Keizer, Siegwart Lindenberg, and Linda Steg, "The Spreading of Disorder," *Science* 322, no. 5908 (December 2008): 1681–5, https://doi.org/10.1126/science.1161405.

3. Katie Liljenquist, Chen-Bo Zhong, and Adam D. Galinsky, "The smell of virtue: Clean scents promote reciprocity and charity," *Psychological Science* 21, no. 3 (2010): 381–3, http://dx.doi.org/10.1177/0956797610361426.

4. Hiroki Kotabe, Omid Kardan, and Marc Berman, "The Order of Disorder: Deconstructing Visual Disorder and Its Effect on Rule-Breaking," *Journal of Experimental Psychology: General* 145, no. 12 (December 2016): 1713–27, https://doi.org/10.1037/xge0000240.

5. Boyoun Chae and Rui Zhu, "Environmental Disorder Leads to Self-Regulatory Failure," *Journal of Consumer Research* 40, no. 6 (April 2014): 1203–18, https://doi.org/10.1086/674547.

6. Kathleen D. Vohs, Joseph P. Redden, and Ryan Rahinel, "Physical Order Produces Healthy Choices, Generosity, and Conventionality, Whereas Disorder Produces Creativity," *Psychological Science* 24, no. 9 (2013): 1860–7, https://doi.org/10.1177/0956797613480186.

7. Ibid.

8. Ibid.

Chapter 14: Creativity

1. Klaus Schwab, "The Fourth Industrial Revolution: What It Means and How to Respond," *Foreign Affairs*, December 12, 2015, https://www.foreignaffairs.com/articles/2015-12-12/fourth-industrial-revolution.

2. Alex Gray, "The 10 skills you need to thrive in the Fourth Industrial Revolution," World Economic Forum, January 19, 2016, https://www.weforum.org/agenda/2016/01/the-10-skills-you-need-to-thrive-in-the-fourth-industrial-revolution/.

3. World Economic Forum, "The Future of Jobs Report 2018," September 17, 2018, http://www3.weforum.org/docs/WEF_Future_of_Jobs_2018.pdf.

4. Gray, "The 10 skills you need to thrive in the Fourth Industrial Revolution."

5. Abigail Hess, "This is the most in-demand skill of 2019, according to LinkedIn," CNBC, January 8, 2019, https://www.cnbc.com/2019/01/07/the-most-in-demand-skill-of-2019-according-to-linkedin.html.

6. James Manyika et al., "Jobs lost, jobs gained: What the future of work will mean for jobs, skills, and wages," McKinsey & Company, November 2017, https://www.mckinsey.com/featured-insights/future-of-work/jobs-lost-jobs-gained-what-the-future-of-work-will-mean-for-jobs-skills-and-wages.

7. Joy Paul Guilford, *The Nature of Human Intelligence* (New York: McGraw-Hill, 1967).

8. Sarnoff A. Mednick and Martha T. Mednick, "A theory and test of creative thought," *Proceedings of the XIV International Congress of Applied Psychology* 5 (1962): 40–7, https://psycnet.apa.org/record/1963-04120-002.

9. Jan Dul, Canan Ceylan, and Ferdinand Jaspers, "Knowledge workers' creativity and the role of the physical work environment," *Human Resource Management* 50, no. 6 (November/December 2011): 715–34, https://doi.org/10.1002/hrm.20454.

10. Christian Kandler et al., "The Nature of Creativity: The Roles of Genetic Factors, Personality Traits, Cognitive Abilities, and Environmental Sources," *Journal of Personality and Social Psychology* 111, no. 2 (August 2016): 230–49, https://doi.org/10.1037/pspp0000087.

11. Jingzhou Pan et al., "How does proactive personality promote creativity? A multilevel examination of the interplay between formal and informal leadership," *Journal of Occupational and Organizational Psychology* 91, no. 4 (December 2018): 852–74, https://doi.org/10.1111/joop.12221.

12. Kris Byron and Shalini Khazanchi, "Rewards and creative performance: A meta-analytic test of theoretically derived hypotheses," *Psychological Bulletin* 138, no. 4 (February 2012): 809–30, https://doi.org/10.1037/a0027652.

13. Ravi Mehta and Rui (Juliet) Zhu, "Blue or Red? Exploring the Effect of Color on Cognitive Task Performances," *Science* 323, no. 5918 (February 2009): 1226–29, https://doi.org/10.1126/science.1169144.

14. Andrew J. Elliot et al., "Color and Psychological Functioning: The Effect of Red on Performance Attainment," *Journal of Experimental Psychology: General* 136, no. 1 (February 2007): 154–68, https://doi.org/10.1037/0096-3445.136.1.154.

15. Mehta and Zhu, "Blue or Red? Exploring the Effect of Color on Cognitive Task Performances."

16. Stephanie Lichtenfeld et al., "Fertile Green: Green Facilitates Creative Performance," *Personality and Social Psychology Bulletin* 38, no. 6 (2012): 784–97, https://doi.org/10.1177/0146167212436611.

17. Anna Steidle and Lioba Werth, "Freedom from constraints: Darkness and dim illumination promote creativity," *Journal of Environmental Psychology* 35 (September 2013): 67–80, https://doi.org/10.1016/j.jenvp.2013.05.003.

18. Angela K. Y. Leung et al., "Embodied Metaphors and Creative 'Acts,'" *Psychological Science* 23, no. 5 (2012): 502–9, https://doi.org/10.1177/0956797611429801.

19. Alex Marin, Martin Reimann, and Raquel Castaño, "Metaphors and creativity: Direct, moderating, and mediating effects," *Journal of Consumer Psychology* 24, no. 2 (April 2014): 290–7, https://doi.org/10.1016/j.jcps.2013.11.001.

20. Michael L. Slepian et al., "Shedding light on insight: Priming bright ideas," *Journal of Experimental Social Psychology* 46, no. 4 (July 2010): 696–700, https://doi.org/10.1016/j.jesp.2010.03.009.

21. Michael L. Slepian and Nalini Ambady, "Fluid movement and creativity," *Journal of Experimental Psychology* 141, no. 4 (November 2012): 625–9, https://doi.org/10.1037/a0027395.

22. Denis Dumas and Kevin N. Dunbar, "The Creative Stereotype Effect," *PloS One* 11, no. 2 (February 2016): e0142567, https://doi.org/10.1371/journal.pone .0142567.

23. Mareike B. Wieth and Rose T. Zacks, "Time of day effects on problem solving: When the non-optimal is optimal," *Thinking & Reasoning* 17, no. 4 (2011): 387–401, https://doi.org/10.1080/13546783.2011.625663.

24. Benjamin Baird et al., "Inspired by Distraction: Mind Wandering Facilitates Creative Incubation," *Psychological Science* 23, no. 10 (2012): 1117–22, https://doi .org/10.1177/0956797612446024.

25. Sandi Mann and Rebekah Cadman, "Does Being Bored Make Us More Creative?," *Creativity Research Journal* 26, no. 2 (2014): 165–73, https://doi.org/10 .1080/10400419.2014.901073.

26. Xiaoqian Ding et al., "Improving creativity performance by short-term meditation," *Behavioral and Brain Functions* 10, no. 1 (2014): 9, https://doi .org/10.1186/1744-9081-10-9.

27. Brian D. Ostafina and Kyle T. Kassman, "Stepping out of history: Mindfulness improves insight problem solving," *Consciousness and Cognition* 21, no. 2 (June 2012): 1031–6, https://doi.org/10.1016/j.concog.2012.02.014.

28. Emma Schootstra, Dirk Deichmann, and Evgenia Dolgova, "Can 10 Minutes of Meditation Make You More Creative?," *Harvard Business Review*, August 29, 2017, https://hbr.org/2017/08/can-10-minutes-of-meditation-make-you-more -creative.

29. Lorenza S. Colzato, Ayca Ozturk, and Bernhard Hommel, "Meditate to create: the impact of focused-attention and open-monitoring training on convergent and divergent thinking," *Frontiers in Psychology* 3 (2012): 116, http://dx.doi .org/10.3389/fpsyg.2012.00116.

30. Matthijs Baas, Barbara Nevicka, and Femke S. Ten Velden, "Specific Mindfulness Skills Differentially Predict Creative Performance," *Personality and Social Psychology Bulletin* 40, no. 9 (May 2014): 1092–106, https://doi.org/10 .1177/0146167214535813.

31. Jon Cohn, "5 Big Companies That See The Big Benefits Of Meditation," Corporate Wellness Program | Fitspot Corporate Wellness Provider, June 12, 2017, https://fitspotwellness.com/blog/5-big-companies-that-see-the-big-benefits-of -meditation/.

32. Schootstra et al., "Can 10 Minutes of Meditation Make You More Creative?"

33. Amishi P. Jha et al., "Minds 'At Attention': Mindfulness Training Curbs Attentional Lapses in Military Cohorts," *PloS One* 10, no. 2 (2015): e0116889, https:// doi.org/10.1371/journal.pone.0116889.

INDEX

ABOUT THE AUTHOR

Thalma E. Lobel is an internationally recognized psychologist who has served as the chair at the School of Psychological Sciences at Tel Aviv University, the director of the Adler Center for Child Development and Psychopathology, the Dean of Students, and a member of the executive board of the university. She has been a visiting professor at Harvard University and a visiting scholar at Tufts University, the University of California at San Diego, and New York University. Lobel has published dozens of articles in some of the most respected academic peer-reviewed journals and has received many prestigious research grants. Her previous book, *Sensation*, was published in fifteen countries.